REFOCUSING YOUR PASSIONS

Don Crossland

REFOCUSING YOUR PASSIONS

Don Crossland

Star Song
PUBLISHING GROUP

Contents

Acknowledgments

The writing of this book has flowed out of the wellspring and passion of my own heart to see people set free to live life passionately through Jesus Christ. Many persons have encouraged me in one way or another. However, it is my joy to express to the following a special "thank you" for their help, either directly or indirectly, in making this book possible.

To my wife, Helen Crossland, who has encouraged me along the way to press through my discouragement and to see circumstances through God's eyes, not my own.

To Frances Davis and Leah Springer, who helped type the original manuscript.

To Greg Graham, who assisted in editing and proofreading parts of the manuscript.

To Joe Sales, who has been sensitive to the needs of this ministry, making it possible for me to have the time to write.

To my parents, A.H. and Dorothy Lamm, who continue to faithfully support us with their love and prayers.

To my pastor, Dick King, whose ministry in person and in the pulpit has continued to remind me of God's grace and the heart of the Father.

To Matt Price, who again has graciously directed the completion of this book, even extending himself in time and effort.

To Stan and Judy Moser, who have received us as friends in their home and hearts, and also into the Star Song family.

Finally, I acknowledge the grace and love of God the Father through Jesus Christ our Lord, who has so kindly redeemed me and given me a new heart to know him and love him passionately. I acknowledge my own inadequacy but his adequacy, my failures but his victories, my shortcoming but his overcoming.

To our daughter and her husband, Tamra and Les Vines, who have illustrated their love and passion for Jesus Christ through their love for one another and others, and especially their forgiveness and care for me during my own healing and restoring journey.

To our son, Rod Crossland, who has helped us not to take everything so seriously, to occasionally laugh at ourselves, and to experience the passion for the day-to-day realities of life.

To our son, Brad Crossland, who went to be with the Lord more than twenty years ago. During his short life of only fifteen months, he taught us that life is so temporal and helped us realize the importance of passion for eternal things.

PREFACE

My wife brought the morning newspaper to our bedroom. I could see a look of concern and worry on her usually cheerful face. "The article is on the front page," she whispered, slowly handing me the newspaper.

There it was, about half way down on one side of the page: the article about my resignation from the pastorate because of my sexual sin. The article had been written by a local reporter who had interviewed me the day before. It was obvious that she had tried to give it a soft edge, but like a Texas storm, it would soon thunder through the area. The article was released to the Associated Press, and soon it landed in newspapers across the country.

I felt weak. I could muster only the strength to pull the bed sheet up over my head, hoping that this was a horrible nightmare I would soon awaken from. That was wishful thinking.

Looking back to that September morning in 1985, when the final walls of my crumbling ministry came falling down, I had no way of knowing the profound effect it would have on my life. The experience was incredibly damaging in the beginning, but it became a source of ministry and help to thousands of people across this country and others who suffer from addictive and compulsive behaviors.

Occasionally, I recall the high profile ministry I enjoyed as pastor of a church with several thousand members, as chairman of a ministry and Christian magazine, and as a representative of other national Christian organizations and ministries. But I do not even attempt to figure out which part of me was serving out of genuine love and which part was searching to belong and perform for acceptance.

Somehow, I knew that my personal struggles with sexual addiction were interwoven with these facets of my life and, like the apostle Paul, I would often cry out: "For that which I am doing, I do not understand; for I am not practicing what I would like to do, but I am doing the very thing I hate" (Romans 7:15). Later, he says, "wretched man that I am! Who will set me free from the body of this death?" (Romans 7:24).

Just as Paul describes the law of the Spirit of life in Christ Jesus that sets us free from the law of sin and death, my purpose in writing this book is to tell my story, relate the story of others, and explain how the restoration process has worked in our lives.

Please remember that this process reflects only how the Holy Spirit has affected my life and that of others. This book is not designed to be the complete work or final word of God's grace in dealing with compulsive behavior.

It is my prayer and hope that it will give you hope and draw you to him. He is our life, our redeemer, and our deliverer.

At this writing, my wife and I live in North Little Rock, Arkansas, where we coordinate Journey Toward Wholeness Ministries. We conduct seminars and workshops on various restorative themes, including a Journey Toward Wholeness, Reclaiming Family and Generational Blessings, and Overcoming the Cycles of Shame and Addiction. The latter workshop focuses on a Christian perspective of sexual compulsive behavior.

I also serve as the national director of the Center for Sexual Trauma and Addiction Recovery at the Living Hope Institute in Little Rock. The Center for Sexual Trauma and Addiction Recovery is being developed as part of the Living Hope Institute. The institute is a biblical-based treatment center with both in-patient and out-patient services.

For further information on these topics, please write to: Journey Toward Wholeness Ministries, Box 1019, North Little Rock, AR 72115.

Author's note: Although the stories in this book are real, names have been changed to guard the anonymity of the people involved.

ONE

SEARCHING FOR A RELATIONSHIP

A few years ago, a friend shared with me a very significant statement. He was in his seventh year of recovery from sexual addiction involving multiple affairs with various women. His words rang through my head for days afterward: "I have noticed that when I have close and healthy relationships, I seem to be free from my problem with lust."

He further explained that his marriage became healthier as he and his wife met with other couples in close and healthy support groups. By healthy, he meant sharing feelings and needs, allowing for accountability, and risking trust. I realized that his addiction, like most addictions, was a search for a relationship—an attempt to fill a void or repair an emotional wound from years past. The addiction explodes in distortion when we try to control it, especially through unhealthy behavior.

The conversation led me to rethink some of my own behavior, and to observe that I too had experienced degrees of freedom from my own addiction when I continued a close relationship with God and others. The problem was that these relationships were transitory, and I too often substituted busyness in ministry for intimacy with Christ. I was more interested in what the Bible said than with who said it, and more concerned with what the Bible said about things than what it was saying to me personally.

My relationships with friends were also sabotaged, though in different ways. My unrealistic expectations of others allowed me to grant them only one mistake. After that, I built walls of isolation. My fear of abandonment and hurt was a lingering sickness from years of emotional wounds and molestations.

My friend's poignant words caused me to focus on the emptiness and isolation I had felt for years. Even though I was involved with hundreds of peo-

11

ple in ministry, I did not allow others to be deeply involved in my life, even my wife. A room in my heart had been so tightly closed and compartmentalized that it no longer seemed a part of me.

This part of my emotions was reawakened after I listened to a videotape from an interview I had done with a Christian minister. The interview, like many others over the past several years, stemmed from my resignation from the pastorate because of a moral and sexual failure and my subsequent process of restoration. Listening to the tape, I was surprised and embarrassed by a statement I had made. I said, "I have never known a time when I have not felt an emptiness and hole inside."

The statement was more of a key to my own wholeness and restoration than most anything else I discussed. Though I did not realize it at the time, my own addictive and immoral behavior was in reality an attempt to deal with the emptiness I felt inside.

To people who had known me, my speaking of feeling empty inside would be almost inconceivable. I pastored a large and fast-growing church, enjoyed the acceptance of my peers, and had a beautiful family and a nice home. Then there was the growing response to my teaching ministry and the demonstration and presence of the Holy Spirit, which seemed to confirm my own maturity and stability. It was enough to satisfy the desires of almost anyone—or so it seemed.

What most people did not know about were the many times I spent in my office, face down on the floor sobbing and crying out to God to fill the emptiness and loneliness I felt inside. The emotional energy it took for me to lead three morning and two evening services on Sunday drained me; they failed to reenergize me. I knew, however, that the longing inside of me stemmed from more than my responsibilities. Even though I had questioned this emotional void during the early years of my college career and marriage, I soon came to accept it as normal. My greatest failure was not my attempt to deal with the void in unhealthy ways, but in not trusting God to heal the wounds and fill the void in his way.

One of the purposes of this book is to help others identify the longings and passions in their hearts and the accompanying distortions and consequences, and to refocus these desires in creative and healthy ways by being restored to the heavenly Father through Jesus Christ. As the prophet cried out in Lamentations (5:22): "Restore us to thee O Lord, so that we may be restored."

We have all experienced longings of the human heart. These longings and desires come from many and varied sources. First of all, God created us with healthy longings, with desires to be the recipient of and channel to his divine grace to others. When these legitimate longings are sabotaged even as early as childhood, false beliefs and deceptions related to their fulfillment set in. They vary from person to person, and they may result in addictive and destructive behavior. They may even span generations through harmful influences and environments.

I have divided our basic needs and longings into three distinct categories for easier understanding:

1. Our being. When God created man in his image, man's sense of being was established through his character and existence. This need for being is first affirmed in childhood by people around us. It is evidenced in the need for nurturing, closeness, being taken care of, unconditional acceptance, and other human responses that ensure the safety and acceptance of our being.

2. Our need for belonging. "God created man in his likeness, male and female created he them." Our gender identity is basic in our need for relationships with those of the same gender and those of the opposite gender. Our gender identity needs affirmation from both parents. The need to be curious in a healthy way, to test and establish boundaries, and to relate properly to authority figures and peers is part of fulfilling the longing for healthy and significant relationships.

3. Our need for becoming. God gave man dominion in the original creation to fulfill the legitimate needs to be fruitful and to replenish, as well as to establish a sense of order so that we can receive blessings and bless others. The need to learn, have proper role models, be organized, affirm our gifts and talents, and fulfill our call and vision are all part of this process.

When one of these basic needs—being, belonging, or becoming—has been sabotaged or distorted, one may search a lifetime to repair and restore the wound of loss.

Though the wounds in the human soul become the primary cause of many and varied sin patterns, the searching mode may begin as early as childhood and end at the grave. The search is usually twofold: to fill the loss or to ease the pain.

God's plan from the creation was for man to relate to himself and others as the basis for fullness. The apostle who was closest to the Lord, John, writes in his first epistle, John 1:3-4: "What we have seen and heard we proclaim to you also, that you also may have fellowship with us; and indeed our fellowship is with the Father, and with His Son Jesus Christ. And these things we write, so that our joy may be made complete."

When disappointments and loss occur over and over again in a person's life, or even once during a very traumatic event, a distrust in God and others may cause that person to enter into unbelief. That person may conclude, "If I'm ever going to get my needs met or keep from being hurt again, I'll have to live life my way because I can't trust others."

13

Once this core belief is established, others quickly fall into place until a trust in God's grace is abandoned for a take-charge attitude of, "I'll do it myself," and an attitude of idolatry that trusts in something or someone other than God.

The search for meaning and fulfillment, or for a quick fix to eliminate the pain, can take varied forms of expression. Some people turn to drugs, work, food, gambling, or unhealthy entertainment until finally the chosen idol becomes a raging, controlling god that demands allegiance to the point of total loss, destruction, and even death.

Sex is one of the most powerful drugs that one searches for to find a relationship. Even though our sexuality is a gift, used outside of God's intended design, the beauty of this gift becomes one of the ugliest and most distorted of all. Researchers have estimated that as many as ten percent of all Christians in the United States now have a sexual addiction (meaning they have reached the state of feeling without choice). Some people believe the number is higher. Still, the estimates are cause for alarm.

Even though the content of this book is designed to deal with the roots of all addictive and compulsive behaviors, I give many illustrations to focus on this particular need.

Through deep repentance from our unbelief in God's grace and through coming to know God intimately and passionately as our Father through Jesus Christ, we are able to expose the lies of Satan about God, ourselves, and life in general and to replace them with the truth. Surely we shall know the truth, and the truth will make us free.

Most of us probably remember being told as children that a pot of gold existed at the end of a rainbow. My own memory of this idea is still vivid; I ran many times through the cotton fields of our Texas family farm after a rain shower, searching breathlessly for an elusive golden treasure. Of course, this was only a childhood game, and the reality soon hit me that it was not possible to find gold at the end of a rainbow. Still, the belief in the possibility of instant riches was magical.

If we transfer this concept to looking for an instant solution to addictive behavior, we will understand the same sense of elusiveness; it will be just like looking for a pot of gold at the end of a rainbow.

Today, many people are still looking for the perfect person to come along and meet all their needs. Perhaps they are waiting for the perfect man to come along and protect them from further pain. Or the perfect woman to assuage their guilt. Unfortunately, the more we look to someone else other than our heavenly Father to meet our deepest longings, we will be hurt and disappointed. God has designed us to be in relationships, and some of our needs may be met through others. However, as David exclaimed in the

Psalms, "My expectations come from thee O God." We should appreciate that someone else can meet some of our needs. However, ultimately, we should trust our other needs to the heavenly Father.

Christ said that if we first seek his kingdom and his righteousness, then all these basic needs would be added to us. In this book, we will discuss some of the basic needs in a person's life. We will also explain that if we focus only on our needs, self-centeredness and lust will result. To focus on God's kingdom and purpose results in finding true happiness and fulfillment. Christ also stated that happiness and blessings would belong to those who hunger and thirst after righteousness, for they would be filled.

Some areas in a person's life need to be healed of wounds, losses, hurts, etc. We must, however, not confuse healing wounds with fulfilling needs. Note that Christ did not say that those who sought righteousness would be healed, but filled. The Lord does heal, and clearly, one of his purposes was to "heal the brokenhearted." But the Lord also fills our lives with his presence and has promised to give us life so that we might have it more abundantly.

Many destructive and addictive behaviors need to be replaced in righteous and healthy ways. This book will describe some of the characteristics behind our unhealthy behavior and how they can be replaced in relationship to Jesus Christ and the Christian community. Of course, the unhealthy behaviors must first be exposed and dismantled.

The apostle Paul describes this pattern in a letter to the Ephesians: "In reference to your former manner of life, you lay aside the old self which is being corrupted in accordance with lusts of deceit, and that you be renewed in the spirit of your mind, and put on the new self, which in the likeness of God has been created in righteousness and holiness of the truth" (Eph. 4:22-24).

The hope of righteousness is not only righteousness itself, which is the result of Christ in us, but the promise that "we be filled." When the passion of our heart is Christ, our deepest longs will be satisfied. Once we are filled sufficiently, we will be able to give to others.

To many believers, this statement may seem like a wish that will never come true. The truth is, it is already true because Christ is in you and you are in Christ. Because of the lies we have believed and the behavioral patterns we are experiencing, we are caught in a cycle of deceit that needs to be interrupted and replaced. In the following chapters, we will examine this process and introduce illustrations of myself and others who have and who are experiencing a new freedom and liberty in Christ.

TWO

PASSIONS OUT OF CONTROL

"Please help me," Keith whispered in desperation. His face was drawn, and I could see tiredness written all over it. Keith slowly began sharing parts of his world that he had never fully shared before. He had shared some details with his wife, but he had never given even her enough information to realize the seriousness of what he was facing.

Outwardly, Keith appeared to be a very successful businessman. He had prospered financially, owned a beautiful home, and apparently enjoyed a wonderful family life. He was a professing Christian who was actively involved in a local church. What was disturbing Keith was the secret world of depravity, secrecy, and hypocrisy that he was now sharing with me. With concern, he began to unravel his story, fearfully wondering if I would expose him and what the consequences would be.

I told Keith that it would be necessary to take the right actions in order to bring wholeness and healing and genuine repentance to his life. As Keith shared from the depth of his being the story of his secret world, I became aware that though he appeared to be a very defeated person, he had developed a very successful life because of his passion and energy and creativity.

But as more details of his story unfolded, he told me that his creativity had almost become nullified. Procrastination was an everyday occurrence. His time was so unaccounted for that he no longer kept schedules, was often late, and missed deadlines. But more desperate than that, Keith had slipped into a world of withdrawal and isolation. His best friends had voiced concern that he was working too much or was under too much pressure.

Keith's story had a familiar sound, and I thought of many other people who have shared their stories with me. His story was similar to my own. Keith was a man of passion. Initially, he felt passion for Christ and his kingdom. His passion and love for his family and his desire to help others contributed to his success in life. But it was now obvious that Keith's passions had been redirected from the kingdom of God to his own selfish ambitions. His passions were out of control.

I told Keith that when our passions career out of control, it is part of a cycle. I explained the cycle of uncontrolled passions that I call addictive behavior. We discussed where this behavior begins and how it flings us into a vicious cycle of sin and death. Unless it is interrupted, unless it is replaced, and unless we get help, we may continue on a treadmill—the cycle of sin and death—that will ultimately bring destruction and devastation not only to ourselves but to those around us.

The apostle Paul talks of the cycle as "the law of the spirit of life in Jesus Christ [that] has set me free from the law of sin and death."

I asked Keith if he would allow me to share some insights on that cycle—one that I and many other people have gone through and couldn't break free of until we had some understanding of how the law of the spirit of life in Jesus Christ could set us free.

I saw hope begin to shine in Keith's eyes. I also saw reservation, because his was a pattern that had developed over a period of years. On many occasions he had tried, by his own willpower, to stop acting out certain behavior. Other times he made vows; he intended to see a professional counselor, but he failed to follow through out of fear of exposure.

I opened up my notebook to a blank sheet of paper and once again I said, "Keith, I'm not here to shame you and I'm certainly not here to embarrass you. I am here to help you. You may have to make some difficult decisions. If you will allow me, however, I'd like to walk you through this cycle that I am talking about and show you how our passions, our desires, and our deepest feelings can actually get so out of control that, though we were responsible for our choices originally, we may get to the point where we feel beyond choice. It seems to be described by Paul as he spoke to Timothy in 2 Timothy, chapter 1, when he speaks of those who have been taken captive by Satan to do Satan's will."

Then I asked Keith, "Do you ever feel that you are doing someone else's will? Do you ever feel like now you're so controlled that you almost have no choice? I'm not saying we're not responsible. We are responsible for our original choices. But Keith, are there times that you pray, you make vows that you'll never do this or that again, and it seems like the cycle just worsens?"

He nodded, looking a little surprised that I seemed to understand some of his deeper thoughts. An expression of hope began creeping over Keith's face as I drew on a sheet of paper the same chart that appears below. As I ex-

Overcoming Cycles of Shame and Addiction

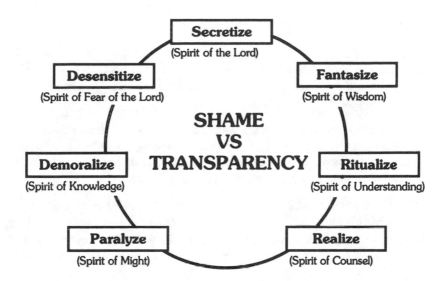

Intervening the Cycles of Shame and Addiction

THE LAW OF SIN AND DEATH
ROMANS 8:12

Secretize
Denial
1 John 1:8–10

Fantasize
Obsessed with thoughts
James 1:14

Ritualize
Establishing behavior patterns
2 Peter 2:12–14

Realize
The acts of sin
James 1:15

Paralyze
Powerless over the addiction
2 Timothy 2: 25–26

Demoralize
Lacks purpose, suicidal
Psalms 88

Desensitize
Seared conscience
1 Timothy 4:1–2

THE LAW OF THE SPIRIT OF LIFE
ISAIAH 11: 1–2

Spirit of the Lord
Convicts sin, righteousness, judgment
John 16:8

Spirit of Wisdom
Discerning the consequences of our actions

from an eternal perspective
Proverbs 1:20–33

Spirit of Understanding
Bringing to light how we behave
Ephesians 5:13

Spirit of Counsel
Knowing God's purpose and will for our life
1 Thess. 4:1–7, Romans 12:1–2

Spirit of Might
Demonstration of God's power
Romans 15:18–19, 1 Cor. 2:4–5

Spirit of Knowledge
Having an eternal perspective of life
2 Peter 1:1–11

Spirit of Fear of the Lord
Awareness of God's presence
Proverbs 16:6

plained the cycle, I painfully remembered my own story. If only I had understood. If only someone had told me about the cycle. Instead of staying in my own deceptive, secret world for so long, I could have been filled with hope much sooner.

The first stage: secretize

I call the first stage *secretize*, though it's really about denial. Anyone who is in a lifestyle of addictive behavior– where it feels that they are out of control–often began by secretizing their needs, their life, or part of their world. This is explained in 1 John 1:8-10.

> If we say that we have no sin, we are deceiving ourselves and the truth is not in us. If we confess our sins, He is faithful and righteous to forgive us our sins and to cleanse us from all unrighteousness. If we say that we have not sinned, we make Him a liar and His word is not in us.

Keith was not admitting to himself his own sin. Like me, he had compartmentalized his life. It was as though the things he did in his secret world that violated his conscience, God's will, and God's way were now contained in some kind of box. On Sundays, and when he was with his family, it was as though they did not exist. Occasionally a knock would come from inside the box of his conscience. But now he had so seared a part of his conscience and so compartmentalized his life that somehow he was able, in his deception and rationalization, to keep that part of his life from integrating with other parts.

Keith's secret world involved hours of pursuing pleasures. He explained how he had become involved in pornography: not all at once, but slowly, at first buying one magazine at a convenience store now and then. Ultimately, he developed an entire secret lifestyle that included not only pornographic bookstores, but acting out his impulses in other ways. It was a world that he was so ashamed of that he dared not share it with anyone, even his wife. This was not the only part of Keith's secret world. There were others.

This is fairly typical; people will often not experience real healing and wholeness and genuine repentance by simply dealing with the acts of their behavior. Deep down inside there are often other secret worlds: a world of shame and isolation; a world that has been hidden; and a world that has been defined in private understanding with lies and deceptions that fuel the wrong behavior.

As Keith talked, I knew there were other issues that were going to be very difficult for him to share. There was the loss of money, the risk, the fear of being exposed, the spent emotional energy, and the occasional misuse of his own expense account. His secret sins and secret world affected every part of his life. It was amazing that he could have kept such a secret and lived with so many unaccounted for hours. Lying had prevented others from discovering his real activity. It became obvious that Keith was deep into denial and deception.

I explained to Keith that when we fail to deal with our secret world, we continue living with the shame and guilt that brings about isolation, and the cycle will only continue to enlarge. Keith, in his desperation to begin breaking the cycle, asked if he could share one other experience with me. His face muscles tightened as he told me that an older cousin had sexually molested him several times when he was nine years old. He was unsure whether this event had anything to do with his present lifestyle and struggles.

Keith began to emphasize his masculinity after those encounters. He stole pornography and showed it to his classmates at school. He tried to become the macho idol of his peers by boasting of his sexual knowledge. In junior high school, he made up stories of his sexual conquests. He became obsessed with his own masculinity, or at least with the idea that others admire his masculinity. In reality, Keith was covering the secret world and shame of a broken heart, of a shamed masculine image, and of a wound that never healed.

The second stage: fantasize

The first stage of the cycle seemed to make sense to Keith, though I told him we can secretize our hidden shame, our hidden needs, and our hidden feelings for only so long. Sooner or later, what we have suppressed will lead to some kind of attachment. As I explained this, I wrote down the second word: *fantasize*. Often we will next take our secret needs and hidden world and fantasize about how we are going to begin meeting, expressing, covering, or living out our doubt and shame.

Up to this point, Keith and I had really not talked about needs. With tears in his eyes, he admitted that he had no close friends. Though he was publicly responsible for a number of people around him, and though they all seemed to like him, there was not one person among his associates whom he could really call a close friend.

I saw the pain grow on his face as he began to realize that he was now living out the needs, the feelings, and the hurts he had covered up for so many years. I explained that we fantasize because part of addictive behavior involves covering the pain and somehow medicating the shame we are carrying.

Even in the days of Noah, the Scripture says, "their thoughts and imaginations were only evil continually." Then I reminded Keith of the words, "Let no one say when he is tempted, 'I am being tempted by God'; for God cannot be tempted by evil, and He Himself does not tempt anyone. But each one is tempted when he is carried away and enticed by his own lust. When lust has conceived, it gives birth to sin; and when sin is accomplished, it brings forth death" (James 1:13-15).

I told Keith that lust is conceived in our imagination, which is the womb of our actions. Actions usually begin with fantasy, with perceiving, and with daydreaming about how we can meet our needs. The fantasy comes from different sources. It can come from something we read or saw in childhood. It can come from a movie, television program, or magazine. We amplify it to make it larger than life. It becomes more than just a picture in a magazine or a scene from a movie. It becomes a part of our thinking, and we continue to play it like a video script in our minds.

In the world of fantasy, people become obsessed with thoughts. Instead of being free to be creative, to think in positive ways that would encourage and build up others and bring success, much of the energy and creativity of our thinking process is directed toward how we can fulfill our own pleasure and cover the pain of our shame. Our secret world gains hold and the cycle becomes a wheel that is going to gain momentum unless it is interrupted.

Keith's concern increased as he realized that his world of fantasy now seemed beyond control. He was obsessed with his fantasies at his desk during working hours. Even with business associates, he seemed to be in a faraway dream world sometimes. Even more disturbing was that these obsessive thoughts would come into his mind during a church service, distracting him from the minister's message or from worship. Fantasizing and lusting after other women, even in a church service, jolted Keith into an awareness of the sickness and depravity he had slipped into. He was responsible for himself and his actions, but he was feeling out of control in his secret world.

Before I continued explaining the seven stages of the cycle, I felt it was important to give Keith this warning: "If we do not interrupt the world of our fantasy and know how to do that, we will live out our fantasy life. When lust has conceived, it will bring forth sin. Once we have put thoughts and fantasy into the womb of our imagination, it is often only a matter of time before they become reality."

The third stage: ritualize

Keith's concern was deepening, so I explained the third stage of the cycle: *ritualize*. At first Keith wasn't sure what I meant. Like a lot of people, he considered a ritual something akin to a church service, holiday, or an initiation event. I told him that in our passion to fulfill unhealthy behavior, we develop a ritual, or a sin pattern. This whole system of behavior guides not only our thoughts but our actions.

At the outset, the behavior is often not full blown in expression. Someone may, for example, drive past an adult theater and later go inside. Or he or she may go there but not fully participate in all that is offered there. I opened the Scriptures and read from 2 Peter 2:12.

> But these, like unreasoning animals, born as creatures of instinct to be captured and killed, reviling where they have no knowledge, will in the destruction of those creatures also be destroyed, suffering wrong as the wages of doing wrong. They count it a pleasure to revel in the daytime. They are stains and blemishes, reveling in their deceptions, as they carouse with you.

Verse 14 got Keith's full attention: "Having eyes of adultery and that never cease from sin; enticing unstable souls, having a heart trained in greed, a cursed children." I emphasized the word *trained* because all of us who have suffered from addictive behavior have trained ourselves. Our passions are out of control, but we have learned to control people, situations, and events for our own pleasure and satisfaction.

In the end, we develop a ritual and a system of behavior that continues carry to us headlong around a cycle that leads to sin and death.

I remember one minister who called me with sadness and concern in his voice. "Don, I was counseling a parishioner, a woman, and over a period of time, it just happened," meaning that they had become involved in an immoral way.

I then said, "I must encourage you to acknowledge something. What you are saying 'just happened' didn't just happen, and you can never be free until you assume full responsibility not only for the acting out of your immorality, but also for your system of behavior and the rituals that you developed."

The minister admitted that he had followed a system not only with this particular experience, but with others; over the last several years, he had had multiple affairs, and they all developed through the ritual of counseling someone. The person was usually a weaker person who expressed great admiration for him as a minister. The first counseling sessions would end with a quick embrace. During the next session, the woman would talk about how her husband did not meet her needs. That session would end with a longer embrace. Generally by the third or fourth session, the minister would admit that his wife failed to meet his needs, and they would show concern and compassion for each other with even longer hugs. After that, an expression of immorality took place in its fullest form.

I asked Keith about the rituals in his life. He had established certain patterns that obsessed him. He found himself going to the same places and frequenting the same bars. He had ritualized his behavior, but never understood how strongly he was being held in the grips of it. This was a revelation to him. He considered only the actual acting out to be sin.

As I began to show him, the natural concepts of hearing, talking, feeling, seeing, and tasting often become a part of our rituals and empower our unhealthy behavior. These rituals become a powerful part of the snare. That is, if those rituals represent certain moods, certain feelings, and certain actions, they are a part of the temptation. When lust has conceived, it brings forth sin.

The fourth stage: realize

I wrote down the next part of the cycle: *realize*. "Keith," I said, "many people have lived a long time in the world of secrecy and fantasy. But sooner or later they will go further. Some people may go through this whole cycle in a very brief time—within a month or a few months. It make take others several years. But the consequences, whether slow or fast, are the same. Realizing is actually the acting out of our wrong behavior. I'm going to call it the acts of sin."

"You see, it isn't just the acting out that is sinful. So is the system that is behind the behavior. In reality it is a lie that we have believed, the lie that God is not able to meet our deepest longings. The lie that somehow the world owes us something. The lie that it can never be better. The lie that if I'm ever going to be happy, I'm going to have to be my own God. The lie that whatever my acting out is, as long as no one else knows it, it isn't going to hurt anyone else. Or as long as I can keep it secret, it will have no consequences. In reality, we are believing the very same lies that Satan shared with Eve in the garden."

Keith looked at me in anguish as he acknowledged the cycle he had languished in without realizing its full devastation. He admitted, "You know, even in my acting out there are times when I realize how damaging it could be, but it seems like the power that now holds me is so strong that I almost can't do anything about it. There are times when I even try to pray, but I feel so much in bondage. I make vows to stop. Sometimes I even go a period of time to prove that I have control. But I only succumb to it again and again."

"In other words," I said, "you feel paralyzed. It's as though now you're held by the cords of your sin as the Scriptures explain."

We didn't have to spend very much time on Keith's acting out. It wasn't necessary for me to know or to understand all the details of his behavior, but it was important for him to understand the ritual. I knew that in time it would be important for him to share with someone, specifically his wife, his systems of behavior so that they could begin to unravel them.

The fifth stage: paralyze

Keith understood the fifth stage of the cycle more clearly: *paralyze*. "Keith," I explained, "the Scriptures tell us we will be held by the cords of our sin. There are actually three cords that hold us." I wrote down the names on the paper as I explained them. "The first cord I'm going to call a psychological cord. By that I mean that when we have unmet emotional and social needs that were never fulfilled or are not being fulfilled in a legitimate way, what we often do is attempt to meet those needs in an illegitimate way. You see, we all have basic needs for our sense of being, of value, our need for belonging in relationships, our need for accomplishment, and purpose. This would parallel our being created in God's image, God's likeness, and God's dominion. The needs that God has allowed us to have are legitimate. But how we fulfill them may become illegitimate or wrong."

When we have unmet emotional and social needs, they may have been sabotaged as early as childhood. I'm not saying this to give you permission to blame someone. We can assume responsibility, release the past, forgive those who have offended us, and get on with our lives. But when these emotional needs are sabotaged, we may suppress them at first, and the suppression may take place over several years. We simply continue to live between secrecy and fantasy. We don't live out the fantasies until ultimately we attach these unmet needs to something or someone through ritualizing the fantasy. Once we do, there is a psychological bonding in which the unmet need, the illegitimate behavior, and the sin pattern become cemented together; we believe that this is the *only* way the need will ever be met.

The second cord of sin, I told Keith, is physiological. Those who have an understanding of science and medicine know that certain chemicals are released in the brain and an actual strand is developed that registers pleasure with our behavior. Once that takes place over a period of time, the scenes and sights and memories of a temptation are registered simply by looking, feeling, seeing, or thinking about something. The acting out is only part of the temptation; we crave the entire high—euphoric feelings that release chemicals in our brain. Now the addiction is no longer simply a psychological need, but a physiological one too.

The third cord is spiritual. By that I mean there are negative spiritual forces at work; there seems to be a demonization of the process. I have talked to so many people who have been held in the bondage of sin and who could not explain uncanny situations and circumstances any other way than to say that some diabolical power was at play. I am cautious of addressing this concept lest someone think I am saying, "The devil made me do it." The truth is, there is a diabolical scheme to destroy, and the demonization of one's heart and mind may well be a part of the pattern that thrusts one further into the strongholds of the enemy Satan.

As I explained these cords to Keith, he realized that he too felt paralyzed even after making vows, praying, seeking, and promising that he would never participate in certain behaviors again. It was as though he was stuck in quicksand, sinking deeper and deeper into the quagmire of addictive behavior. This is what the apostle Paul explained in 2 Timothy 2:24-26.

25

And the Lord's bondservant must not be quarrelsome, but be kind to all, able to teach, patient when wronged, with gentleness correcting those who are in opposition; if perhaps God may grant them repentance leading to the knowledge of the truth, and they may come to their senses and escape from the snare of the devil, having been held captive by him to do his will.

I didn't have to say any more. I knew that Keith felt paralyzed. I knew that he understood, to some degree, what I was saying about the cords of sin. The more I shared, the more I felt some of the pangs of my past. Though I knew I was walking in the grace of God, and that there had been that wonderful deliverance, recovery, and restoration, still the memory of my deception and the pain of those I had hurt occasionally surfaces. How vicious and deceptive the cycle of sin really is.

The sixth stage: demoralize

We progressed to the sixth stage of the cycle: *demoralize.* "Keith, by demoralize I mean that we began to lack purpose. We may even become suicidal. Life will begin to look hopeless. In fact, we may question if there even is a God. Why doesn't he deliver us? We may cry out for help. Our paralyzed world takes on new dimension as schedules are missed and commitments are not kept. We begin to discover that not only are we driven by our self-centeredness and selfish ambition, but we start feeling beyond choice and we wonder, in our state of paralysis, how God could ever use us again."

In fact, we may feel so demoralized and hypocritical that we fear even singing in church would represent a show of hypocrisy. We have had one main goal until it has become all-consuming, and that is to fulfill our selfish desires. We see no further purpose in life. Clearly our passions are out of control and are now controlling us. We may even hear a minister or a well-meaning Christian remind us that we should first seek the kingdom of God and his righteousness, but we have no idea how to begin to do that.

Many men and women have explained to me that, as they have reached this part of the cycle, they feel as far from God as they have ever felt in their lives. They no longer feel a desire to pray. They have absolutely no interest in or hunger for the word of God. Only occasionally does the spirit of God seem to interrupt. Otherwise, they exist in a world of hopelessness and despair.

At this point I read Keith some Scripture and I said, "I really do understand how you are thinking. There were times when I thought the only way out was suicide. And though I was too afraid to commit suicide, knowing the eternal consequences, I certainly wished that my life would hurry up and rush by and the pain and the degradation would end. I would often hope that maybe God would just allow me to have a wreck—that somehow he would take me out of my misery and pain. Though there's pleasure in sin for a season, the consequences and the guilt and shame finally take their toll." I read an entire chapter to Keith at this point. I knew that it would more fully reflect how he felt.

Oh Lord, the God of my salvation, I have cried out by day and in the night before You. Let my prayer come before you; incline Your ear to my cry! For my soul has had enough troubles, and my life has drawn near to Sheol.

I am reckoned among those who go down to the pit; I have become like a man without strength, forsaken among the dead, like the slain who lie in the grave, whom Thou dost remember no more, and they are cut off from Your hand. You have put me in the lowest pit, in dark places, in the depths. Your wrath has rested upon me, and you have afflicted me with all your waves. You have removed my acquaintances far from me; you have made me an object of loathing to them; I am shut up and cannot go out. My eye has wasted away because of affliction; I have called upon you everyday, oh Lord; I have spread out my hands to you.

Will You perform wonders for the dead? Will the departed spirits rise and praise You? Will Your lovingkindness be declared in the grave, Your faithfulness in the place of destruction? Will Your wonders be made known in the darkness? And Your righteousness in the land of forgetfulness?

But I, O Lord, have cried out to You for help, and in the morning my prayer comes before You. O Lord, why do You reject my soul? Why do You hide Your face from me? I was afflicted and about to die from my youth on; I suffer Your terrors; I am overcome. Your burning anger has passed over me; Your terrors have destroyed me. They have surrounded me like water all day long; they have encompassed me all together. You have removed lover and friend far from me; my acquaintances are in darkness (Psalm 88).

The seventh stage: desensitize

The final stage of the cycle, becoming *desensitized*, occurs when our conscience becomes seared. Paul says clearly in 1 Timothy 4:1-2, "But the spirit explicitly says in later times some will fall away from the faith, paying attention to deceitful spirits and doctrines of demons, by means of the hypocrisy of liars, seared in their own conscience as with a branding iron." Whatever our sin patterns, our behavior results in guilt and shame. But we have not been designed to live with guilt and shame. Either we will sear our conscience or we will change the way we believe about God; that is, we will adjust our theology.

Somehow we try to readjust our theology to our lifestyle, resulting in desensitizing our conscience or justifying our lifestyle. We begin to compare ourselves with others. It is revealing that many people in sinful lifestyles will focus on how wrong something else is because it is more *socially* unacceptable. This is another way we desensitize our conscience and try to justify our own behavior.

I knew that Keith had some degree of understanding of the vicious cycle of sin and death. In fact, he said to me, "Don, this is where I am," as he pointed to the last stage.

I explained to Keith that if we do not interrupt the cycle and make a change, we will continue in our isolation, our secrecy, and our addictive behavior. We may at this point attach to other behaviors and try to fulfill the insatiable needs of our deceitful hearts. But the cycle will continue unless precise steps are taken and the grace of God intervenes.

At this point, Keith was ready for change. "Keith," I said, "I'm not trying to give you a quick formula. I am going to give you several steps, amplifying each one, that I believe will make a difference and set you free. It is only in Jesus Christ that we can be free. I am not talking about a quick fix, but rather a process. Are you willing to begin taking these steps?" With intense desperation, Keith whispered, "Don, I have come for help. Please help me! I want to do whatever it takes."

We moved on to the task of outlining and amplifying the steps he would, with the grace of God, need to take to allow the Spirit to intervene.

Study questions

1.) How long have you been stuck in the cycle of addiction—or at least, when did you become aware that you could not break out of it?

2.) What activities do your secret world consist of now? When are you most likely to pursue those activities?

3.) What are the recurring fantasies that you play over and over in your mind to cover the pain of your addictive behavior?

4.) Write down the rituals in your life that obsess you, including your actions as well as your thoughts.

5.) How do you act out your unhealthy thoughts and fantasies?

6.) How do you use the three cords of sin—psychological, physiological, and spiritual—to satisfy your unmet emotional needs?

7.) Are you beginning to break commitments? Miss appointments? Do you have any interest in the word of God? How else has your paralyzed world begun to feel like it is caving in on you?

8.) How have you tried to readjust your theology to your lifestyle to justify your behavior?

THREE

ALLOWING THE SPIRIT TO INTERVENE

Keith was beginning to express hope. His voice conveyed a new sense of life and anticipation. I stressed that this was a process and a journey that would take time—it was no quick fix—and that the vicious cycle of sin and death could be broken if he faithfully applied the word of God to his life.

I opened the Scriptures and read to Keith these words from Romans 8:1-2: "There is therefore now no condemnation for those who are in Christ Jesus. For the law of the Spirit of life in Christ Jesus has set you free from the law of sin and of death."

"Keith," I said, "the law of sin and death that you have been in, the cycle of unhealthy patterns, can only be broken by the Holy Spirit. I began to understand this process by looking back at my own journey out of the vicious cycle of sin and death. I discovered how the Holy Spirit really had helped me in this process."

In order to see how the Spirit of life lifts us out of the vicious cycle of sin and death, it is important that we understand the fullness of the expression of the son of God. Isaiah the prophet explains this.

> Then a shoot will spring from the stem of Jesse, and a branch from his roots will bear fruit. And the spirit of the Lord will rest on Him, the spirit of wisdom and understanding, the spirit of counsel and strength, the spirit of knowledge and the fear of the Lord. And He will delight in the fear of the Lord, and He will not judge by what His eyes see, nor make a decision by what His ears hear; but with righteousness He will judge the poor, and decide with fairness for the afflicted of the earth; and He will strike the earth with the rod of His mouth, and with the breath of His lips He will slay the wicked. Also righteousness will be the belt about His loins, and faithfulness the belt about His waist (Isa. 11:1-5).

As I read these words, it became clear to me that the wicked and wicked ways are dealt with by the sevenfold expression of the Spirit of the living God: The Spirit of the Lord; the Spirit of wisdom; the Spirit of understanding; the Spirit of counsel; the Spirit of strength; the Spirit of knowledge; and the Spirit of fear of the Lord. Through this Spirit we experience righteousness about our waist as we walk in his ways.

I explained to Keith how each expression of the Spirit of the living God interrupts one of the stages in the cycle of our addictive behavior. I should emphasize again that unless *every* stage of unhealthy and addictive behavior is interrupted, the possibility of relapse can take place at any point.

Keith and I reviewed the cycle of sin and death: secretize, fantasize, ritualize, realize, paralyze, demoralize, and desensitize. I showed him how we could parallel the sevenfold expression of God, as seen in Isaiah 11, with the cycle of addiction, and how amazingly the Spirit of the Lord interrupts each stage. This is the process:

The Spirit of the Lord intervenes at the secrecy stage

The first expression is the Spirit of the Lord. It is important to remember that the first work of the Holy Spirit was to convict. Jesus said this about the Holy Spirit:

> And He, when He comes, will convict the world concerning sin, and righteousness, and judgment; concerning sin, because they do not believe in Me; concerning righteousness, because I go to the Father and you no longer behold me; and concerning judgment, because the ruler of this world has been judged. I have many more things to say to you, but you cannot bear them now. But when He, the Spirit of truth, comes, He will guide you into all truth; for He will not speak on His own initiative, but whatever He hears, He will speak; and he will disclose to you what is to come (John 16:8-13).

In other words, the Holy Spirit brings to light all hidden areas of darkness. When Jesus entered the temple, one of the first things he did was cleanse it. When he entered a group in which hypocrisy was prevalent, he exposed the secrets of the hearts of men.

I explained to Keith that in order for us to enjoy freedom, we must break the denial of our secret lives. This may come about in different ways. For some people, it happens after they are arrested for criminal activity.

I remember speaking to one person whom I'll call Earl. Earl had been a prominent minister in a small town. One Monday morning the police showed up at his house and told him he was under arrest because of his sexual activity with an underage member of his congregation. This was a secret world no one knew about except Earl and the girl.

I could feel the pain of Earl's exposure. I could sense the horror of his secret world being brought to light. When I asked Earl how he felt, he said, "Relieved!" I understood those feelings too. It's a relief that gives us the hope that our secret world is over. We can now move on to dealing with the guilt and shame. This played a tremendous part in Earl's recovery. As he discovered, recovery *is* an ongoing process.

Another way our secret world may be brought to light is through unexpected exposure. I remember a man named Lynn, who told me how one of his letters to a lover, a married woman, had been intercepted by a friend of that woman. The situation was brought to the attention of Lynn's local church leadership, and the affair no longer remained a secret.

Illness can break our secret world too. By experiencing stress and strain or a brush with death, we may gain a new perspective on eternity and what has real value in our lives. We may feel a renewed appreciation for the deep love of our family and those closest to us.

Financial difficulty can provide the same type of wake-up call. After spending money in a secret world or mishandling our finances, we may be brought to a place of repentance by means of financial pressure. I have seen people brought to the edge of despair simply by the realization that the road they were on was a costly, dead-end street. They know life can be better. The pleasure of sin lasts only for a season; afterward, there is despair and tribulation.

The same holds true for marital difficulties, which can also splinter our secret world. When we realize how much we really do love our spouse and children, the risk of exposure and the resulting devastation comes into greater focus. Finally, we can confess our sins—the best way to recognize and apologize for our state of denial.

Exposure can take many forms. It's important to remember that God has allowed our sins to be exposed. Even though the attitude or intent of the person or persons who exposed us may be wrongful, God has allowed the exposure to take place to initiate our recovery.

Keith's secret world was exposed through financial and marital problems that brought him to his knees. He too needed to understand that his problems were really the result of God's mercy and judgment—to enable him to seek repentance, wholeness, and healing. Until Keith saw this, he felt only despair.

One very strong caution about exposure: Do not confuse the enormous relief of "coming out" with a sense of wholeness. Exposure is only part of the process of restoration, not the entire thing. To stop at this juncture would place you in great danger. There is a road to be traveled and a journey to be experienced. As we are filled with the Holy Spirit, we must allow him to expose and work through every aspect of our addiction. We need him to lift us out of the hole, not simply point to it.

Establishing a new pattern: Each stage in the cycle of addiction needs to be interrupted and replaced with a new pattern of response and behavior. The pattern of secrecy must be replaced with a new honesty and openness. This will involve sharing with your spouse, a close friend, or a spiritual leader and joining a small support group for accountability. Since the world of addiction is also a world of dishonesty and lies, you must allow those around you to confront you on your secretiveness and dishonesty.

The Spirit of wisdom intervenes at the fantasy stage

People may spend years in a secret world fantasizing about how they can meet their needs, or how they can live out secret fantasies they have read or heard about. Even though they may fluctuate between the first two stages for a period of years, we know it's only a matter of time until they go further; the Scripture says "when lust has conceived, it brings forth sin."

Fantasies occur when the imagination begins to visualize how we can meet our needs. The danger is, if we let our fantasies continue as a basis for hanging on to what we think is pleasure, it will be only a matter of time before we find ourselves back in the vicious cycle of sin and death—back in the same rut that led us into destruction.

How do we interrupt the pattern of fantasy? If it is the Spirit of the Lord that exposes our sin, and if exposure brings judgment upon our secret world, then it is the Spirit of wisdom by which we discern the consequences of our actions from an eternal perspective. Hear what Proverbs 1:20-33 says:

> Wisdom shouts in the street, She lifts her voice in the square; at the head of the noisy streets she cries out; at the entrance of the gates in the city, she utters her sayings: How long, O naive ones, will you love simplicity? And scoffers delight themselves in scoffing, and fools hate knowledge? Turn to my reproof, behold, I will pour out my spirit on you; I will make my words known to you, because I called and you refused; I stretched out my hand, and no one paid attention; and you neglected all my counsel, and did not want my reproof; I will even laugh at your calamity; I will mock when your dread comes, when your dread comes like a storm, and your calamity comes on like a whirlwind, when distress and anguish come on you. Then they will call on me, but I will not answer; they will seek me diligently, but they shall not find me, because they hated knowledge, and did not choose the fear of the Lord. They would not accept my counsel, they spurned all my reproof. So they shall eat of the fruit of their own way, and be satiated with their own devices. For the waywardness of the naive shall kill them, and the complacency of fools shall destroy them. But he who listens to me shall live securely, and shall be at ease from the dread of evil.

To spurn the wisdom of God, then, is to spurn life and to refuse God's way.

Keith was listening with interest. I asked him this question: "Keith, when you were in your obsessive and addictive behavior, did you ever visualize or consider the consequences?" Keith admitted that he did occasionally, but quickly blocked them out. I explained to him that when people fantasize, they do so foolishly, and God warns of how these events of calamity will come upon us. If we do not interrupt our fantasy, it is only a matter of time before we live it out. I could see Keith was confused, so I talked about the Spirit of wisdom using a personal example.

One evening, while driving home from a speaking engagement, I felt deeply disappointed and disillusioned because of the response of the leader of the congregation to some of my needs. I must admit that my reason for speaking there was not the best. I had a bill that was due, so I accepted the invitation primarily for financial reasons.

I had driven almost all night on my way there to save money on their behalf, and I spoke for several evenings. There seemed to be a tremendous response from members of the congregation. Each night, a love offering was taken. However, when I received the check, it was barely enough to cover my expenses. I thanked the pastor halfheartedly and left.

My motivation for accepting the invitation was wrong, but I still felt anger well up inside of me. I was disappointed not only with the pastor, but with the Lord. I remember saying, "But Lord, you have said that you would provide for my needs." It was interesting for me to see how this was a pattern of how I dealt with disappointments.

Disappointments tend to be triggers in my life. By triggers, I mean certain feelings and attitudes that may cause us to respond to a situation with old behaviors. I told Keith that we all have triggers.

Still, that night as I left the congregation, I began to fantasize about behavior from my past. I knew that I was approaching a large city. I also knew that I had used some forms of pornography as pain killers. I began visualizing the possibility of using this old form of medication, of again acting out my rebellion toward the Lord. And even though deep in my spirit I despised my old behavior, in my flesh and carnal mind, the power of the draw seemed to be overwhelming.

I thought about some of the pornographic experiences I'd had in the past—certain scenes and sights that had offered some degree of relief and pleasure that I thought would fix me. It was like sticking a needle in my arm and shooting up with drugs. I experienced a high, a form of medication that erased my pain and disappointment.

Realizing that I was facing life and death choices, I cried out to God, admitting my own powerlessness. I needed his grace desperately. I had to rely upon him because there was no strength within me.

That's when a most amazing thing happened. While I was driving, approaching that big city where I knew unhealthy opportunities would be available, it was as though the Holy Spirit had placed in my mind a very vivid picture I will never forget. It was of three large scorpions. It was as though the Holy Spirit whispered into my heart that if I went to a certain place in this city I would die.

Just as quickly another picture came to my mind. This time it was a picture of me ministering to a multitude of people. There was great joy upon their faces. Many people were being set free. Again the Holy Spirit seemed to whisper into my heart, "If you will overcome this temptation, if you will receive my promise, if you will walk in my way, and rely upon my strength, your joy will not be the temporary pleasure of acting out sinful behavior, but the joy of the Lord in giving an answer and seeing people set free. You will minister to multitudes about my delivering and saving grace."

It didn't take me very long to decide what to do about my fantasy. Once I had the revelation of God's purpose in my spirit, I made a decision based upon God's way and God's word. I bypassed the city, with all its sinful and rebellious temptations.

Since then, whenever I experience fantasies that are overwhelming, I simply bring them to the Lord and expose them to the light. I cry unto the Lord for his grace so that I can see the reality of my fantasies and the destructive power that rests behind them.

God always promises blessings to those who overcome. Faith is believing that God exists and that he rewards those who seek him. And the rewards are always bountiful and eternal. If we do not allow the Holy Spirit to intervene in our fantasy life, we will discover that it is very difficult to abort wrong actions and impossible to reap the rewards.

One of the reasons Keith sought my counsel was because of the exposure of his own sin patterns. It seemed like a good time to ask him this question: "Keith, when you were fantasizing that sin pattern and when you made the decision in your heart and mind to participate in the activity that has brought you to the edge of destruction, did you ever consider the possibility that you would be found out?"

"Oh, no," he said. "I only thought that if I never got caught, if no one knew about this activity, then it couldn't hurt anyone else." It was obvious that Keith did not understand the full spiritual and emotional consequences of his activities.

I asked Keith another question. "Have you ever considered viewing the end results of your fantasy before acting it out?" I knew that Keith's heart was aching for God's best, and we both prayed together for the Holy Spirit to give him wisdom in seeing not only the consequences of his behavior, but the blessings that could be his through overcoming.

Establishing a new pattern: Since our fantasy world is so powerful in activating actions, we must cleanse harmful and destructive fantasies from our minds. This may be done through asking the Holy Spirit to purify our hearts with his word. Also, any harmful materials, such as pornography, should be thrown away. We should begin hiding the word of God in our hearts and minds. We must also begin to look at people as instruments and recipients of God's love, not as objects to be used and taken advantage of. By generalizing people, we see them in their totality; a woman can be a daughter, a wife, a mother, and a person of value. By sexualizing people, we focus only on parts of their body and devalue them as people.

The Spirit of understanding intervenes at the ritual stage

Once we have ritualized, we have established certain behavioral patterns. I explained to Keith about ritualizing and how by the Spirit of understanding this pattern is interrupted. This Spirit of understanding brings to light how we have behaved and requires understanding of our systems of behavior. The Scripture tells us that with wisdom, we get understanding. The apostle Paul says in Ephesians 5:13: "But all things become visible when they are exposed by the light, for everything that becomes visible is light."

There's tremendous power, I told Keith, whenever we begin to expose our systems of behavior. There's something about bringing to light our patterns of wrong behavior that disempowers those systems.

We all have rituals. And part of our behavior is rooted in the high that comes from getting there; it's as important as the actual act.

One illustration I use is that when I drive by a bar or a lounge, I am not tempted in any way. Now, I am not saying that to be boastful. There are other things that tempt me, but the presence or use of tobacco and alcohol do not. When I was a young child, a friend offered me a cigarette and I tried to smoke it. In doing so, I inhaled all the smoke and then blew it out. I almost coughed to death. Later I was introduced to a cigar. It had even greater damaging effects. When I tried to drink liquor, I tried to be manly and drink as much as possible, and I thought I would burn up. Probably the last substance I was introduced to was chewing tobacco. I saw men chew tobacco and spit it out. I thought you swallowed some and what you couldn't swallow you spit out. Operating on that theory, I almost died. To this day I have no desire for alcoholic beverages, for smoking, or for any kind of tobacco. Again, I'm not boasting of my own restraint. It's just that those substances touch off memories of pain and distaste.

In understanding our rituals, or our patterns of acting out, it is important that we understand the role of our natural senses. There are five natural senses: touching, seeing, hearing, tasting, and smelling. The first three are the most powerful. The Scripture says that Lot vexed his soul with all that he saw and heard. Vexed means tormented. That was a feeling. Once we've allowed certain scenes and sights and feelings and words to remind us of a certain mood, it's not long until we find ourselves in that mood. If we were assembled in the dark listening to a Christmas tune and the snowflakes were falling, and if you did not have too many other things on your mind, you could probably get into a nostalgic mood of Christmas fairly quickly.

The same is true of our rituals. When we establish sin patterns, they are not simply the end result of acting out. Part of the high, the euphoric feeling that establishes the pattern, comes from the natural senses generating certain moods within us. If you are visually oriented, certain scenes may turn you on. For some people, the high starts through words or music. For others, it may be feelings of anxiety, disappointment, or anger. Any of the natural senses can trigger this high—the euphoric feeling that reminds us of how we have previously acted out to meet our needs or to cover our pain and medicate our feelings. This is what rituals are about.

Although participating in a behavioral pattern gives us a feeling that all is well, and although we may feel better about ourselves while we are experiencing it, these feelings are false. The end result is devastation and despair.

The ritual itself can take many forms. It may be cruising the streets looking for sexual opportunities. It may be driving to the grocery store to buy chocolates or candies. It may be flying into a rage to keep from facing reality. It may be going on a shopping spree to try to cover feelings of inadequacy.

People who have unhealthy behavioral patterns and systems will discover, if they are willing to look, that they have natural senses that aggravate, emphasize, remind them of, and help create that certain mood that is part of the high they are after. I told Keith that before this happens, it is very important to ask the Lord for the Spirit of understanding so that we can begin to understand how our behavior and our rituals are part of our unhealthy lifestyle.

I'm reminded again of the minister I talked about in the previous chapter, the one who characterized his current affair as having "just happened." He later admitted that it was actually just the most recent of many affairs, all of which had started through the ritual of counseling. He was able to identify and admit to the behaviors that usually led to the affairs.

I explained to Keith that when we expose our pattern to the light—even confess it to a trusted Christian confidante—the pattern begins to lose its power. No longer is the pattern mystical and unknown. Once we let in the light of the Holy Spirit, the Spirit of understanding, we can see our pattern, and we're able to start dismantling our behavior.

I have discovered that people who are willing to expose, understand, and even confess their behavioral patterns to their spouse and to others find tremendous power to replace those patterns with better ones.

I further explained to Keith, "If we don't break the pattern of ritualizing, if we don't have the Holy Spirit to intervene in our fantasies and our rituals, we will never be free. There are those who, though they may have broken out of their addictive behavior, and though they may not be acting out, will continue the fantasy, even going to the edge in their ritual and their patterns without completing their acts. The ritual is still a part of the high. It is like putting the needle in the arm and taking a smaller dose of the drug."

Establishing a new pattern: The first step in dealing with a ritual or pattern of behavior is to expose it to someone. Writing out the ritual and reading it to a safe support group has proven to be of great value. However, it is not enough to simply expose the ritual. New boundaries, with accountability, must be established.

The Spirit of counsel intervenes at the realization stage

The next stage in the cycle is realization. This is the stage characterized by Scripture as "when lust has conceived it brings forth sin." It's the actual acting out, and it's interrupted by the Spirit of counsel.

Many people have told me that as they've come out of destructive behavior and lifestyles, one of the proofs of God's grace that often surprised and overwhelmed them was that at the very point of acting out, the still, small voice of God would speak to them in their hearts and ask, "Is this the reason I have created you? This is not my purpose for you. This is not what I have planned for your life." There always seems to be that counsel of the Lord that keeps reminding us even in our pit of sin that this is not God's purpose for us. The love of God is as deep, it seems, as our own pits of behavior. And though we're in that place of judgment because of our own acts, the love of God seems always to flow—the grace of God always seems to be drawing us unto himself.

The Spirit of counsel, then, is simply this: to have a clear sense of God's purpose and will for our lives. Unless we have a sense of clarity, we will find it difficult to walk in faith. We will lack the power and motivation to do so. The Scripture says "the just shall live by faith." The writer of Hebrews tells us that faith is believing that God rewards those who seek him.

Part of the information we can glean from the roll call of faith in Hebrews 11 includes the information that the walk of faith was not only dependent on people believing that God exists; each person listed seemed to have had a call and a purpose in their life and knew that God was the rewarder of those who sought him. The apostle Peter says that we escape corruption in the world through the exceedingly great and precious promises of God. If we have a sense of God's purpose and will for our life, we are capable of counteracting our own corrupting behavior. Then we can walk in real freedom.

Isn't this what the Spirit of counsel, the fourth expression of the sevenfold Spirit of God, is? Paul says this:

> Finally then, brethren, we request and exhort you in the Lord Jesus that, as you received from us instruction as to how to walk and please God (just as you actually do walk), that you may excel still more. For you know what commandments we gave you by the authority of the Lord Jesus. For this is the will of God, your sanctification; that is, that you abstain from sexual immorality; that each of you know how to possess his own vessel in sanctification and honor, not in lustful passion, like the Gentiles who do not know God; and that no man transgress and defraud his brother in the matter because the Lord is the avenger in all these things, just as we also told you before and solemnly warned you. For God has not called us for the purpose of impurity, but in sanctification. Consequently, he who rejects this is not rejecting man but the God who gives His Holy Spirit to you (1 Thess. 4:1-7).

I have read this verse in the past, but somehow it never gripped me as it does now. I think the reason is because I have recently come to understand that when the Book of Proverbs speaks of sexuality and especially of sexual temptations, they are described in terms of water, streams, rivers, power, and strength. It is very interesting that these are synonymous terms used of the Holy Spirit in the New Testament. Not that our sexuality and our spirituality are the same, for they are distinctly different, but they are so interwoven and related to one another that for a person to be sexually addicted is to be spiritually bankrupt. To suffer from a sexual addiction is to be in spiritual adultery. So we must follow the will of God as the apostle Paul instructs:

> I urge you therefore, brethren, by the mercies of God, to present your bodies a living and holy sacrifice, acceptable to God, which is your spiritual service of worship. And do not be conformed to this world, but be transformed by the renewing of your mind, that you may prove what the will of God is, that which is good and acceptable and perfect (Rom. 12:2).

And so the Spirit of counsel also moves us to get God's approval before we seek it from ourselves or others. This Spirit will help free us from the reality of our own unhealthy behavior.

Establishing a new pattern: As we begin to consider God's call and purpose for our lives, the focus establishes a new way of looking at life. I have often asked people to share an experience of God's call in their lives, or what they believe God's purpose and ministry to be. The more we focus on God's promises, the greater our desire will be to escape our destructive patterns.

The Spirit of strength intervenes at the paralysis stage

By this time, Keith understood the road to recovery was a long one, but hope was surging in his heart, so we continued with the last three stages.

The fifth stage is about paralysis—the feeling of being powerless over our addiction, of having been taken captive by Satan to do his will. I think all of us have, at certain times in our life, felt paralyzed. At these times we feel powerless and as though we live in a mundane world.

However, those with addictive behaviors are people who believe that life should often be a high. Everything must feel euphoric. They do not understand that a high is not necessarily normal. When they feel defeated, they have the tendency to simply give in to obtaining a high in the best way they know how. I have found that at this point of feeling paralyzed, there are three lies that we are willing to believe.

The first lie is: If God doesn't meet my needs now, on my terms or in my way, then I cannot trust him. I will take control of the circumstances myself. The truth is that God is more concerned with our character, attitudes, and inner person than with instances of personal happiness. In fact, he may test us to bring us to maturity. (See James 2:2-4.)

The second lie that we believe is that if we make one mistake, experience temptation, or even begin the process of acting out our addiction, then it's proof that we are basically bad people—"I might as well finish the job; what's the use?" But the truth is, it is always beneficial to resist the devil and to immediately stop acting out. To continue will only bring further ruin and death. To humble ourselves and acknowledge our need for help will result in our receiving grace and power to overcome. (See James 4:6-10.)

The third lie is that if others make a mistake or disappoint us, it only proves that we can't trust them. They will only hurt or betray us again. The truth is that the circumstances of people, places, and things do not make us happy or unhappy. We choose our state by the way we view life. Our judgment of others is a reflection of how we see ourselves. (See Romans 2:1-3.)

As we interrupt our false core beliefs with truth, we need the Spirit of strength. The Spirit of strength is a demonstration of God's power. It is specifically when we feel powerless that we need to be aware of his power and his grace. God's grace, which is spoken of as the Spirit of grace, is that expression and power of the Holy Spirit that interrupts our behavior, that intervenes by meeting our needs in God's way. The apostle Paul gives us an example of relying on God's grace:

> I will not presume to speak of anything except what Christ has accomplished through me, resulting in the obedience of the Gentiles by word and deed, in the power of signs and wonders, in the power of the Spirit; so that

from Jerusalem around about as far as Illyricum I have fully preached the gospel of Christ (Rom. 15:18-19).

I remember an occasion in my life from some years ago when disappointment was surging through me after I had resigned from the ministry. Our bank account was gone. Our savings had evaporated. The old car I was driving was increasingly undependable. I'd been invited to speak in a small community, which meant that I would need to drive about 300 miles. I began my journey early one morning, and I was probably 50 miles into it when the snow began to fall heavily. It was then that I realized that I was going to have real difficulty in continuing the journey.

To add to the snowstorm, the car began to backfire, and black smoke started coming out of the exhaust. It barely made it to a service station before the care died. I had to call my wife and a friend to come get me. I was able to catch a flight to reach my destination, but the whole time I was there, I was worried and concerned about that old, broken-down car and the fact that I had no money to fix it or buy another one. I preached the Sunday service with great difficulty, having this concern and burden of transportation on my heart.

Afterward, as I ate lunch with a couple who had been praying for me, the man turned to me and said, "We had a very unusual experience driving over here today to hear you speak. We felt the Holy Spirit was moving us to give you a gift to buy a van." Now, I'm not even sure if they knew that I was looking for or shopping for a van. But I was overwhelmed at the goodness of God and thanked them for their sensitivity. Their gift was exactly the amount I needed to purchase a van with 47,000 miles on it—at a much lower price than it ordinarily sold for. Today, it has more than 230,000 miles on it and has required no major repairs whatsoever.

That was a point in my life when I was so down and discouraged that I felt paralyzed; it felt like nothing was going right. Then the Spirit of strength intervened.

There are many ways God may choose to intervene. It may be through a supernatural healing. It may be through communication from another person who gives us encouragement at the right time with just the right words. I have found that the Spirit of God intervenes any number of ways in our greatest time of need—not because we're more spiritual then, but because we're more needy. It is then that he will interrupt our feelings of paralysis, our feelings of discouragement, and our feelings of hopelessness. In his grace he interrupts with the Spirit of strength and shows himself strong.

Establishing a new pattern: Since a person who is depressed and feels a strong sense of hopelessness has difficulty experiencing the reality of God, sharing and reading about God's supernatural power provides hope. I have often asked people at this stage to share testimonies and illustrations of God's power and demonstrations of the Holy Spirit. By calling on people to remember evidences of God's power and grace, we begin to stir up the gift of God. Participation in praise services and prayer meetings that demonstrate God's presence is also very important.

The Spirit of knowledge intervenes at the demoralized stage

Keith and I talked next about feeling demoralized, the sixth stage in the cycle. We often feel like this when we lack purpose. We may even become suicidal—caught in the grip of wrong behavior with no way out. We simply despair of life and begin to give up.

At this point, the expression of the Spirit of God that will interrupt is the Spirit of knowledge. It means having an eternal perspective on life. I read to Keith words that the Lord spoke to Peter:

> Simon Peter, a bond-servant and apostle of Jesus Christ, to those who have received a faith of the same kind as ours, by the righteousness of our God and Savior, Jesus Christ: Grace and peace be multiplied to you in the knowledge of God and of Jesus our Lord; seeing that His divine power has granted to us everything pertaining to life and godliness, through the true knowledge of Him who called us by His own glory and excellence. For by these He has granted to us His precious and magnificent promises, in order that by them you might become partakers of the divine nature, having escaped the corruption that is in the world by lust. Now for this very reason also, applying all diligence, in your faith supply moral excellence, and in your moral excellence, knowledge; and in your knowledge, self-control; and in your self-control, perseverance; and in your perseverance, godliness; and in your godliness, brotherly kindness; and in your brotherly kindness, Christian love. For if these qualities are yours and are increasing, they render you neither useless nor unfruitful in the true knowledge of our Lord Jesus Christ. For he who lacks these qualities is blind or short-sighted, having forgotten his purification from his former sins. Therefore, brethren, be all the more diligent to make certain about His calling and choosing you; for as long as you practice these things, you will never stumble; for in this way the entrance into the eternal kingdom of our Lord and Savior Jesus Christ will be abundantly supplied to you (2 Peter 1:1-11).

As I had already explained to Keith, there are several attitudes that may trigger wrong behavior. These are likely to be attitudes or experiences of disappointment, anger, anxiety, loneliness, guilt, or shame. Whatever the experiences may be, if we do not know how to respond to them through God's perspective and God's grace, and if we do not have a sense of the knowledge of God, it is very easy to become demoralized. I told Keith about one of my experiences with feeling demoralized and how the Spirit of knowledge intervened.

My wife and I had faced a very difficult period after my resignation from the pastorate. It was as though our world had become a very silent, devastating wilderness. And during the next year or two, some acquaintances and friends simply did not know how to reach out to us. I would have despaired of life itself had I not understood the ways of God. For it was during that time that I felt the Holy Spirit led me to spend a special time with the Lord.

I was nearly consumed with the Scriptures day and night. I ate very little and spent much of my time praying. I would read a Psalm and then spend most of the day reading through one of the prophets of the Old Testament. The more I read, the more God began to show me his ways.

In the past, I had been almost intimidated by the prophets of the Old Testament. I had a very difficult time understanding some of the Old Testament and specifically with equating the heart of God with the heart of Jesus. To me, they had almost seemed like two different characters. But the more I read, the more I began to know God in a deeper way than I had ever known him before. And I saw that love was the basis of his judgment, firmness, and character.

God has established standards and disciplines and corrections because he loves us, not because he hates us. Through this realization, I also began to see some things about the ways of God regarding my own circumstances. And the more I read about the ways of God and discerned them by his Spirit, the more joy and comfort came to my own heart.

For example, I noticed that one of the ways God corrects his children is by allowing others to judge them, including his enemies. This was the reason Habakkuk was so concerned when he cried out to God; he was concerned that the Lord was allowing a nation more wicked than Israel to judge Israel. On other occasions, the Lord says that certain nations were his arm of indignation. Not that he approved of them, but he worked through them and used them in order to bring correction and judgment to his own people.

I saw in my reading that following a period of judgment, the Lord allowed a nation or a person to go through a period of exile. This wilderness experience was not intended to destroy them, but to bring their heart into obedience and to cleanse them from all idolatry. It is always in that wilderness experience that God seems closer than ever.

Afterward, there is a period of restoration. It is a time when God restores what was lost. It may not be a restoration of *exactly* what was lost, but it will be more in quality and quantity. As I began to see the ways of God, I began to feel a sense of renewed hope. To the degree that I had a sense of knowledge of God and what he was doing in those circumstances, I could interrupt the stage of feeling demoralized.

Isn't this what the Scripture tells us in the book of Romans? "And we know that God causes all things to work together for good to those who love God, to those who are the called according to His purpose" (Rom. 8:28). Interestingly, we often quote that passage and leave out the opening conjunction "and." The Scripture doesn't tell us simply that we know all things work together. Rather it tells us "and we know." That verse is preceded by verses 26 and 27: "And in the same way the Spirit also helps our weakness; for we do not know how to pray as we should, but the Spirit himself intercedes for us with groanings too deep for words; and He who searches the heart knows what the mind of the Spirit is, because He intercedes for the saints according to the will of God." *Then* it says, "And we know . . ."

You see, unless we have sense of the Spirit of knowledge and some discernment of what God is doing, we can end up in despair. This is the reason the Scripture tells us that Job saw the end of the Lord. Job had patience and endurance because he had a sense of the knowledge of God, of what God was doing, and of his purpose and will. James speaks about the very same thing when he says, "Brethren count it all joy when you fall into diverse temptations, knowing this. . . ." James does not ask us to "count it all joy" without having a sense of knowing something.

This important point reminds me of a man who sought counsel from me because he was suffering great distress over his relationship with an in-law. The more he tried to respond in a Christ-like way, the greater his despair became. "What do you believe God is teaching you?" I said. "What does God want you to learn and to develop through this difficult situation?" He said he didn't know, so I answered for him. "Until you have some sense of what God wants to do in and through this situation, it's going to be very difficult for you to count it all joy. I would encourage you to ask God for wisdom to give you understanding and knowledge regarding this circumstance so that he can complete in you that which he wants to."

I have found that I can deal with disappointments, irritations, and other difficulties more easily when I can figure out their purpose and learn from them. Without a Spirit of knowledge of God and his ways—without being able to have some sense of what God wants us to do and accomplish—it is very difficult to respond with great joy.

Daniel endured when he prayed because he knew the ways of God. He knew that Israel would be in captivity for seventy years. And when he prayed on a daily basis, facing Jerusalem, he prayed with faith because he knew the prophetic word of the Lord and the ways of God. This is the way to the Spirit of knowledge.

If we do not look at life's circumstances and situations with the Spirit of knowledge, we may spend a lifetime blaming others for our losses, feeling bitter about difficult situations, lacking trust in God, and distrusting others. If we can respond with this Spirit, even though others may respond to us in a way meant for evil, we can say, like Joseph, "They meant it for evil but God meant it for good." I am not suggesting that God causes everything; I am suggesting that he *works through* everything. When we possess that sense of knowledge, we will have a sense of joy and peace that transcends all understanding.

Establishing a new pattern: The more we know about the ways of God and have a knowledge of his purposes, the less we will despair and give up. To know God's ways is to have hope that when we repent and turn to him, He will turn ashes into beauty and restore the years the locusts have eaten. Knowing God and having a knowledge of his ways gives us a much larger perspective on life. This new pattern should involve emphasizing the eternal perspective of life. When we feel paralyzed and without hope, expression of genuine love in a small support group is necessary. Participating in physical activities and getting out of isolation is also important.

The Spirit of fear of the Lord intervenes at the desensitized stage
Keith and I were ready to discuss the seventh and last stage in the cycle, feeling desensitized. If we continue around the cycle, there will come a time when we will either have to change our concepts of God, reinterpret theology to fit us, or become desensitized in our conscience (which the Bible speaks of as having our conscience seared with a hot iron). We cannot live with guilt that stays unaddressed; it will only thrust us further into isolation and loneliness.

Isolation empowers addictive and sinful behavior. An addiction is really a search for a relationship. But ironically, the more we continue in this vicious cycle of sin and death, the greater our feeling of loneliness and our separation from God and others.

This last stage can be interrupted by the Spirit of fear of the Lord. It is the awareness of God's presence in every circumstance and in every situation, whether it be his presence of judgment or his presence of blessing. It is the awareness of the presence of authority and sovereignty. The writer of Proverbs says in Proverbs 16:6: "By lovingkindness and truth iniquity is atoned for, and by the fear of the Lord one keeps away from evil."

In the book of Exodus (20:20) we read: "And Moses said to the people, 'Do not be afraid; for God has come in order to test you, and in order that the fear of Him may remain with you, so that you may not sin.'" The fear of the Lord *is* the beginning of wisdom.

I explained this to Keith in very simple terms, and he certainly understood it. Then I told him a story from my own life. One day while I was driving, I noticed a flashing blue light behind me. I was being followed by a policeman.

My heart began to thump, and I looked at the speedometer. Relieved that I was not going past the speed limit, I pulled over to the side of the road. The officer explained that my license plate, from out of state, had expired. I had forgotten to renew it. So I was fined, and the next day I got my license renewed. Even now I can see that flashing blue light; it serves as a reminder to me of the presence of the law. The law can actually be the hand of God.

I asked Keith, "Have you ever noticed that in your own life there are, as I call them, special 'flashing lights' that God allows just to give you a warning of danger that is yet to come? In the case I just mentioned, if I had not renewed my license plate that week, it would have cost me an additional six hundred dollars for both of my vehicles. A new law that was being enacted beginning the following month required a special import tax for new vehicles. Looking back, I see my own irresponsibility, but also that God protected me from a greater hardship."

There are times in our lives that God will allow flashing blue lights. He will allow the arm of the law. He will allow certain circumstances and events to make us aware of his presence and to protect us from greater problems and greater failures later on down the road. The Bible calls our awareness of this the Spirit of the fear of the Lord—that awesome, reverential awareness that God is near.

Establishing a new pattern: Part of the behavior in an addictive person is that of risk taking. Sometimes the risk is a way of crying out for help. The more a person continues in the addictive cycle, the greater the risks he or she will take, thereby developing additional addictive behaviors. We must identify the risks we take and the consequences that will result from them, both in our own lives and the lives of those we love. It is also important to establish the relationship with God as the Father. The consequences of wrong behavior are not a result of God's hate or condemnation, but rather the loving discipline of the heavenly Father.

As we finished talking through the cycle, Keith asked, "But how do I apply this? How do I walk in this?"

I gave him the explanation of the apostle Paul. "Have you ever noticed that when Paul prayed for the church in Ephesus, this is exactly what he was praying for? And in the very same way that Paul prayed, you can also pray for this in your own life." Notice what Paul prays for in Ephesians 1:15-23:

> For this reason I, too, having heard of the faith in the Lord Jesus which exists among you, and your love for all the saints, do not cease giving thanks for you, while making mention of you in my prayers; that the God of our Lord Jesus Christ, the Father of glory, may give to you a spirit of wisdom and of revelation in the knowledge of Him. I pray that the eyes of your heart may be enlightened, so that you may know what is the hope of His calling, what are

the riches of the glory of His inheritance in the saints, and what is the surpassing greatness of His power toward us who believe. These are in accordance with the working of the strength of His might which He brought about in Christ, when He raised Him from the dead, and seated Him at His right hand in the heavenly places, far above all rule and authority and power and dominion, and every name that is named, not only in this age, but also in the one to come. And He put all things in subjection under His feet, and gave Him as head over all things to the church, which is His body, the fullness of Him who fills all in all.

"Keith, have you noticed the things that Paul prayed for parallel the sevenfold expression of the Spirit of God?" I showed him that in Isaiah, the prophet speaks of the Spirit of the Lord, of his glory and character; in Ephesians, Paul prays that we will have a revelation in the true knowledge of him. In Isaiah, the prophet speaks of the Spirit of wisdom; Paul prays in Ephesians 1 for the Spirit of wisdom. The prophet speaks of the Spirit of understanding; Paul prays for our understanding. The prophet Isaiah speaks of the Spirit of counsel; the apostle Paul prays that we may know the hope of his counsel. The prophet Isaiah speaks of the Spirit of strength; Paul prays that we may know the exceeding greatness of his power. Isaiah the prophet speaks of the Spirit of knowledge; Paul prays that we may know, or be able to comprehend. Isaiah the prophet speaks of the fear of the Lord; the apostle Paul tells us that he has put all things under his feet, which is an expression of Paul's awareness of God's sovereignty and authority, his reverential fear of who God is and his position.

"The same things can be interrupted in your life as you pray to be filled with the Holy Spirit," I told Keith. "What we are really talking about is asking God to fill you with his fullness." That is why Paul also prayed to "know the love of Christ, which surpasses knowledge that you may be filled up to all the fullness of God." "What," I asked Keith, "could be more full than the sevenfold expression of the Spirit of God?"

Keith bowed his head and together we prayed the same prayer that the apostle Paul prayed in Ephesians chapter 1. We asked that this would become a reality in Keith's life. I explained to Keith that when God interrupts and intervenes at these stages, it might not occur in exactly the same order as the cycle we discussed; it would occur according to his needs at the appropriate time.

As we prayed, it was with a sense of great anticipation and joy that Keith would break free of the vicious cycle of sin and death. There was also a strong sense and a presence of the Holy Spirit that comes from saying—and meaning—"Holy Spirit, I give you the freedom, and I will cooperate with you in your intervention and taking control of every area of my life." This is acknowledging Jesus as Lord.

I stressed to Keith that intervention takes time. Moreover, we must learn how to recognize unhealthy behavioral patterns and ultimately replace them with God's ways.

Study questions

1.) How can you cleanse yourself of a secret element of your addiction, just as Jesus did upon entering the temple?

2.) How has public exposure, illness, or financial or marital difficulties exposed your secret world?

3.) How can the Spirit of wisdom help you see the consequences of your unhealthy actions?

4.) Rituals lose their stronghold on our behavior when we share them with a trusted friend or adviser. Think about someone you can share your rituals with. What is holding you back from doing so?

5.) What is God's purpose and will for your life?

6.) Think about difficult times in your life when God's power and grace have been evident to you. How did his presence help you?

7.) How can you defeat feelings of disappointment, anger, anxiety, guilt, or shame with an eternal perspective on life?

8.) God's purpose is not always clear. Think about an unfortunate event in your life and how his presence protected you from greater problems in the future.

FOUR

RECOGNIZING UNHEALTHY BEHAVIORAL CHARACTERISTICS

How do we change old behaviors that are inconsistent with God's will and contrary to our Christian walk? Tina had asked this question of herself many times, but never seemed to get an answer. She had made inner resolves, promises, even vows, but always seemed to give in to her former behavior of excessive consumption of prescription drugs and eating binges. The internal decision process may, for some people, have value in changing behavior; however, at best, the change will probably last a few months, or maybe even a year or two. By internal process, I mean making an inward commitment to our conscience to behave and act differently.

Unlike Tina, Mark had not made any inner resolves or promises to himself to change his addictive use of drugs and alcohol. But other people, especially his family, had attempted to change him through the use of threats. Mark's father had told him to stop taking drugs and drinking heavily or he would have to leave home. The threat did little to change Mark's behavior. Neither did being arrested, serving a jail sentence, and being stricken from his father's will.

Making an inward commitment like Tina or receiving outside pressure like Mark may have some effect on some people. But it will not produce the ongoing results that will come from replacing old behavior with new attitudes and behavioral patterns. I am not suggesting that behavior modification alone is the road to permanent change; however, I am saying that in the new birth experience (John 3:5), in the inner core (heart), change is based upon new beliefs, new rituals and new responses. The apostle Paul states this same concept in Ephesians 4:21-24:

> If indeed you have heard Him, and have been taught in Him, just as truth is in Jesus, that in reference to your former manner of life, you lay aside the old self, which is being corrupted in accordance with the lusts of deceit, and that you be renewed in the spirit of your mind, and put on the new self, which in the likeness of God has been created in righteousness and holiness of the truth.

We often reason that members of our generation must be different from the believers of the first century church. However, a quick search of Scripture will clearly reveal that the early Christians had also come out of lifestyles—or rather, death styles—and that somehow the ministry of the early church resulted in ongoing and powerful changes in their attitudes and behavior.

> Or do you not know that the unrighteous shall not inherit the kingdom of God? Do not be deceived; neither fornicators, nor idolaters, nor adulterers, nor effeminate, nor homosexuals, nor thieves, nor the covetous, nor drunkards, nor revilers, nor swindlers, shall inherit the kingdom of God. And such were some of you; but you were washed, but you were sanctified, but you were justified in the name of the Lord Jesus Christ, and in the Spirit of our God (1 Cor. 6:9-11).

The purpose of this chapter is to reveal five characteristics of unhealthy behavior and to show how they can be replaced. These characteristics are present in all addictive and destructive behaviors. The early church was designed by the Lord himself so that each characteristic could be replaced with an ongoing and reinforcing one. Even though change begins with an event of regeneration, when God gives us a new heart and a new spirit, this new life must be reinforced by a new walk in the power of his grace.

> Moreover, I will give you a new heart and put a new spirit within you; and I will remove the heart of stone from your flesh and give you a heart of flesh. And I will put My Spirit within you and cause you to walk in My statutes, and you will be careful to observe My ordinances (Ez. 36:26-27).

Tina and Mark and others like them who have experienced the new birth and regeneration through the Holy Spirit have begun to recognize these old attitudes and behavioral patterns. Better still, they have replaced them with new ones.

The five characteristics of unhealthy behavior

When three or more of these characteristics are present, addictive behavior may occur. The five characteristics are listed below and will be discussed individually:

1. A faulty belief system
2. Unmet emotional, physical, and spiritual needs

3. Inadequate and immature responses to difficult life situations
4. A lack of proper boundaries and personal convictions
5. A faulty value system

1. A faulty belief system

Every person I have talked with who has suffered from a personal problem or failure has had, without exception, a faulty belief system. That's not so difficult to understand, really. When our perception of God and his way is distorted, the result will be a distorted view of ourselves and life.

I have often asked myself, "Why did I walk in addictive behavior?" It seemed as though I represented the epitome of success: I had a beautiful family, a large and growing church, and recognition from my peers. Yet what appeared as security and confidence was a deep-seated core of unbelief and insecurity. In the midst of my ministry I would have expressed a belief in all the cardinal truths of Christianity, and I still do. I expressed a sincere belief in the resurrection of Jesus Christ, the power of the blood, the Holy Spirit, and the sovereignty of God.

Yet after my resignation from the ministry I began to realize that even though I had expressed and applied many of the basic truths of Scripture, deep down a part of me did not really believe that God could meet my deepest longings. This unbelief resulted in a distortion of reality. The apostle Paul says, "They exchanged the truth of God for a lie, and worshipped and served the creature rather than the Creator, who is blessed forever. Amen" (Rom. 1:25).

Often as I stood in a pulpit to speak, thoughts of my addictive behavior would flash through my mind. But either through compartmentalizing (refusing to admit to myself that I was acting out my sin), or rationalizing ("It isn't really as bad as others' behavior" or, "It isn't God's best, but I will change in time"), I continued in bondage and defeat.

Should we be surprised that since the purpose of Jesus was to show us the Father (John 14:7-8), Satan would present himself as the father of lies? We can be sure that our faulty belief system is based on a scheme that is diabolic and deceitful. Recovering from addictive behavior involves standing against these schemes of lies and replacing them with the truth in Jesus. Put on the full armor of God, that you may be able to stand firm against the schemes of the devil (Eph. 6:11).

Our faulty belief systems may fall into several categories. I will list the most prevalent ones and the accompanying distortions:

A faulty belief system about God. Since our belief system about God is at the core of and thus influences all other belief systems, I will attempt to show more thoroughly Satan's schemes to distort. Satan does not usually begin with a blatant lie, but a subtle suggestion. He may offer an ounce of lies with a pound of truth to start. Even in the beginning (Gen. 3:1-7) we find Satan's strategies—the same strategies used today. Notice the progression:

1. The strategy of speculations. If Satan can cause us to speculate—that is, doubt God's Word—then the process of deception has begun. The very first words from Satan's mouth were, "Hath God said?" If one is convinced that there are no standards or absolutes about morals and ethics, then man is left to himself to be his own god. The strategy of speculation involves leaving out part of the Word, adding to the Word and changing the Word. Satan left out part of God's Word when he said, "Indeed has God said, you shall not eat from any tree of the garden?" The truth is that God said, "From any tree of the garden you may eat freely; but from the tree of the knowledge of good and evil you shall not eat, for in the day that you eat from it you shall surely die" (Gen. 2:16-17).

Eve continued in speculation on God's Word as she responded to Satan, saying, "From the fruit of the trees of the garden we may eat; but from the fruit of the tree which is in the middle of the garden, God has said, 'You shall not eat from it or touch it, lest you die'" (Gen. 2:2-3).

The pattern of deception continued by adding to the Word "or touch it." If we focus on rules and restraints instead of on God's grace of protection, our carnal and natural senses will be only strengthened, for the law strengthens sin.

The final type of speculation is to change the Word of God in this example from "You shall surely die" to "Lest you die." To add our own interpretation is sure destruction, as the apostle Paul warns those who twist the Scriptures to their own detriment.

Throughout the Christian community are segments of those who are making these very same mistakes of speculation. Even though the Scriptures warn of specific sins and consequences, people are led down the same road of deception as Eve was in the garden when they try to defend lifestyles of greed, immorality, pride, etc., by taking Scripture out of context, interpreting it apart from the light of other Scripture and history, and worse, building Scripture around their lives instead of building their lives around Scripture.

2. The strategy of lies. Even though speculation is an entrance to the whole system of lies, Satan's schemes continue a direct assault against the very knowledge of God himself. Notice how these strategies intertwine and become parallel.

"You shall not eat from any tree of the garden." This lie suggests that if man and woman could not eat from any or every tree of the garden, then their basic needs could not be satisfied. I see this lie behind every sin pattern and addiction. Because we believe that since some of our basic needs (nurturing, relationships, affirmation, security) were not met while growing up,

maybe it's because God wouldn't, or couldn't, meet our needs, or worse, maybe God *isn't*. The motive of this lie is to create an unbelief in God as our Father (see James 1:17) and to keep us from exposing the one who sabotages, kills, steals, and murders: Satan, the father of lies.

Jane was very despondent and angry as she cried out one day, "I can't forgive her because of what she has done to my family." Jane was referring to her best friend, who had become involved with her husband and had left town with him. I tried to understand some of Jane's grief and console her, but I also understood that her bitterness and unbelief would further hurt her and her family.

"Jane," I asked, "do you believe that God is big enough to make this awful event work together for his glory and your benefit?"

Jane hesitantly nodded her head. Then I said, "Have you thought that one reason we don't want to forgive someone is because we want that person to be hurt as much or more than we have been hurt?"

I explained that anger occurs when we have experienced feelings of loss and have placed the blame for the loss on someone else. Bitterness occurs when we nurture our mind and emotions with the thoughts of loss and the one causing the loss. It becomes like roots continuing to spread into every crack and crevice as we recall and relive the pain and hurt. No wonder the writer of Hebrews warns against these roots of bitterness and how many are defiled by them (Hebrews 12:15).

"Jane," I continued, "are you concerned that God is not able to bring justice into this situation, and that if you forgive, only more hurt and loss will occur?" Embarrassed, she stared straight ahead. "Maybe the reason you do not want to forgive is because you have difficulty believing that God really is in control, and you think that if you forgive, then justice may never be accomplished."

"How can God's justice come out of this?" she practically screamed. "The legal system OKs it, and many of our friends continue to be his friends also."

"Have you ever thought that what you are really dealing with is not just about your husband, who has wronged you and your family deeply? The bottom line is, 'Is God big enough to honor his Word?' By forgiving, you are able to let God have control and to pray effectively. Also, concerning justice, it has been dealt with at the cross. Christ has already died for all our sins and injustices, and now we can forgive others on the basis that we have been forgiven. Forgiveness does not mean the offender is released from responsibilities. Accountability and intervention may also be necessary. Vengeance belongs to the Lord, not us. If your husband and friend continue in unrepentance, don't let them stand between you and God. According to Scripture, God will be your husband and provider."

Jane's expression began to change, and I realized that the true fruit of faith, hope, and love was beginning to show itself. That day I began to see more clearly that all destructive emotions of anger, hate, vengeance, etc., are actually the results of unbelief.

"You shall not surely die." The basic lie of this statement is that there are no consequences resulting from choices that violate God's Word and our convictions. Morals are irrelevant, and "doing what feels good" becomes the outgrowth of this error. It is really a lie against the life and ministry of Jesus Christ. "For the wages of sin is death, but the free gift of God is eternal life in Christ Jesus our Lord" (Rom. 6:23).

Nick had been arrested several years ago because he had exposed himself indecently to one of his wife's friends. It was no misunderstanding on the woman's part; Nick walked unclothed from the shower to the bedroom and made lewd expressions to her.

When the woman told her husband, he immediately called the police and Nick was arrested. He was fined and placed on probation. When my phone rang, Nick's pastor shared the information that Nick had once again been arrested and was out on bail. The court case was pending. The pastor urged me to talk with Nick.

Several days later Nick and I sat in a small restaurant. He was nervously wringing his hands and would only occasionally glance up. I felt some of the pain he must have been going through, as well as that of his family and the victim.

We discussed some of the issues he was facing and a possible plan of recovery. During the conversation, I looked straight into Nick's eyes and said, "I would like to ask you a question. This is not to judge you or shame you. I am here to help you. When you exposed yourself this last time, did you consider that you might be reported and arrested?"

Nick slowly responded, "No, I was staying at a relative's home and I really thought the other person involved was playing my game with me. I guess I went too far."

Nick already knew from reading about addictive behavior that our perception can become distorted, and that we can begin to believe that others think and feel like we do. However, he finally admitted that he did not really think the woman would turn him in.

Once again we see the old lie from the garden—that our sin has no consequences. One of the foremost lies behind this lie is that as long as no one knows, or we aren't caught, there is no problem. The truth is that any sinful act and wrong behavior involves spiritual and emotional consequences and risk.

"You shall be as gods." This lie says that if my basic needs are going to be met, I will have to meet them myself, especially since I have not been able to trust God or even my parents. This blatant lie is like a slap in the face of the Holy Spirit, who desires to work mightily in us to accomplish God's will and purpose. The apostle Paul says, "Now to Him who is able to do exceedingly abundantly beyond all that we ask or think, according to the power that works within us" (Eph. 3:20). It is heinous enough to fall prey to idolatry, but to become the idol is even more serious. The epitome of Satan is the man of sin who will sit in the temple of God, displaying himself as being God (2 Thess. 2:4).

My heart was crushed when Mike shared with me that he no longer professed Christianity and was now agnostic. I experienced feelings of sadness like huge waves crashing against my heart. I had been close to Mike for several years, and had the joy of seeing him surrender to full-time Christian ministry and even complete college and theological seminary training. Even though we had lost contact with each other for a few years, he attended one of the seminars I was conducting in the city where he lived. He had come to see my wife and me again, and we agreed to meet after the service for a short time.

Mike's parents had divorced since I had last seen him, and during a recent divorce from his own wife and disastrous financial problems, he had felt the assault of Satan and disappointments. "How could there be a God?" he kept muttering. His mind seemed so made up and distorted. He had plunged into studies of various non-Christian religions. Mike admitted that he had not become an atheist, but he no longer believed that one could know God in a personal way.

My wife and I knew that we shouldn't argue with Mike, but be channels of God's love to him and to pray often for him. Our conversation ended and as we said good-bye for the evening, I couldn't help but notice the faraway gaze in his eyes. The old joy and vitality were gone. I did not try to figure out the theological whats and ifs about his present position, but I couldn't help but realize after our conversation that Mike had never known God as Father. Somehow, his limited and distorted view of God had left him disillusioned.

Philip the disciple said to Jesus, "Lord, show us the Father, and it is enough for us" (John 12:8). The Gospel that Mike had believed, the God he had trusted, were not enough; Mike had become his own god. The subtlety of unbelief always seems to either deny God altogether or to so vaguely define him that one can easily accept any god, including self.

3. The strategy of diversion. Once we have believed Satan's lies and do not believe that God can meet our deepest longings and needs, we attach our unmet needs to something or someone. This diversion is a scheme to distract us from God's purpose and divert us to temporary causes and pleasures. This scheme of diversion is so subtle that one can often mistake it for legitimately meeting needs. The strategy of diversion actually is an appeal to natural senses, but always outside of God's timing or his way.

In the garden experience in Genesis 3:6, a clear description is given of the natural sense appeal: "When the woman saw that the tree was good for food, and that it was a delight to the eyes, and that the tree was desirable to make one wise, she took from its fruit and ate; and she gave also to her husband with her, and he ate."

The strategy of diversion continues as Satan's ploy and can be related to each of our own garden experiences. A parallel to this scheme is illustrated in the temptation of Jesus in the wilderness and in the epistle of John the Apostle.

Genesis 3:6	Matthew 4:1-11	1 John 2:15-16
The tree was good for food.	If you are the son of God, command that these stones become bread.	The lust of the flesh.
It was a delight to the eyes.	If you are the son of God, throw yourself down.	The lust of the eyes.
The tree was desirable to make one wise.	All these will I give you, if you fall down and worship me.	The boastful pride of life.

"The tree was good for food." At first glance, the taking of food seems to be the right thing to do. Even the Lord had made this provision:

> And out of the ground the Lord God caused to grow every tree that is pleasing to the sight and good for food; the tree of life also in the midst of the garden, and the tree of knowledge of good and evil. . . .

> And Lord God commanded the man, saying, "From any tree of the garden you may eat freely; but from the tree of the knowledge of good and evil you shall not eat, for in the day that you eat from it you shall surely die (Gen. 2:9,16-17).

A careful reading of this Scripture reveals that God has provided for basic human needs with aesthetically pleasing, tasteful food. The problem was not in the provision, but in going beyond God's boundaries. The tree that was forbidden was the tree of knowledge of good and evil. The Lord never intended man to know the distinction between good and evil by experience, but rather by the spirit within man.

The word *lust* means a strong desire or drive. When one attempts to fulfill a legitimate need in an illegitimate way– that is, outside of God's will–then sin and death will occur. The legitimate need becomes illegitimate, not just by an act, but by exaggerating the need and its fulfillment as more essential and necessary than is true.

Satan tempted Jesus to turn stones into bread after Jesus had fasted for forty days and was hungry. The legitimate need for food was right, but the source of it and the timing were wrong. Thus Jesus said, "It is written, Man shall not live on bread alone, but on every word that proceeds out of the mouth of God" (Matt. 4:4). More important than immediate satisfaction of food was obedience to his Father.

The lust of the flesh. It is the apostle John who refers to the "lust of the flesh." Certainly there are basic human needs that have been designed by God that can be righteously and gloriously satisfied. The basic drives for food, relationships, intimacy, fun, creativity, family, provisions, etc., are all God given and God provided.

However, when we begin to believe the lies of Satan and divert our deepest need for relationship with God our Father to the tangible needs for things that perish, then our focus has been diverted; it has become lust to fulfill selfish desires and not God's fuller intent.

During the years I walked in sexual addiction, I believed that if I could meet the right person, have the right experience, enjoy the right relationship, the deep hole inside of me would be filled. The search for fulfillment became a raging lust and consuming fire. God never intended my deepest need to be filled by something or someone else. Jesus said that when we seek first the kingdom of God and his righteousness, all these things will be added to us.

It was when I began to discover God as my Father that the deep hole of me began to be filled, even overflow. Instead of simply receiving, I became free to receive and to give. This new passion for the Father and his unexplainable love toward me released in me a new passion for my wife, my family, and others.

The lust of the eyes. "It was a delight to the eyes." The Lord's creation was meant to be enjoyed. All of us have probably marveled at the beauty of a sunrise or sunset, the grandeur of the Grand Canyon, the serenity of an ocean shore on a still day, or a newborn baby. It was never a sin for the basic provisions to be a delight or to be enjoyed. The sin was the result of looking to the wrong provision, and at the wrong time.

The temptation of Jesus in the wilderness was an appeal to the lust of the eyes; that is, the sensational and unusual. When the Devil tempted Jesus to throw himself down from the pinnacle of the temple to illustrate in a visual way that God was with him and that the angels would bear him up (Matt. 4:6-

7), Jesus responded from Scripture, "You shall not put the Lord your God to the test." Jesus cut to the very heart of this attempt to appeal to the "lust of the eyes" and later amplified his warning: "An evil and adulterous generation seeks after a sign" (Matt. 16:4). The preaching of the Gospel in the early church was accompanied by signs and wonders—not as ends in themselves, but to confirm and demonstrate the power of God in bringing men to Christ.

The eyes are called the "windows of the soul." I would also call them the binoculars of the soul. Not only are we able to see deeper into a person's character and attitudes by looking into his or her eyes, but our view of life and other people often stem from the way we perceive and interpret them visually. It is said in the prophetic scriptures in Isaiah 11:3 concerning Christ that "He will not judge by what His eyes see, nor make a decision by what His ears hear." And the *ministry* of Christ should not be interpretted by an outward image or what appears to be real, but through the "eyes of the Spirit" and an inward discernment, as he would interpret life's circumstances.

The lust of the eyes is not, therefore, an enjoyment of the beauty of creation and the wonder of human creativity. It happens when we interpret life and its meaning and our meaning through the natural and not the spiritual. David said, "My eyes are continually toward the Lord" (Ps. 25:15). David is not saying that he literally looks up to the sky, but that his interpretation and perception of events flow from a spiritual discernment that comes from having the same view of life that God has.

In the Gospel of John, chapter 6, we read that Jesus lifted up his eyes on the vast multitude and saw their needs, both physical and spiritual. His view of people was not toward how he could use them or get something out of them, but how he could give to them and meet their deepest need—a need for the food that will satisfy the soul. On a number of occasions, the Scriptures record that Jesus looked upon a person or persons and was moved by compassion. His perspective of truth was from his heavenly Father.

On the contrary, the apostle Peter speaks of those "having eyes full of adultery and that never cease from sin; enticing unstable souls, having a heart trained in greed, accursed children" (2 Peter 2:14). Earlier in the same chapter Peter says, "... And many will follow their sensuality, and because of them the way of the truth will be maligned; and in their greed they will exploit you with false words; their judgment from long ago is not idle, and their destruction is not asleep" (2 Peter 2:2-3). The distinction between the ministry of Jesus and that of false leaders is that Jesus ministered to give while false leaders minister to get.

The "lust of the eyes," then, is not an enjoyment of the aesthetic beauty of the created. It occurs when we look to the created as our fulfillment or life source. The apostle Paul describes this as "serving the creature rather than the creator." When one focuses on meeting a basic need as the end result or most important aspect of life, then the "need" becomes lust and its object of fulfillment becomes an idol. Real freedom and joy come from seeking first the kingdom of God and his righteousness; fulfilling basic needs becomes a secondary resource. In doing so, we become fulfilled, "and all these things will be added to you."

The pride of life. The pride of life is based on "what we do, who we know, and what we have." The appeal of Satan to Jesus in the wilderness temptation was to offer him all the kingdoms of this world if Jesus would fall down and worship him. Jesus responded, "Be gone Satan! For it is written, 'You shall worship the Lord your God, and serve Him only'" (Matt. 4:10). This diabolical appeal attempted to place the significance and purpose of existence on position and power rather than on a relationship with, and obedience to, God the Father.

One day a friend called with an emptiness in his voice that seemed to say, "I just don't know who I am anymore." Since becoming a Christian, he had begun to break the addictive patterns in his life, including promiscuity and multiple affairs. After some discussion, he began to realize that for most of his life his self-worth had been based on attractive women responding to him. His concept of self had become based on who he knew and who knew him rather than on knowing God the Father and his acceptance by Christ.

I explained that "who we are" includes our inward character and integrity since Christ has become to us "wisdom from God, and righteousness and sanctification and redemption" (1 Cor. 1:30). To violate this truth is to deny who we really are; therefore, we cannot reckon ourselves "dead to sin but alive unto God" (Rom. 6:11). Even though this discussion did not produce a "quick fix" in my friend's life, it did begin a process that allowed him to rediscover his true identity in Christ. His being, identity, and purpose were not based on others, but in Christ. Others might enhance and affirm him, but ultimately his life was hidden with Christ in God (Col. 3:3).

The pride of life is actually man's attempt at existence and self-preservation apart from the grace of God. Pride is putting ourselves at the center of our universe and using others, even our false concept of God, to make sense out of and add meaning to life. Thus Jesus' warning: "For whoever wishes to save his life shall lose it; but whoever loses his life for My sake shall find it" (Matt. 16:25).

As we looks at these three strategies—speculation, lies, and diversion—we can more clearly understand why the apostle Paul instructed the believers: "For the weapons of our warfare are not of the flesh, but divinely powerful for the destruction of fortresses. We are destroying speculations [the strategy of speculations], and every lofty thing raised up against the knowledge of God [the strategy of lies], and we are taking every thought [the strategy of diversion] captive to the obedience of Christ" (2 Cor. 10:4-5). The word for "destroy" in this verse means "to take by force" and denotes a definite plan to dismantle and replace. I believe that one can do this in the following way:

Exposing to the light—Eph. 5:13
Laying aside falsehood—Eph. 4:25
Replacing perceptions with the truth—Eph. 4:23-24

Let's examine this process. When a system of lies about God and his Word has been implanted and received as truth, then our entire life outlook is affected, and even infected, by lies. This system of lies is further discussed in chapter 5 of my first book, *A Journey Toward Wholeness*. Here is a list of the most prevalent lies:

*About self: I **am** a mistake versus I **made** a mistake.* When we view ourselves through unhealthy shame, our conclusion is, "I am a mistake." It is one thing to admit making a mistake, assume responsibility, and acknowledge sin; it is far different to believe the lie that we are second-class citizens, marred and not even worthy of having been born. It is especially an error for a Christian to accept this lie. A mistake can be corrected, a sin can be confessed and repented, and irresponsibility can be changed to responsibility.

About life: Life isn't fair. Therefore, I can't be fair either if I am to make it. The truth is that life *isn't* fair. We are warned over and over that Satan, our adversary, is a murderer, a thief, and a liar, and that the "whole world lies in the power of the evil one" (1 John 5:19). But whoever is "born of God overcomes the world; and this is the victory that has overcome the world— our faith" (1 John 5:4). As believers, we can trust the living God who is sovereign, and by his grace he will work everything together for his good, to those who love him and to those who are the called according to his purpose (Rom. 8:28). To believe that we, too, have to follow the spirit of this world into dishonesty, scheming, manipulation, and deception in order to get by is a blatant lie of the enemy. Through our acts of righteousness and kindness, we can expose the lies of the world's system and that which is unfair. God will make things "fair" for his people through his righteous judgments and supernatural power.

About past failures: I am the sum of my past. Many believers are still held in bondage, believing that because of past failures, either on their part or on the part of someone else, life is forever limited or scarred. Though we are certainly affected by past events, we are not delineated by those events. Those who were sexually molested as children are deeply affected *by* that experience (as I and many others were), but we are *not* that experience. To live life as though a past event will determine who we are and what we can or cannot do is to suffer even greater abuse by our own minds and emotions than by the original abuse. The glory of God's grace is to take even what may have been meant for evil or destruction and use it for his glory and our benefit. Past failures can become the basis of our greatest strengths and ministry.

About happiness: Happiness, peace and joy are based on circumstances and others. To believe this lie is to be trapped forever in the labor of trying to change those around us. Yes, circumstances may need to be changed, and those around us may need to be confronted, but our peace and happiness is not based on outward changes, but inward resolve. Jesus said, "Peace I leave with you; My peace I give to you; not as the world gives, do I give to you. Let not your heart be troubled, nor let it be fearful" (John 14:27). Again, Jesus said, "These things I have spoken to you, that in Me you may have peace. In the world you have tribulation, but take courage; I have overcome the world" (John 16:33). The peace that Jesus is talking about is the inward serenity that comes from knowing that God is in charge and that he can work every circumstance for his glory, for our benefit, in his timing and in his way.

True peace is interrupted by fear. It may be fear of the unknown, fear of death, of failure, of rejection, or even of fear itself. James the apostle says that fear torments. Most of us have probably amplified our thoughts, especially at night, and allowed them to run the gamut of destruction and pain. The opposite of this behavior is faith. Faith is not denying the problem, but asking the Lord how to respond to the situation, and then doing so with a deep, abiding peace. It is knowing that worrying about the problem will not change it, but that praying about it will change us and our response to the problem. Peace is knowing that whatever happens, God will use it for his purpose and for our good. He is our Father and we can trust him.

About relationships: The need for a meaningful relationship with another person or persons who are significant to us is one of the most important needs in our life.

We assume that real love involves being consumed with each other's time, schedule, plans, etc.—behavior that is, in reality, possessive. Another assumption is that real love means that we try to protect the relationship from any possible danger, which is really controlling behavior. Finally, we assume that real love involves the constant intenseness of intimacy and sharing of emotions without restraint, which is really lust, not love.

These are some of the most common faulty beliefs and the erroneous assumptions behind them. Once a faulty belief system is in place, every aspect of our life will fall into error. This is why we must be most vigilant against this first characteristic of unhealthy behavior.

2. Unmet emotional, physical and spiritual needs

Anne was the fourth of four girls, born to dedicated Christian parents. Even though she was raised in a Christian home and still attended church regularly at the time she came to talk to me and my wife, she could hardly speak between sobs as she shared her secret world of promiscuity.

Anne's parents had desperately wanted a boy when she was born, and she had often heard them talk about it while she was growing up. Still, as far back as she could remember, she had been closer to her father than the other girls. In fact, Anne said she was like the little boy he never had. He taught her how to catch a softball, cast a fishing line, and wear a baseball cap.

As Anne reached puberty, her father began to pull away from her emotionally. It was as though he did not know how to affirm her in her womanhood. Worse, when she wasn't doing family chores, Anne's mother tried to spend her time with the other girls. It was her way of compensating the girls for the time Anne's father spent with Anne.

Any attachment or connection that Anne had experienced now seemed to be gone. In her desperate search to belong, she became easy prey for some of the older high school boys who showed her special attention, but for the wrong reasons. She got involved in a lifestyle of promiscuous sex that lasted into her mid-fifties.

As we talked, Anne admitted that it wasn't the sexual experiences that she really wanted. In fact, sometimes she was repulsed by the sex itself. But her need to be needed seemed overwhelming. What Anne was partially crying out for was for someone to affirm the "little girl" inside of her. She had been her daddy's little boy, but she had never been anyone's special girl, wife, or mother. Her promiscuous behavior was a false attempt to affirm her womanhood. She made herself into a pathetic sex object crying out for affirmation.

Anne attempted to meet her needs through tragic methods. Whether we attempt to meet our needs in an illegitimate way, or to cover the pain of unmet needs with addictive behavior, the results are the same: guilt, shame, and death.

God's design. In order to understand Anne's search, and the search of many people like her, we need to understand God's design in creation. The Genesis account (Gen. 1:26-31; 2:18-25) describes Adam as being created in God's image, according to his likeness, and being given authority to rule over earth's domain. But because of Adam's fall, his own sons were born in his likeness and lost God's original plan for them.

Even after the fall of man, in which all have sinned and come short of the glory of God, the reflections of God's creation still exist in man's being: "For the wrath of God is revealed from heaven against all ungodliness and unrighteousness of men, who suppress the truth in unrighteousness, because that which is known about God is evident within them; for God made it evident to them. For since the creation of the world, His invisible attributes, His eternal power and divine nature have been clearly seen, being understood through what has been made, so that they are without excuse" (Rom. 1:18-20). What is the truth that man suppressed? It is clearly described in the creation—that Adam was created in God's image, according to his likeness and given dominion.

God's image is his glory and character and has to do with our **being**.

God's likeness is his order and has to do with our sexuality as male and female. Our gender identity is at the core of relationships and is related to our sense of **belonging**.

God's dominion is his purpose and has to do with our sense of destiny and **becoming**.

When any one of these steps is sabotaged and wounded, the process of distortion and destruction is set in motion. This is precisely what has happened to man since the fall. Any remaining reflection of God's glory has been so blinded by Satan that without regeneration and the grace of God, man can never be restored to wholeness. Even after regeneration, the old patterns and systems that were attempts to meet basic legitimate needs must be laid aside as falsehoods and replaced with the truth as it is in Jesus (Eph. 4:17-25).

God's standard for wholeness. The verse we originally mentioned, 2 Corinthians 3:18, says that God's standard for maturity and wholeness is Jesus Christ. The apostle Paul further states in Colosians 1:15-16, "He is the image of the invisible God, the first born of all creation. For by Him all things were created, both in the heavens and on earth, visible and invisible, whether thrones or dominions or rulers or authorities—all things have been created through Him and for Him." Again, Paul says in Colosians 2:9-10, "For in Him [Christ] all the fullness of Deity dwells in bodily form, and in Him you have been made complete, and He is the head over all rule and authority." Clearly, our standard of wholeness is Christ, and even though through the new birth we are a new creation, our mind, will and emotions are in need of being conformed to this image (Rom. 12:2).

What is this process for healthy spiritual, emotional, and physical growth? The process of maturing and growing into wholeness is illustrated in the life of Jesus Christ as described in Luke 2:52: Jesus grew in wisdom (spirit), and in stature (physical and chronological), and in favor (psychological and personality) with God and man. This process included and was dependent upon healthy relationships with God and man.

Likewise, our well-being and growth as believers needs the same process of an intimate relationship with God the Father through Jesus Christ and the fellowship and affirmation of the body of Christ through his church. When this process has been interrupted, even in childhood, recovery and restoration may be hindered unless we acquire proper understanding and healing.

The results of woundedness. "A brother offended is harder to be won than a strong city, and contentions are like the bars of a castle" (Prov. 18:19).

When the relationships affecting our spiritual and emotional growth are interrupted through overt or covert activities, a wall is built and the relationship is hindered or sabotaged. Anne was deeply wounded by her father's rejection of her femaleness and her mother's refusal to respond to her needs. Additional hurts from others reinforced this wall, preventing further relationships and hindering growth.

Think of the wall as a high, invisible brick structure that was surrounding Anne's life. It had been built, brick by brick, with each hurt and disappointment. It represented Anne's attempt to keep from being hurt again, but it also imprisoned her by keeping her from developing healthy and meaningful relationships. The additional hurts that reinforced the wall came from the men she became sexually involved with but who only used her and boasted to others about it.

Often, feelings of hurt or offenses are transferred to God, causing further isolation and loneliness. We ask, "Why did God let this happen? Why didn't he give me a different family?" On and on we struggle for answers until our heart becomes hard and cold toward God. Sadly, many people stay in the prison of hurt and bitterness forever.

The apostle Paul describes this process in Romans 1:21: "For even though they knew God, they did not honor Him as God, or give thanks, but they became futile in their speculations, and their foolish heart was darkened." Why would a person not give thanks to God? Because of unfulfilled expectations. Our anger and bitterness is not only directed toward those who have hurt us, but may also be directed to others who look, act, or remind us of those who hurt us.

Results of a traumatized personality. Sometimes a wall is built around a person, not through a series of remembered offenses, but through severe trauma. A person who has been severely traumatized through abuse and molestation (physical, sexual, or emotional) may close off himself or herself in an attempt to eliminate pain through loss of memories. Some of the characteristics of the traumatized personality include a total or partial loss of memory, especially of childhood, if that is when the molestation occurred.

I would caution at this point to not assume or try to imagine childhood molestation just because of loss of memory, as this might lead to blaming someone without evidence. Trust the Holy Spirit to bring clearly to your mind any events that should be recalled and, with the help of a good and competent counselor, sort out imagination and fiction from reality. Through imagination and false accusations, innocent people and families can be destroyed. The purpose of restoration is not to cause further emotional or mental abuse to innocent parties. However, where molestation in childhood has occurred, seek out helpful reading resources and an experienced counselor to guide you through the process of healing for yourself, the perpetrator, and any other people involved.

A deep sense of shame and self-hate may also be prevalent when a person has a traumatized personality. For years, Betty lived in an isolated world of shame and self-hate. Even though she had not remembered childhood molestation, neither could she remember many events from the past. A long, dark space blanked out her history, as if someone had turned off the light in her mind. Actually, Betty had turned off the light to keep from seeing and feeling the pain and hurt from sexual molestation from an older brother and her stepfather over a period of several years.

During a seminar about releasing unhealthy shame, it was as though someone turned on a light for Betty. As she learned about God's fatherly love and how to trust him in his grace and mercy, her restoration and healing began.

A distrust of others and a fear of abandonment may also characterize a traumatized personality. A person may not even be aware of why he or she doesn't trust people. Once when I ministered to a congregation about restoration to wholeness, a middle-aged man came forward for prayer and ministry. I reached out to touch him on the shoulder as I prayed. To my surprise, he pulled away with a look of terror on his face. I withdrew my hand and continued to pray softly for him, especially that the Holy Spirit would bring to light any hidden area in his life that was unresolved.

Later, after being counseled by a Christian counselor, he shared how the ministry time had led him to seek further help that resulted in bringing to light the hidden memories of having been sexually molested by older neighborhood children for nearly five years. Distrust of others, especially men, had kept him isolated from meaningful friendships.

Results of a fragmented personality. Unlike someone with a traumatized personality, the fragmented person may remember most past events and personal history, but a specific area or areas of his or her life may seem splintered and unattached.

The arresting of personality growth may occur in one specific area (sexuality, relationships, trust, finances, etc.), and while other areas will be affected, it will not be to the same extent. A person may feel fragmented and splintered in the most affected area. That person may also exhibit instability. A double-minded man will be unstable in all his ways (James 1:8).

A reparative drive. All of creation exhibits a restorative and reparative drive. When Mount St. Helens erupted, the earth began to replenish vegetation and other life from within itself (and also with the help of government agencies). When the skin is broken to the point of bleeding, a reparative drive takes place in the body to prevent further bleeding. The apostle Paul alludes to this reparative process: "For we know that the whole creation groans and suffers the pains of childbirth together until now. And not only this, but also we ourselves, having the first fruits of the Spirit, even we ourselves groan within ourselves, waiting eagerly for our adoption as sons, the redemption of our body" (Rom. 8:22-23).

This is true not only in nature and creation, but in our broken and damaged emotions. A reparative drive seems to seek to replenish that which was lacking. However, it is at this point that most problems involved in meeting or repairing those unmet needs occur. Without the ministry of the Holy Spirit in this process, a person may very easily resort to his or her own understanding in an attempt to repair, thus resulting in deception and a system contrary to God's will. (For further reading on this subject, see chapter four in *A Journey Toward Wholeness*.)

3. Inadequate and immature responses to difficult life situations

Van and Joyce sat across from each other in our living room, hardly looking at each other but projecting an attitude that said, "This is it. I've had it. It will never work." It wasn't anything like marital unfaithfulness or financial problems that was plaguing their marriage, they said. It was the pressure of everyday life.

"He acts so immature," Joyce blurted out. "He'll never sit down and discuss a problem, and when the least difference of opinion comes up, he gets in the car and leaves for two or three hours." I could tell Van was uncomfortable in the session and probably wanted to leave.

I asked Van and Joyce a question that they had never linked to their present conflicts. "How did your family respond to pressures when you were growing up? This could be the pressures of finances, of adjustment, of minor irritations, or anything else that seemed to push you out of your routine or comfort zone."

I asked Van and Joyce to think about this for a moment and, if helpful, to write down any of their thoughts. Van responded first. "Well, I remember my dad being gone most of the time. In fact, I never thought very much about it before, but he had a job that kept him away from the home most of the time." Van's voice began to quaver and hurt began to show on his face as other memories surfaced. Van admitted that on weekends his father left his six children for long periods of time and usually came home drunk.

"What were some other ways that your family responded to pressure?" I said.

"Well, when things went wrong, we never talked about it."

"How was it dealt with?"

"All I can remember is that whoever was causing the problem was told to leave. If it was during a family meal, it was, 'Leave the table.' If it was in the house, it was, 'Go outside' or 'Go to your room.'"

Van began to see the pattern. He explained that in times of pressure, which was most of the time, the family used any opportunity available to leave the home for as long as possible.

It was obvious to Van and Joyce that the pattern of his past was linked to his present responses. "I have another question to ask you," I said with an awareness that they already knew the answer. "How do you respond to pressure in your life now?"

"Well," he said, "I guess that I am doing what my family did. I leave."

Unlike Van's family, Joyce's family dealt with pressures by working harder. Fighting back tears, she said her family celebrated only two holidays: Christmas and Easter. They were Christians, and they celebrated for short periods of time, but then they went right back to work. "We worked all the time," she said. "On other holidays, such as the Fourth of July or Labor Day, when other families took time off, we worked on our family farm so we would be ahead of everyone else."

At this point, Joyce anticipated my next question: "And how do you respond to pressure?"

Van answered for her. "She works. She works all the time."

"It's true," Joyce said. "When Van leaves in one of his moods, I don't take time to grieve; I just work harder. Sometimes, I work almost all night long."

Van and Joyce saw that they were perpetuating the patterns they had learned as children. Fortunately, over a period of time, they both began to change their immature responses and develop new ways of communicating their feelings to each other, as well as responding to the promptings of the Holy Spirit in their actions.

I have asked many people to describe how their families responded to pressure. The answers vary, but these are the most common:

Getting drunk
Going into a rage
Getting sick and going to bed
Eating and watching television
Arguing and fighting
Becoming silent
Taking prescription drugs

When I ask the next question—"How do *you* respond to pressure?"—the response is predictable. Almost always, present behavior mirrors family systems of behavior.

The apostle Paul said, "When I was a child, I used to speak as a child, think as a child, reason as a child; when I became a man, I did away with childish things" (1 Cor. 13:11). The difference between childishness and mature responses is the order of responding. A child speaks and acts before he or she thinks and reasons. It is often true in our adult lives that we still act out of our childish responses. At first thought, these systems of response may seem harmless; however, we soon find that if we don't learn to respond to difficult life situations in mature ways, we may end up in a shipwreck in our personal life, our marriage, and our job.

John was a man whose life clearly illustrated this possibility. He had flitted from job to job but was presently without one. His family was suffering, his home had been foreclosed on, and he was about to have his car repossessed. John told me that his father had dealt with work pressures or reprimands by quitting and finding another job. John remembered moving from town to town, sometimes leaving in the middle of the night to avoid detection from people he owed money to. John's father had never learned how to deal with pressure, and neither had he. In the following chapters we will examine how to create new memories and new responses to life situations.

When we develop a habit of negative responses to ongoing situations, the negative responses tend to become stronger and stronger as life goes on. My own experience and observation has been that addictive behavior is the result of responding to the pressure of pain in an inadequate way. A satisfied addiction is actually a mood altering experience. The mood is the feeling and the altering experience is the drug of choice, either a substance or a process, by which we try to cover or divert the pain. Part of this addictive system exists in the way we have learned to deal with our feelings of pain. This is precisely what Paul discusses:

> This I say therefore, and affirm together with the Lord, that you walk no longer just as the Gentiles also walk, in the futility of their mind, being darkened in their understanding, excluded from the life of God, because of the ignorance that is in them, because of the hardness of their heart; and they, having become callous, have given themselves over to sensuality, for the practice of every kind of impurity and greediness (Eph. 4:17-19).

The word *callous* means to feel no emotion. When we ignore feelings and turn them inward, destructive and addictive behavior will surely follow in an attempt to cover the pain, which is still there. Paul gives us another clear warning about our unresolved emotions in 2 Cor. 7:9, revealing that godly sorrow produces a repentance unto life, but the sorrow of the world produces death.

Some students of psychology have pointed out that most eating disorders are the result of unresolved feelings. Overeating is likened to packing down our feelings, bulimia is likened to purging our feelings, and anorexia is likened to rejecting our feelings.

Feelings retain power because they are associated with people, places, things, moods, and natural senses. When we are in contact with these stimuli, the association with the repressed feelings in our mind can be overpowering. These associations become like anchors in our lives that keep us stuck in the same recurring patterns.

The process of sorrow that is not dealt with begins and continues as follows: When one experiences loss, the result is feelings of sorrow. One can receive God's wisdom to view the loss through his eyes as an opportunity to learn and develop character, or as an opportunity to learn to minister and comfort others in the same situation. But if meaning and positive purpose cannot be attached to the loss, then anger will develop.

Anger is directed toward someone (even God) who is seen as responsible for causing the loss, along with an inward desire to see that person hurt as much or more than we were because of the loss. Anger comes from the same root word as "orgy," and is often behind many sexual sins and addictions. Anger is dealt with in the wrong way when we use it to cover up our feelings or act it out against others.

Bitter judgments grow out of anger as one rehearses over and over in the mind the details and cause of the loss. This is spoken of as "roots of bitterness" in Hebrews 12:15, and can soon consume other emotions. "But if you bite and devour one another, take care lest you be consumed by one another" (Gal. 5:15).

Unbelief regarding God's grace and purposes is fostered in the heart by bitterness until one begins to believe the lie: "I can't trust God to bring about justice, so I'll do it myself." Vengeance is really assuming God's responsibility, the Scripture says: "Never take your own revenge, beloved, but leave room for the wrath of God, for it is written, 'Vengeance is mine. I will repay,' says the Lord. 'But if your enemy is hungry, feed him, and if he is thirsty, give him a drink; for in so doing you will heap burning coals upon his head.' Do not be overcome by evil, but overcome evil with good" (Rom. 12:19-21).

The sad and ongoing effect of unbelief is best described in Hebrews 3:12-13: "Take care, brethren, lest there should be in any one of you an evil, unbelieving heart, in falling away from the living God. But encourage one another day after day, as long as it is still called "today," lest any one of you be hardened by the deceitfulness of sin."

4. A lack of proper boundaries and personal convictions

What is a boundary? Let us define it as the area of responsibility that we have for our life and behavior. I was raised on a farm in western Texas, and we had livestock and other farm animals. One way that we established a boundary was by building fences to keep our animals in and other animals out. Between the various farms, small dirt roads or fences divided the properties. One never questioned whether to violate someone else's boundaries where they were clearly defined. We humans have boundaries; however, they are often not as clearly defined in a society, a community, a family, or in an individual as they are on a farm.

When I helped repair or build a fence on our farm, I would first place posts in the ground to hold the fence upright and then connect each post with wooden boards or wire. Even today I like to think of boundaries like that; the posts are the convictions (the values we will talk about later) and the decisions and choices connected to our values are the boards or wire. Together they form a boundary.

Some personal boundaries are too strict and limiting while others are too loose and poorly defined. The following examples illustrate boundary problems:

Physical boundaries. Dan can't remember ever being hugged by either of his parents while he was growing up, though he does remember being spanked and sometimes slapped. Though he desired physical closeness and intimacy, he became like his family; he did not know how to show affection. Dan's physical boundaries were too strict and limiting.

Jan, on the other hand, often saw her parents and older brothers walking in the nude from the shower to the bedroom. They would watch television in the family room with only their underclothing on and thought nothing of it. Jan also remembers sleeping with members of her family, both male and female, and feeling uncomfortable with the arrangements. As an adult, Jan often took abuse from her colleagues at work because she had not clearly defined her physical boundaries. Jan's physical boundaries were too loose and poorly defined.

Emotional boundaries. Linda was raised in a foster home where very few emotional expressions were shared. She desperately wanted someone to say "I love you" and to be called pet names like "honey" or "precious." There was a void of emotional sharing, but Linda assumed this was normal and, in adulthood, continued to respond the same way toward others. Linda's husband was frustrated and did not understood her apparent coldness; he judged it as a lack of love on her part. Linda's emotional boundaries were so rigid that she had been left with emotional needs in her own life and was unable to give much to anyone else. Linda's emotional boundaries were too strict and limiting.

Jeff was raised by his divorced mother. Jeff's father had left the family for another woman when Jeff was twelve years old, and his mother turned to him for emotional support. Jeff became so entrenched in his mother's emotional stress that he felt guilty about dating or participating in a school activity that would prevent him from being with her.

I met Jeff when he was in his early thirties. He was married and had been active in the ministry, but was forced to resign because of his involvement with several women. Jeff lacked convictions and acted irresponsibly, but change began to come about when he realized that his relationships with women were too emotional and without boundaries. Jeff's need, among other things, was to establish some clear and healthy boundaries and convictions. Jeff's emotional boundaries were too loose and poorly defined.

Spiritual boundaries. Ned was an angry college student. He had stopped going to church during his first semester; he said he was tired of having religion "pushed down his throat." As I talked with Ned, I was surprised at how sensitive he was to spiritual issues, and that he seemed to have a deep hunger for God. I realized that Ned wasn't lacking spiritual interest after all. He had been raised by a "strict, authoritarian father who insisted that he alone was right and he would like to see who could prove otherwise."

Though Ned's definition of his father was probably a little extreme, it was obvious that his religious boundaries had been severely restricted to a small, authoritarian group which, like those of his family, didn't allow honest investigation of and questions about their rules. Ned had been forbidden to play high school sports because practices and games were held on church nights, and his family demanded loyalty to their church.

Ned's understanding of Christianity and God as his Father had been deeply marred and affected by the severely strict limits and boundaries his parents imposed on him. Instead of protecting him, which I trust was their intent, they drove him away. Eventually, Ned was able to forgive his parents and establish the true boundaries that were given by the Holy Spirit in accordance with God's Word. Ned expanded his spiritual boundaries, which were too strict and limiting.

Billy had no religious background of any kind. When his brother was killed in a motorcycle accident, Billy attended the service at the funeral home, but had no idea what the preacher was talking about. Several years later, Billy was introduced to Christ and responded enthusiastically. By this time, he was in his late thirties and his own family had become "pretty messed up," to use his words. His fourteen-year-old son had been arrested for taking drugs, but then, Billy had used them too.

With tears in his eyes, Billy shared some of his unresolved anger with me. "I can't believe that I was raised without anyone taking me to church, instructing me about God, or at least doing something to give me some kind of a moral and spiritual foundation." Unfortunately, he had failed to give his own children these gifts. I reminded him that God can restore the years the locust has eaten, but I too felt the pangs of his loss. Billy's spiritual boundaries were too loose and poorly defined.

God has boundaries that are very clear and defined. His own creation has the boundaries of laws and principles. He has also given us personal boundaries and convictions. How do we know when these boundaries are healthy or unhealthy, appropriate or inappropriate? I believe that one way to tell if something is unhealthy is to know what is healthy. The following list contains some of the characteristics of healthy boundaries. By studying them, we can begin to determine what might be inappropriate in our lives and respond accordingly.

Healthy boundaries grant the power to say no even when others expect a yes. Mitch had been artistic since he was a child. As he developed his talents, friends asked him to take on special projects. At first he was encouraged by their need for him, and he sometimes worked until late in the evening to complete the projects. Mitch's friends never asked about his work schedule and time commitments; they just assumed he would say yes to whatever project they handed him. Mitch began to feel like he was being taken advantage of, and he resented it. He learned through a Christian counselor that part of the solution was to establish some healthy boundaries and to learn to say no, even when he felt like saying yes.

Healthy boundaries help us assume responsibility for what is ours. A year after joining a Christian ministry, Jay began to feel a sense of disillusionment. At first he tried to ignore it. He reasoned that since organizations are made up of people and people are human, one has to expect human weakness in organizations. Jay was reluctant to share his thoughts with a counselor because he worried about being "disloyal." But when his feelings intensified, he decided to open up.

Jay was bothered by a rule requiring parents and relatives to obtain permission from the ministry before visiting. And he was troubled that he could make no personal financial investments without the leadership's approval, even though he was not in debt and had an immaculate credit record. Jay was married, had children, and once pastored a fast-growing church. He was confused about why he should now "give his rights" and ownership to the Lord. Jay was reprimanded for not trusting the Lord to work through the leaders of the ministry to meet his family's needs.

Jay realized through counseling that he had turned his anger inward, and that he did indeed need to forgive and give his "rights" to the Lord. However, in giving his "rights" and "ownership" to the Christian ministry, he had gone beyond reasonable bounds by releasing his own responsibilities to someone else. He soon left the ministry and established healthy boundaries in his own life and family.

Healthy boundaries help us develop the ability to negotiate. To negotiate means to reconcile differences that prevent a solution to a contract, an agreement, or a problem. Many people simply sign on the bottom line of an agreement even though it may be to their disadvantage. They often feel anger and bitterness later. Other people lack negotiation skills and are unable to work out solutions, so they refuse to agree to anything.

I fell into both camps, sometimes agreeing to something by giving in to a stronger person, and sometimes refusing to do anything, even though the situation called for some kind of action. Sometimes I would take my car to a mechanic to be repaired, and even though it would not be fixed when I picked it up, I would pay the bill anyway. It was after learning from several friends and reading helpful resources that I began to negotiate on the basis that others were blessed, and that I too could be blessed in the process.

Healthy boundaries help us understand the difference between being nice and being used. Several of these characteristics may overlap, but responding to situations simply because we want to "be nice" may cause more harm than good. It is commendable to be nice and kind and gentle; these are Christian qualities. Yet sometimes the absence of confrontation or forthrightness can result in our being used.

Lynn was the pastor of a very large church in his denomination that had many prominent businessmen as members. He soon learned of an organization that was being promoted as a "Christian businessmen's group for wise investments in order to give to the kingdom." The only problem was that many new Christians and prosperous men who were joining the fellowship were being used to finance the ventures and were losing money.

Lynn had a gentle spirit and usually dealt with church problems by "being nice." But the truth was that he was being used by unscrupulous men who were trying to financially ruin new Christians. Lynn began to assume his responsibility as a pastor. He could model the positive attitudes of kindness and gentleness, but he had to become tough and forthright to protect healthy boundaries for himself, his family, and his congregation.

Healthy boundaries mean establishing standards of priorities. Glen was the town favorite. Married, in his fifties, and the grandfather of three, Glen could be counted on whenever anyone needed him, and that was most of the time. He served as a church usher, taught Sunday school class, worked with the Boy Scouts and the volunteer fire department, and gave his time to any organization that clamored for his skills. When his wife left him, everyone in their small town was shocked.

Glen had failed in his early life and marriage to establish clear boundaries of priorities that included not only his devotion to God's kingdom through good works for others, but to his wife and children. This illustration underscores the poignancy of the question: "What should it profit a man if he gained the whole world and lost his own soul?" In a more limited sense we could say: "What profit is there when a man gains the approval of those around him, and loses his own family because of misplaced priorities?"

Healthy boundaries enable us to deal with criticism and accusations in a positive way. How do you deal with slanderous or harmful accusations? Someone with a lack of personal boundaries may say nothing and allow others to project their own guilt and shame. Someone with restrictive personal boundaries may overreact to criticism or accusations from others.

Leonard was a Christian counselor and was devastated when he heard some gossip and slander about himself that had supposedly come from another counselor. At first, he did nothing and decided to "bless those who would curse him." This seemed to work until he learned the gossip was reaching other people too.

Leonard went through a process I believe was very healthy. First, he called the source of the information. Then he asked the person spreading the false statements to talk to the other person involved to clear the misunderstanding. Most of the slander faded into oblivion.

This was a new, empowering experience for Leonard. He established a healthy, personal boundary that had long been missing in his life—the boundary that protected personal integrity for the cause of God's kingdom. It enabled him to deal with criticism and accusations in a positive way.

Healthy boundaries help us establish a strong sense of morals and ethics. Boundaries involve morals and ethics. When people post a sign that says, "Thank you for not smoking," they are, in a kind way, expressing a boundary that reflects their convictions. The clothing we wear, the materials we read, and the social groups we belong to reflect the boundaries that we have established through our moral and ethical choices.

Jeanne was a premed student at a prestigious university. She had come from a small village and had grown up with the teachings of a church. From the start, Jeanne's convictions were challenged at the secular university. In dating and social relationships, she had to make choices that would reflect her moral and ethical values.

Although she experienced many hurts and rejections from others because of the boundaries she established, today Jeanne is a prominent pediatrician in her community. She recently shared with me how grateful she is that she grew up in a Christian home and church that embraced moral and ethical boundaries. Even though she questioned them at times, she was ultimately protected and blessed by them.

5. A faulty value system

A value is a measure of how important we consider something to be. When the Scripture speaks of the reins of our heart, it is really speaking of our passions or our value system. When Jesus said that "where a man's treasure is, there will his heart be also" (Matt. 6:21), he was referring to a person's values.

Values are determined by our belief system. When someone believes that something is necessary and essential for happiness (or whatever results are being sought), then the means necessary for reaching that result become important. For example, a person may say that his or her greatest desire is for love, but may have experienced a feeling of being loved through sexual expression. If love and sexual experiences are equated, then sexual experiences become one of the most important things in life, resulting in a faulty value system.

The apostle Paul describes a faulty value system in Romans 1:21-25:

> For even though they knew God, they did not honor Him as God, or give thanks; but they became futile in their speculations, and their foolish heart was darkened. Professing to be wise, they became fools, and exchanged the glory of the incorruptible God for an image in the form of corruptible man and of birds and four-footed animals and crawling creatures. Therefore God gave them over in the lusts of their hearts to impurity, that their bodies might be dishonored among them. For they exchanged the truth of God for a lie, and worshiped and served the creature rather than the Creator, who is blessed forever, Amen.

In this section of Scripture it is clear that because one dishonored God (because he judged him as weak), and did not give him thanks (because of unfulfilled expectations), that which was important was transferred from the incorruptible God to another which, even though corruptible, was considered more important. This faulty value system stems from a faulty belief system that was reinforced by unmet needs, a wrongful response to difficulties, and inadequate boundaries and convictions.

How does one determine a value and how is it measured? By weighing the following considerations:

Priorities of time. We have all heard the saying, "We do what is important to us." This is really true; we all do what we want to do deep down, unless we are hindered by time, finances, health, or other obstacles. But even if we are prevented from doing something important to us, we still *want* to do it.

Some time ago a friend and I agreed to have lunch together on a weekly basis. After he missed our scheduled lunch date several times, I shared my disappointment with him. During our discussion, we realized that we both placed the same value on our friendship; however, my value of the scheduled time together was greater because I saw it as an opportunity for mutual encouragement and sharing. I was disappointed because I had judged his value of our friendship as less than mine.

He apologized, and the following week he arrived for lunch fifteen minutes early. Now I realize that his value of the spiritual significance of our friendship is as deep as mine, if not deeper. Moreover, to him, missing a lunch appointment did not make or break our relationship. The priority of time expresses our value of something or someone and is one of the hallmarks of what we consider important.

The things we choose to invest in. The investment of time, money, and energy gives value to what we are doing. I consider personal restoration of the fallen not only a calling, but of great value in general because I believe that it is the heart of God and one of the fullest expressions of love. "Brethren, even if a man is caught in any trespass, you who are spiritual restore such a one in a spirit of gentleness; looking to yourself, lest you too be tempted. Bear one another's burdens, and thus fulfill the law of Christ" (Gal. 6:1-2).

When we spend our time, money, and energy on what we love and consider important, we don't count the cost as a loss, but as an investment in something we value. If our child contracts a serious illness that will result in tremendous medical bills, we would not make decisions based on our bank account, but on the value of the child. Somehow we would find a way to pay for the treatment.

True values are enduring. How long something lasts or how much something means to us reveals its value. What about a baby who died at birth? If we believe that a baby has an eternal spirit, then the cessation of the physical being does not determine our value of it. If a person does not believe that a baby in a mother's womb has a spirit, then the value system allows termination of its life and gives it little meaning or significance. However, if we believe that the unborn baby has a spirit, then the value of that life is as great as that of a small child, a teenager, or an adult.

It is not only a sense of eternal life that imparts value, but also acknowledging the difference a choice or action will have on something five years from now, ten years from now, and even twenty years from now. What difference will my actions and choices make to my children and my children's children? Endurance imparts value.

Something worth living and dying for. Freedom, liberty, family, and country are worth giving our lives for, and we grant them importance and value. But even more value is given to that which is worth living for.

Ministers, evangelists, missionaries, teachers, and a host of other Christian servants give their lives in difficult and trying circumstances with grace and joy because of the value they grant to God's kingdom and his righteousness.

The decisions we make. When people have difficulty making a major decision, either their value system is not clear or they are mulling in their own hearts how, when, or where the decision will line up with their values. If they value security, then they will most likely avoid any decision that would result in insecurity.

A faulty value system would support gain for self, or what James the apostle called selfish ambition: "But if you have bitter jealousy and selfish ambition in your heart, do not be arrogant and so lie against the truth. This wisdom is not that which comes down from above, but is earthly, natural, demonic. For where jealousy and selfish ambition exist, there is disorder and every evil thing" (James 3:14-16).

Some might say that the values of God, family, ministry, finances, etc., are really the way to a deeper value—that is, to be loved, to experience joy and peace, to feel happiness, etc. The deeper value should be to bear fruit in other people's lives and to lay up treasures for eternity. To be loved, to feel joy, and to have peace and happiness are not values, though they are valued when we observe them in people's lives. They are really motives that move us to lay down our lives for others. Love, joy, and peace are not the products of our fruits; they are among the fruits of the Holy Spirit in us that motivate us with God's grace to serve.

> But the fruit of the Spirit is love, joy, peace, patience, kindness, goodness, faithfulness, gentleness, self-control; against such things there is no law. Now those who belong to Christ Jesus have crucified the flesh with its passions and desires. If we live by the Spirit, let us also walk by the Spirit. Let us not become boastful, challenging one another, envying one another (Gal. 5:22-26).

The deepest value is to know Christ and for him to be our life. "When Christ who is our life is revealed, then you also will appear with Him in glory" (Col. 3:4). Any value system is false when it substitutes temporal values for eternal values, death for life, the false for the true.

How are these five characteristics of unhealthy behavior replaced with healthy behavior? I believe that the early church, as recorded in the book of Acts, illustrates how this process begins.

> So then, those who had received his word were baptized; and there were added that day about three thousand souls. And they were continually devot-

ing themselves to the apostles' teaching and to fellowship, to the breaking of bread and to prayer. And everyone kept feeling a sense of awe; and many wonders and signs were taking place through the apostles. And all those who had believed were together, and had all things in common; and they began selling their property and possessions, and were sharing them with all, as anyone might have need. And day by day continuing with one mind in the temple, and breaking bread from house to house, they were taking their meals together with gladness and sincerity of heart, praising God, and having favor with all the people. And the Lord was adding to their number day by day those who were being saved" (Acts 2:41-47).

A careful study of this section of Scripture will impart many insights regarding the life of the early church. Notice that the continuing reinforcement of new patterns, accompanied by joy and transparency, resulted in the transformation of lives and gave a new sense of mission and purpose as more believers joined.

I believe this same pattern reflects the process of restoration today. Members of the early church did not view Christianity as an event or a one-time experience; they knew that it began with the event of regeneration that was expressed through baptism and remained a continuing experience of change and growth from glory to glory. This continuing process included teaching, fellowship, breaking bread, prayers, and mission. Mission was the ongoing fulfillment of the great commission to "make disciples of all nations, baptizing them in the name of the Father, and the Son and the Holy Spirit, teaching them to obey all things he commanded" (Matt. 28:19). When growth and experience are not shared to help others, then the process becomes stagnant and stops.

The first characteristic: A faulty belief system
The process of change: Teaching
The purpose: To replace false belief systems with truth
The result: Reframing, or looking at life experiences with God's interpretation

The second characteristic: Unmet emotional, physical, and spiritual needs
The process of change: Fellowship
The purpose: To replace wrongful relationships with meaningful and pure relationships
The results: Rebonding, or giving God our whole heart

The third characteristic: Inadequate and immature response to difficult life situations

The process of change: Breaking bread
The purpose: To replace memories of guilt, shame, and hurt with forgiveness, peace, and joy
The results: Reanchoring, or experiencing new memories through experiences, rituals and identification

The fourth characteristic: A lack of proper boundaries and convictions
The process of change: Prayer
The purpose: To replace temptations to fulfill selfish ambitions with the kingdom of God
The results: Rebuilding, or giving reality to life situations and establishing God's convictions

The fifth characteristic: A faulty value system
The process of change: Mission
The purpose: To replace a lack of eternal purpose and joy with a new vision and enthusiasm
The results: Redirecting, or changing priorities and plans to fulfill God's will.

The next five chapters will discuss how each unhealthy behavioral pattern can be replaced.

Study questions

1.) Our beliefs about God influence all of our beliefs in life. How do Satan and his lies try to undermine God's glory in your life?

2.) Lust of the eyes is a powerful human appeal. How can you better enjoy the beauty of creation in a spiritual way?

3.) Think about a past failure or traumatic event in your life. How can you free yourself from that experience and use it to enrich your future?

4.) Healthy spiritual, emotional, and physical growth depends upon a healthy relationship with God and man. How does God work in your own life to assure growth in these areas?

5.) Everyone has their own way of dealing with pressure and stress. How do you cope with it? Does your response usually help to resolve or camouflage the problem?

6.) Think about the emotional boundaries your parents lived by as you grew up. Do you still live within those boundaries? Are they comfortable for you today?

7.) Healthy boundaries allow us to establish healthy priorities for family, church and work commitments. When you priorities become jumbled and cause friction in your life, how could you reset your boundaries?

8.) We are all guilty of placing importance on something we later realize was unhealthy. How have you replaced that tendency with a healthy and productive value?

FIVE

REFRAMING

Looking at Life Experiences with God's Interpretation

We have all heard the saying, "time heals." Actually, it isn't so much that time heals, but that our perspective of events and circumstances changes over a period of time. We have all met people who have not healed over time. The hurt, the pain, and the difficulty they experience in their heart and mind is just as real today as it was when the event that triggered the pain, be it ten, twenty, or thirty years ago. So it should be obvious that time alone is not the healing agent; it is a matter of change in our perspective, our frame of reference, and the way we look at an event that allows healing. And although such changes usually take time, we have probably met people who have gone through painful events in the recent past but who continue to walk in joy and peace.

One of the outstanding characteristics of my wife Helen is her ability to walk in incredible peace. She did not develop this ability all at once, but over a period of years. As it developed, I began to realize that her perspective on events led her to expect a healthy, positive outcome. When I questioned her out of my own curiosity about her ability to walk in this sense of peace and joy, I discovered that it was not based upon gritting her teeth or denying or refusing to admit the reality of a situation. Her ability to walk in peace was based upon her perspective of the event or circumstance itself.

I believe that all negative and positive emotions are the result of our perspective. I began to ask questions of other people who I sensed had an ability to respond to difficult life situations in a meaningful way. In each case I discovered the same truth: These people had an ability to reframe situations and events in their minds and emotions by interpreting them in a positive and meaningful way. That is, they tried to see events as beneficial, and from God's point of view.

An example of this was clearly illustrated to me one day when I returned home after conducting seminars in various parts of the country. I was tired, depleted of emotional and physical strength, and faced a mountain of work on my desk that demanded immediate attention. When Helen brought several more letters to my attention, my stress level peaked, and I burst out in anger. "Don't you know I can never get this all done?" Feeling the pressure of having to travel again in two days, I blurted out, "I am just overwhelmed."

Helen quietly left the room with a look of surprise and hurt, but still that unusual sense of peace was there. "Oh God, please help me," my soul was crying out inside. "Why am I like this?"

In the past my pattern would have been to give up, put everything on hold (only to have the pressure mount), and kill my pain by spending the rest of the day eating hamburgers, snacking, drinking malts, reading several newspapers, and then feeling even worse about the situation and myself. Sadly, this response to stress was my typical pattern.

This time, however, I bowed my head and asked the Lord to give me wisdom (James 1:5), revelation, and the ability to see my circumstances through his eyes (Eph. 1:17). It was as though the Holy Spirit exchanged the words in my mind. Instead of saying, "I am overwhelmed," I tried "I am challenged." At first this seemed to be just a play on words or simply a psychological game that would lead nowhere, but in quest of a solution, I repeated to myself aloud: "I AM CHALLENGED to complete this task." Not only did I say these words, but inside I felt the sense of joy and peace that would result from completing the task. I felt a new sense of energy and creativity as I began sorting out the subject matter and prioritizing my workload. Even my posture improved; I was no longer slumped over. I found myself ready to charge forth in an important battle.

I nearly completed my "overwhelming task" with enough energy and creativity left over to complete another task I had been put on hold. What had happened? Was this a one-time experience, or was this a pattern that could be repeated over and over with the same results?

I have seen many people experience similar life changing results by beginning to reframe situations and circumstances in their lives through picturing the event or scenes differently through word or phrase exchanges.

Second Kings 6:8-17 describes how the servant of the prophet Elisha prayed that his servant's eyes would be opened to the spiritual reality of what had been causing him great fear. The servant had just gone outside and seen an enemy army circling the city. When he cried out in fear, "What shall we do?" Elisha the prophet answered, "Do not fear, for those who are with us are more than those who are with them."

When Elisha prayed for the servant's eyes to be opened, the servant saw the mountain full of a heavenly army of horses and chariots of fire. Now the servant saw, by the Spirit, the reality of the situation. The Lord allowed him to see the same scene in a new way. He was able to respond with confidence where he had previously responded with fear. Even so, when we pray for the eyes of our heart to be opened (Eph. 1:18), we may expect to see circumstances as God sees them.

In Mark 5:35-42, reframing through word exchange is illustrated.

> While He [Jesus] was still speaking, they came from the house of the synagogue official, saying, "Your daughter has died; why trouble the Teacher anymore?" But Jesus, overhearing what was being spoken, said to the synagogue official, "Do not be afraid any longer, only believe." And He allowed no one to follow with Him, except Peter and James and John, the brother of James. And they came to the house of the synagogue official; and He beheld a commotion, and people loudly weeping and wailing. And entering in, He said to them, "Why make a commotion and weep? The child has not died, but is asleep." And they were laughing at Him. But putting them all out, He took along the child's father and mother and His own companions, and entered the room where the child was. And taking the child by the hand, He said to her, "Talitha Kum!" (which translated means, "Little girl, I say to you, arise!") And immediately the girl rose and began to walk; for she was twelve years old. And immediately they were completely astounded.

How interesting that Jesus refused to speak of the little girl as dead, but asleep. This exchange of words is not intended to deny reality, but to express God's intent. Neither is this an illustration of trying to change the will of God by speaking words, as though words alone could dictate God's sovereignty. Rather, this is an illustration of aligning the correct word or words to release the will of God as he intended.

We need to be reminded of the power of using and speaking the right words in harmony with his will, instead of using words and phrases that hinder his will in our lives and circumstances.

How well I remember the day Ray called me. Despair and concern were evident in his voice. It seemed to him as though his world was crashing around him. As we talked, I began to understand that Ray's perspective was not only centered on himself, but limited by his interpretation as to time and outcome. I began to ask Ray certain questions, and my intent was to help him gain a larger perspective.

Ray's despair centered on a financial crisis. The more he thought about it, the more he imagined that there would be no way for him to meet the needs of his family in about a year or two. Not surprisingly, Ray's entire perspective focused on finances. I'm not suggesting that finances are unimportant; I'm saying there are other values that are even more important and have more meaning and purpose.

I read to Ray from Hebrews 11 about the men and women of God who were willing to forfeit their every material belonging. They were willing to have taken from them that which was temporal, and they still retained joy and meaning and purpose in life. They were even willing to die for the kingdom. Ray began to realize that his focus was more on the temporal than on the spiritual. He also came to realize that he had believed the lie that financial security alone could make him happy. I believed that if his perspective on financial matters changed, then his response to life's situations would change too.

After about thirty minutes of conversation, Ray's voice began to change. His responses began to take on a new tone. After some guidance, Ray was able to refocus and gain a new perspective on money: it is important, it is necessary, but happiness and joy are not based upon how much or how little we have, but rather on how we see our financial life fitting into a larger picture. Ray was gaining a new perspective, a new way of looking at circumstances as part of a larger picture. He learned that the key to reframing situations and events, whether they are past, present, or future, is to see them as part of a larger picture.

I saw the same truth illustrated in a person I shall call Lee. He had just recovered from alcoholism, and had been through drug rehabilitation. He had made a new commitment to Jesus Christ. Lee had come from what seemed to be a very committed Christian home. His parents were deeply religious and well respected in the community, but there had been a long-standing conflict between Lee and his father. Lee had never really felt close to his father, yet one of his deepest desires was to please him. After Lee became a Christian and entered recovery from drugs, alcoholism, and other addictions, he wanted to return home to live with his parents. His hope was that since he was free from drugs and alcoholism and became a newly committed Christian, perhaps the closeness he had hoped for with his father would become a reality.

Lee lived at home for six months. Instead of experiencing joy, Lee was slipping into a low-grade depression. The day we met, he was at such a point of despondency and despair that he was considering returning to his old lifestyle. After I asked him several questions, Lee began to realize that he had the wrong perspective on his father. His passions needed to be refocused by changing his perception of events and reframing the way that he looked at things. It was obvious that Lee was basing his happiness upon his father's response to him. Lee began to realize that his father did not make him unhappy; it was the way he perceived his father's response that caused him unhappiness.

I explained to Lee that his father might never change, that years could pass and the closeness that he longed for with his father might never occur. And though I hoped that it would, and I certainly knew that this was Lee's desire, his sense of happiness, joy, and peace could not be based upon someone else's actions or reactions. His peace and joy in life were based upon his perceptions and perspective. I asked Lee what he believed God was doing in this situation in order to produce in him eternal qualities. Lee readily admitted that he was more responsive to people who were hurting, that it seemed that people who had difficult life circumstances were drawn to him for counsel. And as he walked more and more in a committed Christian life, he was able to give them meaningful answers, and that brought him even greater joy. Lee began to understand that his happiness should not be based upon someone else's response, but his own responses and his own relationship with Jesus Christ.

How do we, like Lee, see the larger picture? How do we begin changing our perceptions? I suggest that we enlarge our frame of reference by looking at events from our past, our present, and our future.

Let's talk about looking at the past. There are many people today who, because they experienced painful, difficult situations growing up, feel that their lives have been permanently scarred. I meet people almost on a weekly basis who believe they are second-class citizens, marred for life because of a childhood event. I would venture to say that all of us probably have painful events and circumstances in our past. But if we continue to live in the hurts and wounds of past events, they will forever prevent us from reaching our goals, from becoming what God wants us to become. *We will be believing a lie.* Paul says, "And we know that God causes all things to work together for good to those who love God, to those who are called according to His purposes" (Rom. 8:28). In other words, as we look at difficult past events and damaging circumstances, we're not saying that God caused them to happen. We're saying that God is big enough to turn circumstances that were life damaging and life destructive into meaningful experiences and even occasions for his glory and for our benefit.

This is precisely the lesson that we learn from the life of Joseph in the Old Testament. Joseph, as we know, was envied by his brothers because he was the favorite son of his father. He was later thrown into a pit by his brothers and left to die. But instead of dying, he was sold into slavery. As a slave, he ended up in the house of Pharaoh in Egypt. There he was falsely accused of rape and thrown into prison for two years.

Despite all those traumas, his perspective was this: "Man meant it for evil but God meant it for good." What difference did this make in Joseph's life? Joseph probably experienced more difficulty than many of us do. We're not talking about a couple of days in jail, but two years in bondage, two years that could have ended in his death. And yet Joseph was able to rise to such a place of understanding that eventually he became the second leader in all the kingdom of Pharaoh. God used his life to minister to the people who had originally sold him into slavery. It was the way that he looked at past and present events that enabled him to muster the resources he needed to minister to his own countrymen. He was able to look toward future resources, at future experiences, and see the broad perspective of why God had brought him to Egypt.

And the larger picture is this: God was not just dealing with Joseph, but with a nation through which Jesus Christ was to be born. In a prophetic sense, Joseph's life was not just his. It involved a nation, a kingdom, prophetic events, and even the birth of the Messiah many years later. Now, few people have a prophetic sense of understanding the future. But we can gather some sense through the Scriptures that God takes every event in our lives and works it together for his good, for our benefit, in his way, and in our time.

So as we begin to reframe our past, we ask certain questions: What does God want me to do with this circumstance? How will God use this event in my life to build character in me and to benefit others? When I talk to people who have experienced destructive events in their past, I ask them, "Do you believe that you are more sensitive to people because of this event? Do you believe that this event, through the eyes of God and the spirit of God, has helped to develop in you a quality that makes you a better person or could make you a better person?" Without exception, I have always received a positive response. In looking at the Scriptures, it is clear that often out of great failure comes great ministry. Often in our greatest weakness, God's strength is perfected in us.

It was the apostle Peter who was always putting his foot in his mouth. It was Peter who said he would never deny the Lord. Peter is the only man I know of in Scripture who was interrupted three times, once by God the Father, once by the Son, and once by the Holy Spirit. And yet it was Peter who denied the Lord. But he came to conviction and repentance, and out of that experience, he became the spokesman at Pentecost. He was the one who received the keys to open the door to the Gentile believers. And yet his greatest failures included his denial of the Lord, his anger, and his cursing.

How should we view past circumstances? By looking at them through the eyes of God and the interpretation of the Holy Spirit. If we do not look at our past from a conviction that God can use all events for his glory and our benefit, we will be bound in shame and guilt for a lifetime. I am not suggesting that repentance is unnecessary. Nor am I suggesting that we should not feel sorrow over past events. But sorrow is an emotion we should work through as quickly as possible. It is only by looking at our past and applying God's perspective that we can see the larger picture.

We must ask ourselves some questions: Is God in control? Is God able to use even our mistakes for his glory? Is God able to use present circumstances? Is God working in us now? What quality is God trying to build in us? We will not become bitter from an experience to the degree that we can learn from it.

Remember Ray, whose focus was entirely on money. He was temporally focused rather than eternally focused. Could it be that God was using circumstances to build a larger perspective in Ray, so that his values would be transformed from temporal to eternal? Ray had a tendency to hoard riches and was unable to share them. I explained to Ray that there is a difference between being rich and being prosperous. Being rich is when we hoard things and keep them for ourselves. Being prosperous is when we allow God to bless us and, with wisdom, use financial and material blessings to meet the needs of others.

So we reframe our life by perceiving it in broader terms of time. We also enlarge our frame of reference by looking at life in terms of other people. The Scripture tells us that no one lives to himself and no one dies to himself. We may be considering actions that would be unbelievably destructive. But we often think about such acts without considering how they would affect others. That's why we should ask ourselves some tough questions: What is this present circumstance? How is it going to affect my children? How is it going to affect my wife? How is it going to affect my family? If we look at a circumstance only in terms of how it affects us, we have narrowed our perception of life—and dangerously so.

After I resigned from the pastorate in 1985, the news of my resignation was released to the local paper and then to the Associated Press. My wife and I had just gone to a friend's home to pick up the key to his condominium in Florida, where we were going to stay for two or three weeks. As we walked through the front door, I saw the afternoon paper and the front page story about my resignation. It felt like a knife had been plunged deep into my heart. My legs became rubber and I could hardly stand up. I could barely even talk.

I will never forget how he quoted 1 Corinthians and prayed that God would use this awful circumstance, which had just happened about two or three days before, so that I could comfort others in the same way I would be comforted. Now, I have to admit that at the time, I saw absolutely no possibility of that happening. My frame of reference was simply based upon the circumstances of exposure, despair, shame, and the humiliation I was experiencing. But there was something about those words about being able to comfort others that caused hope to spring in my heart. You see, as I began to look at my situation in terms of others, it began to change. I realized in the following days that not only was there a possibility that I would be restored, however long that would take, but that afterward I would have the opportunity to restore others.

I also began to consider what the situation meant to my family—that healing would come not only to me, but to the people who shared my situation. Perhaps I would even be able to help them. Suddenly my perspective began to change. And over the next few months and years, it continued to change dramatically as I began to enlarge my frame of reference in terms of others and how they were affected by my actions.

I felt great despair in those days because of the disappointment I had brought to the kingdom of God and the body of Jesus Christ. I knew that my own sin had been a great betrayal of those who had trusted me. But at the same time, as I received God's forgiveness, I asked forgiveness of others and purposed to make things right, however long that would take. I also knew it was possible (and time proved me right) that there were many people in the kingdom who were in situations similar to mine. If I would submit myself to the hands of a loving God to help me walk in restoration, not only could I be restored, but I could possibly be an instrument to restore others who had been in similar situations.

It was by looking at the present and the future in terms of others that I began to reframe a situation that originally seemed unbelievably hopeless. We're able to reframe our life circumstances and gain a larger picture if we think in terms of others, such as our family and the kingdom. I knew that my message would begin to change. And it has. Not because my old message was invalid, but because now there is a new emphasis in my life. This change came about as I began to view things in terms of others.

One day a minister friend named John called me with a greatly disturbed heart. He had just been, he believed, falsely accused of an impropriety. As he poured out his heart about this accusation, I could hear the frustration in his voice because the accusations were inaccurate and potentially damaging. I asked John several questions. First I asked, "John, was the accusation partially true?" As he shared the details with me, it certainly seemed clear that the person who aired the accusation was either trying to slander and cause damage, or had projected their own guilt upon John.

I asked John another question: "John, even though these events may be untrue and the accusation is false, is there anything that you can learn from this experience?" John was almost in despair, troubled that the words that were spoken could be so used against him. John had been in a lay counseling ministry. And as he reflected on the situation, he admitted that as a result of that accusation, he was going to change his entire method of counseling. At first his intent was to stop making himself available to people. But as he reconsidered, he began to see that though the accusations were false, there were some lessons he needed to learn from them.

First, he realized that he met with people in a questionable place—a place where he could easily be accused of harboring improper motives. Second, John realized that it would have been smarter to employ a team to counsel a person with this type of problem. In this case, it dealt with sexuality. Third, he realized that there were questions he had asked this person that could have been misconstrued as too intimate. As John began to look at the circumstances in terms of others, he began to gain a new perspective. Even though the false accusations had no lasting effect on his character, it had the deeper effect of enabling John to reframe that situation in terms of his counseling.

I will never forget the evening Mark came to see me after I had conducted a seminar in his church. At the time, he was separated from his wife. This beautiful couple, married with all kinds of dreams and hopes for their Christian walk, now saw their dreams and plans shattered upon the floor of damaged emotions and an inability to communicate. I realized that Mark was looking at this situation only in terms of himself. He was not able to see it in terms of others, especially his wife.

We are all guilty of this lapse at some point, but we must interpret an event in terms of others. That means interpreting an event from the standpoint of what they're saying. We need to see the situation through their eyes—to try to feel the way they may feel and understand the way they may perceive it. This allows us to see an opportunity for reconciliation.

That evening I asked Mark to write down what he believed were the negative problems in his life from his wife's point of view. He had never done this before. He saw her as an incessant complainer, someone who always pointed out his problems. And he underlined the word "always." Nevertheless, Mark wrote down seven problems. Using his wife's words, the first problem was, "Don't block me out. You're not listening to me." His second notation was, "I don't do the things she asks me to do—simple things such as taking out the trash." The third problem, she would say, was, "You're always changing the subject. Don't change the subject. Let's talk through what we're dealing with." The fourth was, "Don't lie or hide the truth."

91

The fifth problem, from her point of view, was that Mark showed more sensitivity and compassion to the people he worked with than to her. The sixth problem, she would say, was, "You don't respect me." The seventh problem was the most painful for Mark: "Don't punish me. You punish me by your silent treatment. Whenever we have a disagreement, you get quiet or withdraw." These seven problems seemed to be at the root of their estrangement. And there was so much pain that Mark wasn't sure they could ever get back together. Their communication was now limited to weekly conversations by phone.

I asked Mark, "Why don't we ask the Holy Spirit to give a discernment to reinterpret or to reframe so that you can look at what she is saying from her perspective? Mark, don't just listen with your head; listen with your heart." After we prayed for wisdom and understanding, we took each problem and tried to reframe it from the standpoint of how Mark could meet his wife's needs. For example, when she said, "Don't block me out," she was really asking him to listen to her. She wanted him to believe that her thoughts were important.

Mark believed the second problem—doing things she asked him to do—stemmed from his wife's bossiness. Reframed, maybe what she was really saying was, "My needs are important. I need to know that I am of value." Mark viewed the third problem—"You're always changing the subject"—as another attempt by his wife to control him, this time through conversation. Perhaps his wife's real need was to be cared about, to know that her feelings were of value to him, and that he would be interested in resolving her issues.

Instead of insisting that she was "always" accusing him of falsehoods, Mark needed to see that his wife's fourth problem stemmed from her need to trust him. He had clearly violated her trust. Mark had considered the fifth problem—him showing more devotion to his coworkers than to his wife—as a sign of self-centeredness and possessiveness. He now began to see that what his wife really craved was intimacy.

When she said, "You don't respect me," what she was really saying was, "I want you to be consistent. I need to feel worth." And when she said, "Mark, don't punish me," what she meant was that she needed him to honor her, grant her a sense of dignity, and encourage her.

It was astonishing how Mark's own responses began to change. That night, he called his wife and they talked for three hours. He asked for her forgiveness for the way he had treated her. He now knew that she was really trying to share her heart, not control his life through unfair demands. He declared a new willingness to be the husband God wanted him to be. He promised to begin ministering to her needs. A short time later, their marriage was restored and rebuilt and they reunited. Mark learned that instead of interpreting his wife's problems in purely a negative way, he would use them as opportunities to hear her heart crying out to him. Moreover, Mark and his wife now help other couples rebuild their marriages.

How exciting it is that by reframing a situation, by enlarging our picture in terms of others, we can see something not just the way we would normally look at it, but the way they look at it. In the end, we are able to change our perceptions.

Finally, and perhaps most important, we gain a larger perspective by looking at situations in terms of God's purpose for our character. How many times have we interpreted an event from the standpoint of our own personal needs, and not from the standpoint of God's kingdom? We harbor the wrong perception of what happiness is, then we decide that our life is ruined and that our purpose is shattered. Most of us fail to ask for the insight to understand God's purpose in such circumstances.

It is interesting that the apostle Paul wrote many of his letters in prison. Most of the churches he started, as far as we know, are no longer in existence as local congregations. But the words he wrote continue to minister and serve as the foundation of churches throughout the world.

We often look at change as something that ruins our lives. I am not suggesting that every change is God's intent. Man can intend things for evil purposes. I am saying that God can take whatever he has caused or whatever he has allowed and work it together for our good, for our benefit, and for his glory. We need to look at circumstances in terms of God's purpose—God's purpose for our lives, God's purpose for ministry, and God's purpose for others.

A geographical change, for example, will lead us to form new friendships. If our children are young, the change will affect who their friends will be and maybe even who they will marry. That's why we should make changes with prayer and spiritual warfare—because negative consequences can occur whenever we walk outside of his purpose and outside of the shadow of his wings.

When I resigned from the ministry in 1985, I saw no purpose for the future. I wished I had died. I realized that I had brought on the consequences of my sin. I knew what Peter meant when he said that it isn't very profitable to suffer for our own sins; there is no great profit when we suffer for that which is false. It was then that the Lord spoke the words to me that forever will be written on my heart: "You will be an example of my mercy and my restoration."

When we suffer for sin, there isn't very much profit except that we can let God take a broken vessel, use it for his glory, and then minister out of the brokenness according to the grace that he has given us. But when the Holy

Spirit spoke those comforting words to my heart—"You will be an example of my mercy and my restoration"—I never dreamed that the Lord would release me to a seminar ministry. I never dreamed that I would write books and other materials.

As I look back, I realize that it was certainly not God's purpose for me to sin. But out of my failure, and because of my repentance, God in his grace took a heart that was willing to repent and used it for his purpose. I understand more about the grace of God today—and I stand in it more—than I ever have in my entire life. Yes, God is able. Whatever your circumstance, whatever your disappointment, look at it from the perspective of his kingdom, and also in terms of your character.

God is more concerned about our character, eternal perspective, eternal healthiness, and spiritual wholeness than any one event in our lives. To what degree may God allow circumstances to happen in order to release his grace in us? As we look at situations in terms of God's purpose for his kingdom and our character, we can give a new interpretation to life events. As we are able to reframe life situations, perhaps the most difficult thing we will face is maintaining the proper basis for doing that, for the Scripture warns about those people who would lean to their own understanding. And yet the Bible is filled with men and women of God who were able to give new perspective to difficult circumstances. They were able to do it by the grace of Jesus Christ because they had a sense and an understanding of Scripture.

The basis for enlarging our frame of reference has at least two major guidelines: the Word of God and prayer. It is vital that we etch the Word of God in our hearts. It is not enough to look at life's circumstances from our own human reasoning or understanding. We might hit on what is right, but often what passes for reasoning is distortion and selfish ambition. The Scripture and prayer should always be the basis of our perception of time and eternity.

Study questions

1.) What is your typical response to stressful situations? Do you shirk from them or try to confront them? How might you improve your response?

2.) Think about a time when you have felt particularly overwhelmed. How could you have changed your perspective to feel challenged instead?

3.) What other words or phrases could you use as a substitute for "overwhelmed" when you sense yourself starting to procrastinate? What words will energize you?

4.) Reflect on a situation or circumstance that causes you considerable distress, in and of itself. How can you reframe that situation in terms of the bigger picture of your life?

5.) Joseph's perspective on life was a tremendously optimistic one: "Man meant it for evil but God meant it for good." How can you reframe a traumatic experience in your life from Joseph's perspective?

6.) Seeing the larger picture requires us to step back from the frame. Try to imagine what a presently unpleasant situation might mean to you years from now.

7.) Think about an unhealthy action you have contemplated or are contemplating now. Perhaps you have thought about how that act would affect you. Now consider how it would affect your spouse, your children, and your family.

8.) Reflect on a change in your life that caused you some upheaval or distress. How can you reframe that experience to see that it was for your good, for your benefit, and for God's glory?

SIX

REBONDING

*Giving God Our Whole Heart and Committing Ourselves
to Those He Commits Us To*

Ron, a former minister, had resigned from the ministry because of sexual problems. He was now on a course of self-destruction. Having separated from his wife, Ron was visiting topless lounges and massage parlors on a regular basis. Desperate for help, he called me, and we agreed to meet for lunch the next day. Sitting across the table from me, he looked gaunt and tired as he poured out his story of shame and guilt. During our conversation, I asked Ron the same question I have asked many other people: "What do you believe you are searching for when you go to those places?"

Pausing, he replied almost in a whisper, "I guess I'm trying to belong. I never really thought about it before, but come to think of it, it's not just the sexual excitement, but feeling a part of the crowd—the smoking, the rowdiness, the feeling of being one of the guys." Embarrassed, he continued, "You know, even growing up I never had a close guy friend. The only way that I knew how to belong was to brag about my sexual conquests, often exaggerating for approval."

Tears were glistening in Ron's eyes as he painfully recalled some childhood events, including a molestation by an older boy. Recounting his shame and guilt after the molestation and further alienation from an emotionally distant father, Ron began to understand his desperate search for a meaningful connection, especially for a male friend.

Though Ron's history did not include homosexual feelings, his legitimate need for male bonding was a force behind his addictive sexual behavior. The ministry had not fulfilled this need because of his continuing shame and

97

guilt. He believed the old lie: If someone really knew me, they couldn't possibly love me.

Ron's recovery involved a long, hard road of breaking the cycle of addiction and shame. It has required regular participation in a support group that specializes in recovery from sexual addictions. His restoration has been reinforced and enhanced by building trust and confidence with the men in his group. Bonding with other men has been a healthy way to replace his old behavior.

This example may sound extreme. However, I believe it highlights the need for true fellowship and bonding in the body of Christ. Some researchers have suggested that as many as ten percent of all believers in the United States suffer from some form of sexual addiction. This statistic alone should awaken the church to one of the deepest needs of the human heart: the need to belong and have meaningful relationships.

The apostle John seemed to understand this need from his own human experience and relationship with Jesus. "What we have seen and heard we proclaim to you also, that you also may have fellowship with us; and indeed our fellowship is with the Father, and with His Son Jesus Christ. And these things we write, so that our joy may be made complete" (1 John 1:3-4).

Of course, sexual addiction is not the only expression that develops from a lack of bonding. A host of other expressions are attempted by people as substitutions for the ultimate relationship and bonding with God our Father through Jesus Christ, as well as for meaningful and fulfilling relationships with others.

What is bonding?

In his book, *Changes that Heal*, Dr. Henry Cloud says that "bonding is the ability to establish an emotional attachment to another person. It's the ability to relate to another on the deepest level. When two people have a bond with each other, they share their deepest thoughts, dreams, and feelings with each other with no fear that they will be rejected by the other person" (46).

Dr. Cloud's definition of bonding is excellent. I believe that we can further define the levels of bonding that take place between two people:

Fellowship. Fellowship occurs when the spirit of Christ in one person touches and communicates with the spirit of Christ in another person. The spirit of Christ, in union with our human spirit, is able to respond without measure, dependent, of course, upon one's sensitivity, discernment, and anointing. In this sense, we can bond in the spirit with any individual believer or a group of believers.

Friendship. Friendship occurs when expressions of our soul (mind, will, and emotions) connect and relate to those of another. Thus, bonding can take place at various limited, guarded, or intimate levels:

1. The mind or intellect. Friendship or bonding at this level usually involves commonalty in realms of mutual agreement, such as politics, religion, world events, social and moral issues, etc. Though intellectual needs may be satisfied, deeper emotional needs may still lack fulfillment.

2. The will or volition. Friendship or bonding at this level goes further than simply sharing intellectual interests. It involves doing things together, spending time on common interests, and making decisions that affect each other. Though this level is deeper than the first, it may still be void of deeper emotional sharing or expressions of concern.

3. Emotions or feelings. Deepening levels of bonding and friendship occur when both people begin to share feelings, needs, histories, and intimate details of their lives. It would seem that the healthiest bonding takes place progressively, beginning with spiritual oneness, and develops with time.

Comradeship. Comradeship is a bonding together and commitment for ministry. It seems that God first calls men together in relationships before he calls them together in ministry. This seems to have been his own pattern with the twelve disciples. It was also evident in the New Testament order among the early leaders, such as Paul and Barnabas, and Peter and John. The souls of David and Jonathan being knitted together is probably one of the best examples of comradeship. This type of friendship is perhaps the one most men desire but never achieve.

Companionship. Marriage without bonding at all these levels, including the expression of sexual intimacy, is in reality only a mirage of what God really intended. When a marriage is based only on emotional and physical intimacy, true bonding is interrupted by the lack of spiritual development and friendship. Conversely, marriage including spiritual oneness and friendship but lacking physical and sexual intimacy may also lack the deepest expressions of closeness and intimacy.

We need to bond

The creation experience itself reveals the most basic need of bonding, first with the God of creation, then in the relation of man and woman (Gen. 2:18-25). This expression of bonding is mentioned in the last book of the Bible: "And the Spirit and the bride say, 'Come.' And let the one who hears say, 'Come.' And let the one who is thirsty come; let the one who wishes take the water of life without cost" (Rev. 22:17). This deep experience of bonding is God's plan for his disciples and is so illustrated in the teachings of Jesus:

> I am the true vine, and my Father is the vinedresser. Every branch in Me
> that does not bear fruit, He takes away; and every branch that bears fruit, He
> prunes it, that it may bear more fruit. You are already clean because of the
> word which I have spoken to you. Abide in Me, and I in you. As the branch can-
> not bear fruit of itself, unless it abides in the vine, so neither can you, unless

you abide in Me. I am the vine, you are the branches; he who abides in Me, and I in him, he bears much fruit; for apart from Me you can do nothing. If anyone does not abide in Me, he is thrown away as a branch, and dries up; and they gather them, and cast them into the fire, and they are burned. If you abide in Me, and My words abide in you, ask whatever you wish, and it shall be done for you. By this is my Father glorified, that you bear much fruit, and so prove to be my disciples. Just as the Father has loved Me, I have also loved you; abide in My love. If you keep my commandments, you will abide in My love; just as I have kept My Father's commandments, and abide in His love. These things I have spoken to you, that My joy may be in you, and that your joy may be made full. This is My commandment, that you love one another, just as I have loved you. Greater love has no one than this, that one lay down his life for his friends. You are my friends, if you do what I command you. No longer do I call you slaves; for the slave does not know what his master is doing; but I have called you friends, for all things that I have heard from my Father I have made known to you (John 15:1-15).

A careful reading of this Scripture will clearly reveal several important truths about bonding. Bonding involves commitment, a sense of connection, a sense of belonging, allowing oneself to be pruned (or corrected), and love for one another, even to the point of laying down one's life for another. Bonding also involves trust and the sharing of intimate information. Some of the results of bonding include creativity (bearing fruit) and feeling joy. These characteristics are only a few listed in this section of Scripture.

Jesus so deeply understood the need of his disciples to bond that in his prayer to the father in John 17:26, he says, "And I have made Thy name known to them, and will make it known; that the love wherewith Thou didst love Me may be in them, and I in them."

Bonding depends on our psychological and spiritual growth

Students of childhood development understand that a child bonds first (or should bond) with its mother in the womb, then bond again with her after birth. At this stage a child may have no real perceptions of others except a sense of oneness and bonding with the mother. It is during this period of development that the child experiences either well-being, no well-being, or worse, a feeling of non-being.

From about eighteen months old, the child will attempt to bond with the father or another caregiver, in addition to the mother. During this period, the child develops a sense of others and relationships. The need for belonging begins to be satisfied. The lack of bonding during either of these two stages leaves a child with a feeling of emptiness and abandonment. The search for bonding to fulfill these needs may take many different forms.

It is later during group activities involving games, sports, school, or work experiences that group bonding develops. Group bonding instills a sense of confidence, power, and accomplishment in a child. Not only is the need for belonging reinforced, but the need for becoming what God has intended is starting to come into focus. When this stage is interrupted, however, feelings of inadequacy, passivity, or boredom develop.

These three stages coincide in an interesting way with God's plan for creation:

> Then God said, "Let us make man in Our image, according to Our likeness; and let them rule [have dominion] over the fish of the sea and over the birds of the sky and over the cattle and over all the earth, and over every creeping thing that creeps on the earth." And God created man in His own image, in the image of God He created him; male and female He created them. And God blessed them; and God said to them, "Be fruitful and multiply, and fill the earth, and subdue it; and rule over the fish of the sea and over the birds of the sky, and over every living thing that moves on the earth" (Gen. 1:26-28).

God's image is his glory and character and involves our sense of *being*. God's likeness is his order and involves our sense of *belonging*. God's dominion is his purpose and involves our sense of *becoming*. Even though Adam fell from this original design, in Christ we are being transformed back into his image from glory to glory (2 Cor. 3:18).

In man's fallen and unredeemed state, the basic needs of our being, belonging, and becoming are still valid. Man without the Holy Spirit will attempt to meet these basic needs in his own way. The search for bonding and meaningful relationships to fill these unmet needs may be attached to any number of things, persons, or processes. In man's attempt to either fill the vacuum left in his soul or to cover the pain of loneliness and shame, his wrong choices in relationships and bonding will be at the core of addictive behavior.

An addiction is, in reality, a search for relationship. An authority on the subject of recovery from sexual addiction (and a recovering addict himself) once told me that when he enjoyed meaningful relationships with other men, his addictive behavior of multiple affairs with women subsided altogether. I pondered this statement for some time and realized that, if true, there are powerful implications to rebonding with the appropriate people. I have also come to realize in my own experience that the need for appropriate bonding is, indeed, one of the necessary steps to freedom.

Bonding priorities

No relationship and meaningful bonding experience can take place without first entering a proper relationship with God our Father through Jesus Christ. John the apostle clarified this point when he said, "But if we walk in the light as He Himself is in the light, we have fellowship with one another, and the blood of Jesus His son cleanses us from all sin" (1 John 1:7).

The apostle Paul instructed a husband to love his wife "just as Christ also loved the church and gave Himself up for her" (Eph. 5:25). "So husbands ought also to love their own wives as their own bodies. He who loves his own wife loves himself" (Eph. 5:28). Paul concludes by saying, "This mystery is great; but I am speaking with reference to Christ and the church" (Eph. 5:32).

This is indeed a great mystery with far more implications than I could share here. However, I believe it starts with acquiring a deep appreciation for the tremendous, eternal love that the Father has for his Son, Jesus Christ (John 17:26). It is only when a man has received the love of a father that he can love himself properly and, thus, truly love his wife as Christ loves the church.

The second bonding priority should be our family—our spouse and our children. It is adulterous to look to others to meet the emotional and physical needs that God has designed to be met in marriage. Our spouse should be our best friend and companion. A bonding relationship with our spouse will lead to other relationships that are balanced, accountable, and meaningful.

Hindrances to bonding
One of the deepest longings of the human heart is to be in a relationship with another person. This longing is often never fulfilled because of hindrances that sabotage the bonding process. These hindrances worked in my life and the lives of many people I have ministered to. True bonding will occur only as these hindrances are removed. The three most prevalent hindrances to bonding are:

Fear of rejection. This fear often stems from past experience. The reasoning? "If I don't get close to someone, then I can't be rejected." This is a self-defense mechanism to prevent more pain. However, when our basis for approval and happiness is man's acceptance instead of God's acceptance, then the final result will always be fear. "Perfect love cast out fear," I John 4:18 says. As we come to know and experience God's love, we are more fully able to be a channel of his love to others. We are able, by his grace, to give without expecting anything in return, since like David of old we can say, "My expectations come from thee, oh Lord." Whatever another person can give or not give to us is enough. Our sufficiency is in the Lord.

Lack of forgiveness. When we have not resolved past hurts and offenses, our relationships with others will at best be guarded and reserved. Innocent people and potential friends are blocked out of our lives because they look like or in some way remind us of someone who has offended us. When the spirit of unforgiveness is present in our hearts, it is easier to become disappointed by present relationships, thus compounding the hurt.

Even unforgiveness is based on unbelief. We are basically saying, "I don't believe that God is big enough to bring justice, and if I don't take matters into my own hands, the person offending will not be punished or hurt for the hurt I've been caused." Yet the Lord does work everything together for good for those who love him and for those who are the called according to his purposes. What is meant for evil, God can make good.

Possessiveness. Possessiveness is really a form of jealousy. The desire to control another person is not love; it's rejection. It is more than a refusal to allow another person to be what God has designed and called that person to be. It is demanding and pressuring that person to be what *we* think he or she should be. It is a basic rejection of God's purpose for another, and thus a rejection of that person.

Possessiveness will always prevent meaningful bonding, for it demands acceptance and cannot result in the joy and fulfillment of receiving God's grace unconditionally through another. Possessiveness does not lead to a relationship with another person; it is an extension of a relationship with ourselves. It results in insecurity, loneliness, and unfulfillment.

The twelve steps to bonding

My own journey into meaningful bonding has been a slow and sometimes painful experience. Sometimes I paused along the way because of past fears, other times I rushed matters in an effort to meet my needs. The following steps have helped me shed some of the most painful emotions: loneliness and isolation. This process has not been without its pitfalls. It has involved one-and-a-half years of Christian psychotherapy, participation in a sexual addiction clinic and support groups, and the kindness and understanding of—and sometimes confrontations with—my wife.

On occasion, my journey began taking on the characteristics of my old addictive behavior. At other times I vowed never to trust anyone, much less let someone else into my life. Today I can say, from the bottom of my heart, that the journey has been worth it. I have come to realize that the loneliness and pain that I felt for much of my life was abnormal. The friends God has brought into my life have set me on a new course of learning. To my wife, my best friend, and others who I have learned to relate to and share with, I am deeply grateful. I trust that these steps will assist you on your own journey.

Take the initiative. A friend pointed out to me that Jesus chose his disciples. Most of my relationships had been with people who I felt needed *me*, and so I felt I *ought* to befriend them. Part of bonding means reaching out—making a phone call, inviting a person for a meal—and taking the initiative. Sometimes another person may be unable to fit us into their schedule or, for their own reasons, might fear a relationship. Usually after a conversation or two, one can determine if mutual interest exists. At the same time, pray for guidance. People who are coming out of addictive behavior and relationships must recognize their susceptibility to deception. Accountability is important.

Risk vulnerability. Sharing our feelings and needs too quickly can be destructive. However, never sharing anything can also be destructive. Therefore, these steps should be taken with discretion and at the right time. I have learned to be more vulnerable with my wife and in a ministers' support group. My openness with my wife about my feelings and temptations has not produced a barrier, but a greater sense of oneness. She has often told me that it is not the information that hurts her; the secrecy and dishonesty does. Risking vulnerability results in greater acceptance and closeness.

Learn about the interests of others. Sometimes we simply assume another person shares our interests. In some cases we may be right, but in others we may be wrong. I learned this lesson from my wife. I assumed that on her birthday or on our anniversary she wanted to go out to dinner and then see a movie. It was only after asking her what she wanted to do that I realized I had made plans to do what *I* enjoyed doing. Had I been more observant, I would picked up on her interests much earlier. If you start observing what other people do for others, you will often learn what they would like done for them. You can also ask them about their interests. Then keep a mental or written note and make an effort to make them happy.

Express gratitude and appreciation. Taking someone for granted is one of the easiest ways to wound a relationship. Showing genuine appreciation is a key ingredient to bonding. One of my biggest weak points was my failure to express appreciation to others. Once when I was pastoring, a man who had volunteered his electronics experience to my church told me he was leaving for another one. He said that he enjoyed the work—didn't even mind getting up early on Sunday mornings to cover several services and then performing the same tasks on Sunday evenings. But never once had I or anyone else said a simple thank you to him. He had felt used and unappreciated. Though I certainly was appreciative of his services, I had failed to express it. I learned my lesson. A simple note or card doesn't take long to write. It's one of the smallest ways we can say thank you.

Show respect. One of the best ways to show respect to anyone is to follow the biblical injunction to think more of others than ourselves. This doesn't mean we should lower our self-esteem, but recognize that every person we meet has been taught by God or has learned something through life experiences that we could benefit from. Learn to ask questions and receive. Receiving information, instruction, and even direction from another person gives that person honor.

Allow for shortcomings. Believing that you can't trust people if they make a mistake is one of the best ways to prevent bonding. Though we may not condone shortcomings, we must expect that, sooner or later, we will see flaws and be disappointed in others. Everyone has a threshold of tolerance. Habits like being late, exaggerating, forgetting to return borrowed items, interrupting conversation, etc., can be possible reasons to end a friendship. Genuine love is based on accepting people for who they are and, at the same time, loving them enough to help them change—not for our sake, but for theirs.

Share blind spots. We have all known people who seem to have almost everything going for them, but one problem stands out like a sore thumb. That person considers it a blind spot. As I conversed with a minister friend one day, he reminded me to refrain from sharing some information with a certain person. Later I realized how sad this was, because though the person he asked me not to share the information with was a wonderful person, he could not keep a confidence. In fact, he had developed a reputation as a gossip. I could not help but think, "Why hasn't someone pointed that out to him? It could only help him."

After this experience, I realized that I too probably had blind spots, but no one except my wife had taken time to love me enough to share them. Interestingly, we usually seek our spouse's counsel last since we reason that most people don't see us the way he or she does. One day I invited a friend for breakfast and during the meal I asked, "I know this may be difficult for you, but I know that most of us have blind spots. Would you help me by pointing out any of mine?" To be honest, I thought he would probably be too hesitant to say anything, or say they were too insignificant to mention. To my surprise, he responded, "Yes, there are three." Then he proceeded to explicate them. Though it was painful to hear, I realized that these qualities were the very ones my wife had talked with me about. Most likely, other people had seen and commented on them too. Bonding involves the sharing of blind spots and honestly working to change.

Experience the power of touch. By the time a baby is born, it has experienced for months the power of closeness in the mother's womb. The power and comfort of human touch continues to contribute to the child's development. Documented studies have revealed the importance of human touch in a child's emotional and physical development. Jesus practiced this expression by laying his hands on sick people, by blessing little children, and by allowing one of his own disciples, John, to recline on his breast. Bonding is enhanced by human touch. A handshake, a pat on the shoulder, a hug, and an embrace are all legitimate forms of physical closeness. Of course, we must respect other people's physical boundaries, especially those whose backgrounds include childhood molestation, rape, or other forms of physical and emotional abuse.

How well I still remember when, in the first years of my own recovery, a friend embraced me upon leaving. My arms were locked tightly against my body and my only response to this warm and expressive hug was coldness. My friend responded, "Don, you're not healed, you're dead." He was right. I had stopped acting *out*, but was now acting *in* by closing down my emotions and the expressions of them. It is not my purpose here to discuss the boundaries, cautions, and limits of legitimate touching, except to note that as it becomes comfortable and when it does not have sexual energy or overtones, the human touch is a big part of the bonding process.

Learn to bless others. Blessing others is very similar to expressing appreciation, but goes further in that it empowers and encourages. To bless is to thank a person for how he or she has benefitted our lives. On several occasions people have approached me after a seminar and thanked me for allowing God to use me to bless the body of Christ. To me, this is more than a form of appreciation; it is being blessed and empowered. Blessing others may be extended by giving financial gifts as well as by affirming the friend in his or her own gifts, callings, and direction in life.

Develop loyalty and trust. Ron, the minister I mentioned in the beginning of this chapter, had a difficult time believing that he could trust a friend, especially with information about his past and present failures. However, loyalty involves commitment not only when a person is popular and being blessed, but in the dark times of crisis, financial failure, moral relapses, and other distress. These are times when the true test of friendship begins. I am not suggesting that you overlook unrepentance and blatant rebellion, but I do believe that loyalty is walking with a person through the dark times of the soul—not just the good times. Loyalty is being there for a friend when the friend is not emotionally, physically, or spiritually capable of being there for you.

Loyalty also involves trust and confidence. A minister friend committed himself to helping my restoration when I resigned from the ministry in 1985. He invited me to attend his fellowship, accompany him on occasional speaking engagements, and have dinner with him and his wife whenever I was visiting their church. As other people heard of his actions, they warned and even rebuked him for reaching out to me. Since his ministry was just beginning to receive recognition, I watched with great interest and admiration as he received letters canceling tape orders and threatening to return tapes if he continued to help me. I was overwhelmed by his loyalty in doing what he believed God was calling him to do: remain my friend. I feel a very deep bond with that minister. He taught me the meaning of loyalty.

Give a relationship space. One of the distinctions between bonding of the soul and bonding of the spirit is that of anxiety and peace. People involved in soulful bonding who have not experienced spiritual bonding may feel anxiety when they are separated. They may constantly need to know where the other person is, who he or she is with, etc. Friends who are spiritually bonded will be concerned but not anxious about each other. The security they feel allows a continuance of oneness and sharing. True bonding means giving other people space to pursue and develop their own identity. Relationships should be inclusive, not exclusive.

Help fulfill another's goal and calling in life. True bonding is having a mutual interest in someone else's goals and purpose in life. In reality, we are talking about the characteristics of love mentioned by the apostle Paul in 1 Cor. 13. Love does not seek its own, but the good of the other. Genuine love desires success for the other and rejoices in the other's blessings and promotions.

We will now turn to the value of reanchoring, the process of experiencing new memories through our experiences and rituals.

Study questions

1.) Why is it necessary to form a strong bond with another human being? How can it help you overcome your sexual addiction?

2.) We all fear rejection at times. Think back to when you failed to pursue a healthy relationship because you feared rejection. How might you have harnessed your fear and developed that relationship?

3.) We cannot always expect people to reach out to us. How might you take the initiative in forming a relationship based upon mutual respect and trust?

4.) How can you learn about the interests of someone you would like to form a bond with? How can you use that knowledge to develop a relationship?

5.) Think of at least four ways you can regularly show appreciation and gratitude to someone important to you.

6.) We are often more capable of accepting our own shortcomings than those of others. How can you make a concerted effort to overlook the shortcomings of someone you genuinely care about?

SEVEN

REANCHORING

Establishing new memories and responses

Several years ago, Helen and I sat in a marriage counselor's office and admitted that we no longer loved each other. In fact, we admitted that we didn't even like each other. It was as though our negative emotions and experiences had anchored us in past memories so that we had become stuck in old responses. But during the ensuing months, something began to happen. We became best friends and our love for one another started growing. As a new friendship and love emerged, the old anchors rusted away and we became reanchored in a new relationship. It was only in retrospect that I began to discover what had happened. This same discovery can apply to almost every aspect of our lives, and we will discuss this phenomenon in this chapter.

There are three basis stages in a relationship: the romance stage, the disillusionment stage, and the transformation stage.

Romance stage

During this stage, usually courtship, most of our memories are very positive. In fact, there may be only a few bad memories, which probably indicates a state of denial. We usually want to spend most of our time together and can hardly wait for the wedding day with dreams of rapture and ecstasy. Even the wedding can be a part of this stage, with all the pictures of family and friends, the honeymoon, and our first house or apartment. We conjure up entirely good and positive memories that anchor our emotions and thoughts in a positive way.

Disillusionment stage

Time has a way of eroding our dreams as reality sets in. By now not all of our memories are good ones. There are the pressures of unpaid bills, staying up all night with a sick baby, each spouse feeling entitled to spend more time with old friends, and wanting a break away from it all. The honeymoon is over. We are now making the transition to the next stage.

Instead of wanting to be with our spouse, we find that his or her presence reminds us only of recent arguments. We keep fresh wounds open, remind each other about unfinished tasks, and argue about how to divide domestic responsibilities. Our memories are now becoming anchored in negative thoughts, not positive ones.

Sometimes infidelity enters the marriage, causing even deeper wounds. "What went wrong?" we may cry to ourselves in agony. Looking at old wedding pictures seems a lot like reading a fairy tale. Surely our spouse has changed—not us. He or she is not the same person we married. "If only there were a way out," we might groan. "Maybe I can wait it out until the children are grown, or I can receive training for a job to support myself." Caught in a quagmire of hurt and bad memories, our marriage is anchored in what seems like a whirlpool of confusion and unhappiness. Sadly, many of us never make the next transition to transformation and genuine love.

When Helen and I sat in the marriage counselor's office and admitted that we neither loved nor liked each other, the counselor seemed almost horrified when we told her we were leaving on a three-week vacation and ministry trip. Her only response at that time was, "You are either going to become best friends or get a divorce." What transpired during the next three weeks and the following year was actually a reanchoring of our memories to more positive experiences with each other.

Everything had been carefully packed the first day of our vacation when we pulled out of the driveway. Helen and I both were walking on eggshells, knowing that at anytime the wrong word or statement could erupt into a volcanic reaction of emotions and memories. Two years had passed since my resignation from the ministry. The shame and hurt from that experience had not yet healed, and it seemed that every scene between us served as another vivid reminder of hurt.

We were both trying to be sensitive and even began our trip with a brief prayer. At first, only silence was shared between us. Finally, Helen shared a joke from a magazine she was reading and we both laughed. Hours and miles slipped by with occasional conversation and the reading of several more jokes from the magazine.

Since our destination was Seattle, Washington, we passed through the mountain pass of New Mexico and encountered a feathery-like snowfall that began covering our windshield. We enjoyed the sight, and I realized that during times of hurt and disillusionment, we start to miss the small delights of God's handiwork. Stopping in Phoenix, Arizona, we had lunch with friends.

The quaint little restaurant gave us a romantic and refreshing feeling that we had been missing for a long time.

We left our friends after a wonderful visit and had just enough time to reach the Grand Canyon by sunset. The breathtaking view was another reminder of God's handiwork, and life began to take on a larger dimension than just our own little world. Several other positive events took place and, though our marriage was not suddenly transformed, the process of reanchoring from memories of pain and hurt began on this trip. God's grace was there even when we didn't recognize it.

During the next few months we were invited to move to the state of Florida to help a Christian leader begin a ministry to restore fallen leaders. Helen and I both sensed the hand of God in this invitation and placed our house on the market. The quick sale and other factors were confirmation that we were making the right decision. I had gone to Florida earlier for a speaking engagement, and spent one day looking for a place to live. To my surprise, the first place the realtor showed me was a beautiful condominium on the Atlantic Ocean. Even more surprising was that the condominium overlooked the very place on the beach where Helen and I had gone after my resignation from the ministry. There, while walking on the beach, the Lord had spoken to my heart, "You will be an example of my mercy and restoration." I was reminded of God's faithfulness each day I looked over the balcony onto the beach. Little did I know at the time that the Lord was now giving me new memories and experiences to replace the old ones. Our lives and marriage were beginning to be reanchored.

We leased the condominium at a reduced price from the owners and recognized it as a real blessing from the Lord. We spent the next two to three weeks cleaning one room, decorating it, and then starting on another. Probably one of the most memorable experiences in our new home took place the day I was cleaning an upstairs bathroom. The room had a beautiful white tile floor, but it had been badly marked after the former renter had tracked in tar from the beach. I was excited when I sprayed on a chemical, and with the swoosh of a sponge, the mark was gone, leaving a beautiful, gleaming floor. "Hurry, hurry," I cried out to Helen.

Running up the stairway to the bathroom where I was cleaning, she was partially out of breath and partially frightened by my excited cry. "What's wrong?" she asked. I could hardly contain my excitement. "Look!" I said. "Watch how by just spraying a little of this stuff on the floor, it only takes a moment to clean it." I was really proud of the gleaming white bathroom, with its large bathtub overlooking the Atlantic Ocean. Helen response was less enthusiastic. "Don, that's been on the market for twenty-one years." We both laughed, but I realized that for twenty-one years I had never helped her clean a bathroom, not to mention other rooms of the house.

We did not recognize the transformation that was taking place in our marriage, or at least we did not yet understand why it was happening. But it continued. During the later evening hours, we would walk together on the beach to watch the giant sea turtles come to shore to lay their eggs. Sometimes in the morning we walked across the street to the Blueberry Muffin Restaurant. When I went on ministry trips, I started missing Helen when she wasn't with me, and I always looked forward to being with her again. Our home didn't seem like a cage anymore, and I didn't want to escape from it. I wanted, and needed, to be there.

Transformation stage

By this time, we were entering the transformation stage of our relationship—the stage where we were able to face the reality of each other's faults and strengths and begin experiencing new memories. When we have more positive memories than negative memories of another person, we have reanchored the relationship. The transformation stage is where we release the painful and damaging anchors of old memories to establish new ones. So how do we go about doing this? By releasing the past, forgiving, making a heartfelt decision to release and forgive, sharing, and creating new anchors.

Releasing the past. By releasing the past, I do not mean forgetting the past. That's impossible for most people. However, the pain, hurt, shame, and any other negative memory associated with the past can be released.

The first time I returned to visit the old family farm where I was raised as a child, I was filled with a lot of memories, both happy and sad. It was interesting how certain scenes immediately brought about old memories and often the same emotions that I had felt at the time. Scenes, sights, sounds, voices, and even smells may call up feelings from the past.

Once we strongly associate our memory and our senses with a feeling or emotion, we become anchored in that emotion. That is why bitterness is spoken of as a root in Hebrews 12:15: "See to it that no one comes short of the grace of God; that no root of bitterness springing up causes trouble, and by it many be defiled."

A root is like an anchor that holds a plant in place. As long as the plant is held in that particular place, it will continue to receive the nutrients present in that particular location year after year. A plant is really no better than the soil it is planted in. A plant in poor soil has to be replanted in a new location or in new soil. It must be reanchored. If it is a bad plant—a weed—then it must be cut at the root.

This symbolism is used by the writer of the book of Hebrews: "For ground that drinks the rain which often falls upon it and brings forth vegetation useful to those for whose sake it is also tilled, receives a blessing from God; but if it yields thorns, and thistles, it is worthless and close to being cursed, and it ends up being burned" (Heb. 6:7-8).

A variant of this symbolism is used in the same chapter when the writer talks about being patient for God's promises, which we have as an "anchor of the soul, a hope both sure and steadfast and one which enters within the veil where Jesus has entered as a forerunner for us, having become a high priest forever according to the order of Melchizedek" (Heb. 6:19-20).

Forgiving. Our souls can be anchored in Christ, in our hope of glory and his promises, or we can be anchored and rooted in bitterness and lack of forgiveness. It depends upon our perception of and response to the Holy Spirit. Lack of forgiveness and bitterness are the foremost reasons that many people are anchored in a negative way to the past. True forgiveness involves forgiving from the heart, not just the mind. It is more than putting intellectual forgiveness on top of our shame and pain. It is fully releasing others from bitter judgments and allowing the Holy Spirit to reanchor us in his faith, hope, and love.

I like to think of the ministry of Jesus as prophet, priest, and king as it relates to forgiveness. Therefore, the first stage of forgiveness would involve the prophetic ministry of Jesus—that is, the bringing to light the hurts, offenses, and lack of forgiveness that is in our heart.

1. Recognize and acknowledge your feelings. In order to heal the wounded heart and deal with a lack of forgiveness, it is important to allow the Holy Spirit to expose our heart and any hidden matters. I was in my late forties before I could finally deal with the childhood molestation I suffered at the hands of an employee of my father. It was during a dream that the memories began to resurface, but even then shame and embarrassment kept me from actually acknowledging them. Maybe, I thought, I was just imagining the event, or had read something that I had projected onto myself. Some people do make up events and convince themselves that their fantasies are factual. But as other memories surfaced, it became apparent that I actually had been molested. My background in a macho, Texas cowboy culture produced an unspoken rule: men don't feel, and they especially don't cry or show emotion. It is essential in the restoration process that we allow the Holy Spirit to bring to our minds and hearts every unhealed emotion and memory. Only then will healing and reanchoring occur.

2. Don't minimize feelings. When Jan first began sharing details of her past with me, she would say repeatedly, "Now I know that I'm probably making too much of this." It was as though she kept trying to minimize her emotions so she wouldn't have to deal with them. It is a sin of pride to keep back what the Holy Spirit brings to light. It may be a risk for a person to exaggerate past hurts for attention, but I believe the greater danger is not sharing them or dealing with them.

Another way we may minimize our feelings is with statements like, "Well, that's just a part of growing up," or "Nobody has perfect parents," or "We're all human, aren't we?" During a break in one of my seminars, a man came to me and said he had been sexually molested as a youth by older neighborhood children. The molestations occurred at least twice a month for about five years. Even though he had tried to block out the memories, the unhealed pain and shame were resurfacing in destructive and damaging ways. Fortunately, during the seminar, he was able to share this information with his wife and a small group of male friends, who have since helped him forgive and start healing.

3. Allow your feelings to be as deep as they need to be. When I began sharing details of my own molestation with a support group, I kept apologizing for my tears and emotions. With each sniffle came a new apology, until one member of the group put a hand on my shoulder and said, "Don, that must have really been painful." It was as if a floodgate opened up inside of me and years of emotions began pouring out. The depth to which I acknowledged my feelings was the depth to which my healing occurred.

Sharing your feelings. We often think of the priestly ministry of Jesus as his praying on our behalf. This is a very important function, but another vital part of the priestly ministry of Jesus includes sharing feelings. "For we do not have a high priest who cannot sympathize with our weaknesses, but one who has been tempted in all things as we are, yet without sin. Let us therefore draw near with confidence to the throne of grace, that we may receive mercy and may find grace to help in time of need" (Heb. 4:15-16).

Share with Christ. At one point, I could not imagine that God would be interested in my feelings. But as I studied the Scriptures, I found that many men and women of God often poured out their hearts to him. The Psalmist David knew that the Lord hears our cries. During a period of dealing with sorrow and unresolved hurt in my own life, it was as though one day the Holy Spirit asked in that small, still voice, "Do you believe that the heart of God was broken because of your sins against him?" Since this experience took place a short time after my resignation from the ministry, I was quick to answer yes. How well I remember reading about the prophet Nathan approaching David about his adulterous affair and telling him forthrightly that he had both despised the word of the Lord and the Lord himself. I had already spent some time weeping before the Lord, and more and more I realized how my sin was against him. In 2 Cor. 7:10 the apostle Paul explains how this kind of godly sorrow will produce a repentance unto life.

Soon after this experience, the Holy Spirit again seemed to ask in that small, still voice, "Do you believe God's heart was broken over your sins against others?" "Oh yes," I answered. I began to realize this one day when an overwhelming sorrow filled my heart. I literally had to lie on the bed because of a lack of strength. It was as though I could feel some of the pain and loneliness my wife had suffered for several years because of my selfishness and addictions. Though I could never feel all that she had gone through, the Lord allowed me just a taste of it to bring me to a place of godly sorrow that works repentance. I had similar experiences regarding my daughter and son. Once we truly understand how our own sins affect others in very negative ways, we will not want to hurt them again, and this will result in deep change.

One Sunday morning after I spoke in a church, a group of students who had attended the church I had pastored before my resignation approached me. Because of the large size of the congregation, I had not seen them during the service. They explained that they had driven seven hours the day before to be there. Their first words were, "Don, we just want you to know that we have not lost respect for you, and we will always appreciate what you taught us." I was, of course, deeply moved by their encouragement. Even though I had asked forgiveness from their church, from many individual members, and through a letter in the local newspaper, I still felt prompted to ask them to forgive me personally for my hypocrisy, pride, and deception. "Oh, we have already forgiven you," they responded quickly.

Then, hesitantly, one of the young women said, "Don, I have also forgiven you, but I need to say something. I do not mean to hurt you, but please understand that when we attended the church you pastored, it cost us something. Because it was a church in renewal, we were made fun of and became the object of jokes. That really didn't matter, though, because of the joy and fulfillment of being a part of that church. But do you realize the jokes and remarks that we also had to hear when your sin was exposed?" I saw tears in her eyes, and I felt tears well in mine. God used this experience to help me more fully realize the hurt and shame that affected others in the body of Christ because of what I had done. Godly sorrow was certainly being engendered in me in ways I had not expected, but I realized that it was God's way of bringing me to a deeper level of repentance.

Believing that most of the grieving period was over, I was surprised to hear the Holy Spirit ask again in that small, still voice, "Don, do you believe that God's heart was broken because of sins against you?" I was honestly shocked. I couldn't imagine that God had even considered my hurts. Then I asked, "You mean all those years as I went through event after event?" "Yes," he replied, "all those sins against you broke the heart of the Father on your behalf." I was stunned. But somehow the Holy Spirit was showing me the heart of God the Father that I had not understood or known. Waves and waves of tears seem to wash my soul as I cast my burdens on him.

For anyone dealing with unresolved hurts and feelings, it is of great benefit and healing to share these with the Lord. After all, the Scriptures tell us that he bore our sorrows (Is. 53:4). Who else has the authority and ability to turn our sorrow into rejoicing and our sighs into psalms and songs of victory?

Share with others. The Christian community has been called a kingdom of priests, a holy priesthood, and a royal priesthood. This means that our responsibilities include praying on behalf of others, and also, like our Lord, being touched by their feelings of weakness. "Therefore, confess your sins to one another, and pray for one another, so that you may be healed. The effective prayer of a righteous man accomplish much" (James 5:16).

As we share our feelings and hurts with appropriate people in the body of Christ—our spouse, a counselor, or in a small group setting—it is in this atmosphere that we can begin to assert our responsibility to respond to an offense and begin to experience the healing of a wounded and broken heart through the prayers of others.

When Margie began sharing details about the physical and emotional abuse she suffered from her stepfather, her support group helped bear the burden that she had carried alone for years. Sobbing, she began experiencing a new freedom as shame was released and a sense of bonding took place. Up to this point, Margie had been unable to trust anyone and thus isolated herself from relationships. As she shared her sorrow with members of the group, they helped her, in deep love and compassion, to see how her sin of bitterness and unbelief affected her Christian life. Margie then asked God's forgiveness for her lack of forgiveness and began to assume responsibility for taking hold of her life and allowing the Holy Spirit to lead her.

Sharing with someone else also creates a sense of accountability. It should not done be to gossip, shame others, or to accomplish other destructive goals. As we, like Margie, begin to assume responsibility for our sins and release others from our blame, we finally enter into the third stage of forgiveness: acknowledging the lordship of Jesus Christ as king.

Making a decision. After we acknowledge our feelings and share them with others, we are ready to make a decision from the heart to forgive and release from bitter judgment. Matthew 18:21-35 gives one of the clearest examples in Scripture of forgiving someone else. Part of this section discusses a king whose servant owed him ten thousand talents (about ten million dollars in silver content) but was unable to pay. Because of this inability, he was designated to be sold, along with his wife and children and all that he owned. The servant fell down asking for mercy and cried, "Have patience with me and I will repay you everything." The king felt compassion, released him, and forgave him the debt. We can learn from the king's threefold example of forgiveness.

Perhaps you are ready to begin to fully forgive someone. This is not a matter of simply saying, "Lord, help me to forgive so-and-so." Rather, it is making a decision: heavenly Father, I ask you to forgive me for my unbelief, my pride, and my unforgiving attitude. In the same way that you have forgiven me because of your grace and mercy, I also fully forgive (fill in the blank) from my heart and release him/her from my bitter judgments. Thank you for your forgiveness through the blood of Jesus Christ and in his name.

Additional insights on forgiveness. When we forgive someone else and even ask their forgiveness, when necessary, they may change—or they may not. Our peace and joy should not be dependent on someone else's response. David said in Psalm 62:5, "My expectations come from thee, O God." Even so, we should continue to pray for the one forgiven, but we should no longer expect anything from him or her. Whatever he or she gives or doesn't give will be enough. God is now the one we depend upon.

Someone asked me, "How do you know when you have forgiven someone?" I believe that the degree to which we can express gratitude for how God is going to use the offense for his glory and our benefit will be the degree to which we have forgiven. The key to forgiveness is to have learned from the experience and to allow it to benefit you, not destroy you.

One reason we find it difficult to forgive is because of the loss and hurt we have suffered. Somehow we feel justice isn't served until the person who has offended us has been hurt as much as or more than we have. It is vital to remember that justice for our sins and the sins against us were taken care of at the cross when Christ bore our sins.

Creating new anchors in our life. We begin to nullify the old anchors and belief systems of the past by creating new memories and releasing the past through forgiveness. Whether we intend to or not, we will continue to create anchors. These anchors will either hold us back from God's intended purposes and plans or they will put us in a position to receive his blessings and grace. Anchors are established when we cement decisions, ideas, observations, etc., together with our value system.

We develop values based upon gain or loss. That is, we make choices to experience gain or avoid loss—to receive reward or escape punishment, to fulfill pleasure or avoid pain. These motivations are the basis of human choices. For the believer, there is a higher motive of love. However, we all make decisions at some level based on these two basic motives: gain and loss. The lowest level of gain is for selfish ambition and the highest is for God's kingdom.

Bill admitted to me his apparent powerlessness to avoid adult bookstores during business trips. He had noticed that his greater temptations occurred when he felt tired, discouraged, or disappointed. On some occasions he would drive into the parking lot and work up the willpower to leave, only to return again later and succumb to temptation. After some discussion, Bill began to see how his addiction to sexual temptation had developed in his life.

When he felt emotional pain, he attempted to cover the pain with sexual pleasure, which brought temporary relief. After making these same decisions several times, there was an automatic connection in his mind and emotions between relieving pain and sexual activity. The scenes, sights, and feelings associated with the bookstores were now part of the high of his addiction. The feelings and memories of the sexual activity associated with the book store had become an anchor in his life. He was able to change this anchor through the grace of God, to understand how to make decisions that last, and to develop new anchors in his own behavior and values.

Like Bill, Sue had created unwanted anchors in her life too. Having been rejected by her stepfather while growing up, Sue began to relieve her pain by eating. Obesity was not only a detriment to her health, but kept her isolated from others. For Sue, the pleasure of eating was greater than the pain of isolation. She had so anchored this belief system with the sights, smells, feelings, and taste of food that she could not imagine replacing it with something better.

If someone had told me that in the process of my own addiction I could reanchor my soul, I would have been doubtful. The book of wisdom, Proverbs, chapter 4, suggests the following steps to create a new value system that will anchor us securely in God's will and purposes. These steps will give us the power to make lasting decisions:

Give new value to a decision. Our decisions are based upon our belief system, which allows us to weigh the loss or gain of a decision in terms of the kingdom of God. Jesus said that where our treasures are, our heart will be too. Our decisions and actions will likely be guided by a desire to guard our treasures. Therefore, in order to establish new anchors or a basis for making value decisions, we must model our values and beliefs in accordance with God's. Ultimately, this can be done through a revelation of the Holy Spirit.

Hear, o sons, the instruction of a father, and give attention that you may gain understanding, for I give you sound teaching; do not abandon my instruction. When I was a son to my father, tender and the only son in the sight of my mother, then he taught me and said to me, "Let your heart hold fast my words; keep my commandments and live; acquire wisdom! acquire understanding! Do not forget, nor turn away from the words of my mouth. Do not forsake her, and she will guard you; love her, and she will watch over you. The beginning of wisdom is: acquire wisdom; and with all your acquiring, get understanding. Prize her, and she will exalt you; she will honor you if you embrace her. She will place on your head a garland of grace; she will present you with a crown of beauty" (Prov. 4:1-9).

Notice in this first section of Proverbs 4 the value that is placed on wisdom. Wisdom is seeing and understanding the loss and gain of your choices and actions from an eternal perspective. It is seeing more than the immediate pleasure of a situation, but the long-term results. When Bill, who I have already mentioned, began to understand this process, it literally changed his behavior. He never considered his value system when he visited adult book stores. I pointed out to him that his sexuality and spirituality were interwoven, and that to be sexually addicted is to be spiritually bankrupt. Together, we went through the Scriptures and began to see the results of purity, and that his sexual impurity was resulting in tremendous loss in his physical, mental, and spiritual life. By receiving the truth in Scriptures and allowing the Holy Spirit to make this truth come alive in his spirit and heart, Bill's value system began to change. He began to reanchor his soul in truth. However, it is not enough to stop at this step. The next two are just as important.

Make a commitment to the value system. If I knew that by participating in a certain activity I would die, and my value system is to live, then my commitment to participate or not participate is based on my values. This kind of commitment is, again, based on eternal perspectives of loss and gain, pain and pleasure. Notice the next section of Proverbs 4, verses 10-19:

> Hear my son, and accept my sayings, and the years of your life will be many. I have directed you in the way of wisdom; I have led you in upright paths. When you walk, your steps will not be impeded; and if you run, you will not stumble. Take hold of instruction; do not let go. Guard her, for she is your life. Do not enter the path of the wicked, and do not proceed in the way of evil men. Avoid it, do not pass by it; turn away from it and pass on. For they cannot sleep unless they do evil; and they are robbed of sleep unless they make someone stumble. For they eat the bread of wickedness, and drink the wine of violence. But the path of the righteous is like the light of dawn that shines brighter and brighter until the full day. The way of the wicked is like darkness; they do not know over what they stumble (Prov. 4:10-19).

Not only are we told to make a commitment to our value system (wisdom), but our decisions also are to include new boundaries and limitations. This is shown in statements like, "Do not enter the path of the wicked," "Do not proceed in the way of evil men," and "Avoid it, pass by it." The result of the decision to walk in wisdom is that our path will be like the light of dawn that shines brighter and brighter until the full day.

So many of our decisions are based upon temporary pleasure and believing there are consequences only if we get caught or exposed. The basis of these beliefs is deception, and it causes shortsightedness. But knowing the truth will set us free. Many of the concepts that are included in this book became clear to me as the result of facing some of the greatest temptations since beginning my recovery process. In the midst of these temptations, the Holy Spirit spoke to my heart and said, "If you will overcome this temptation, I will give you insights and understanding that you have not had heretofore to walk in purity."

One of my value systems and anchors is to walk in truth. Now, understanding and believing deep in my heart, by revelation, that knowing the truth will set us free, my commitment to this value gets stronger and stronger. It is important to link our actions and values and the resulting effects.

Reinforce values and commitments. Continue to review your values, reinforce them by studying the Scriptures, and observe in everyday life how these values prove to be true results in the blessings of God. The third section of Proverbs 4 reveals this:

> My son, give attention to my words; incline your ear to my sayings. Do not let them depart from your sight; keep them in the midst of your heart. For they are life to those who find them, and health to all their whole body. Watch over your heart with all diligence, for from it flow the springs of life. Put away from you a deceitful mouth, and put devious lips far from you. Let your eyes look directly ahead, and let your gaze be fixed straight in front of you. Watch the path of your feet, and all your ways will be established. Do not turn to the right nor the left; turn your foot from evil (Prov. 4:20-27).

Unless we continue to reinforce our new anchors of values, we can easily be deceived into false ways. However, over a period of time the values and commitments become such a part of our heart that we are able to set our face like flint without turning to the right or left in departure from his truth. We can reinforce our values and commitments by:

• Hiding the word of God in our heart, especially the Scriptures that relate to the values and truths that we are enforcing. The word of God works mightily within us, and James says that by receiving with meekness the implanted word, we save our souls (James 1:21).

• Making a decision to obey the word of the Lord, especially when it is quickened and made alive in our spirit. Again, as James says, "But prove yourselves doers of the word, and not merely hearers who delude themselves" (James 1:22).

• Continuing to meditate and intently consider that we are a new creation in Christ, and that having his nature and life, we also have his values and truth. Paul says in 1 Corinthians 1:30 that Christ became to us wisdom from God, along with righteousness, sanctification, and redemption. And James again says, "For if anyone is a hearer of the word and not a doer, he is like a man who looks at his natural face in a mirror; for once he has looked at himself and gone away, he has immediately forgotten what kind of person he was. But one who looks intently at the perfect law, the law of liberty, and abides by it, not having become a forgetful hearer but an effectual doer, this man shall be blessed in what he does" (James 1:23-25).

The law of liberty is really the law of love; we should love the Lord our God with all our heart, all our mind, all our soul, and all our strength. The love of God has been shed abroad in our hearts by the mighty Holy Spirit, who has been given to us (Rom. 5:5). To look at him, our Lord Jesus, is a reminder of who we are. We shall be like him for we shall see him just as he is (1 John 3:2). "But we all, with unveiled face beholding as in a mirror the glory of the Lord, are being transformed into the same image from glory to glory, just as from the Lord, the Spirit" (2 Cor. 3:18).

Christ is our truth and value system. As we intently continue to have fellowship with him and behold him, then all our false value systems will be nullified and we will be reanchored in him in our relationships, our finances, our morals, our disciplines, etc. Christ is our hope and our anchor. The writer of Hebrews says that he has entered within the veil (Heb. 6:19), which is the holiest of the holy. The place that the world cannot see, we can now enter through the blood of Jesus Christ.

Even as our soul becomes firmly anchored in Christ, we will still face temptations—perhaps even more—because our adversary the devil is like a roaring lion going about seeking whom he may devour. We must learn how to gird, or rebuild, our loins with truth to face the crisis of temptation.

Study questions

1.) To truly forgive someone, you must recognize and acknowledge your own feelings of hurt and disappointment. Write down on a piece of paper all of your feelings, even angry statements you might never articulate to the one you must forgive.

2.) The king mentioned in Matthew 18:21-35 served as a model of genuine forgiveness. He showed compassion, released a servant from prison, and forgave him a huge debt. How can you copy the king's example in your own life?

3.) Remember that when we forgive someone, he or she may not change. To cope with that possibility, what prayer will you say for the one you have forgiven?

4.) To be sexually addicted is to be spiritually bankrupt. Think about your own way of acting out your addiction and how it may conflict with your value system.

5.) How can you make a meaningful commitment to your value system so that you can walk in truth?

6.) Map out your own personal plan, in calendar form, for reevaluating your values and studying the Scriptures. Your goal should be to reinforce your values at least twice each month.

EIGHT

REBUILDING

Defining life's boundaries according to God's will and standards

It was late when I left the church meeting that hot Tuesday evening. I had driven for nearly eight hours to keep a speaking engagement that I had accepted in place of a minister friend who had become sick. The services were well attended by several hundred people, and after the two-day schedule, I was leaving to drive back home. The trip would take most of the night. I was terribly confused by the lustful thoughts from old memories that were pounding in my mind. Why would such thoughts follow a service that seemed to have been so mightily anointed by the Holy Spirit?

As I prepared to leave, the pastor handed me an envelope with an offering for my ministry. As I opened the envelope in his presence, I prepared to thank him for his generosity. He looked embarrassed, and before I could lift the check from the envelope, he said, "I wish it could have been more, but I hope it will help you with your expenses." Actually, the amount did not cover my expenses. I realized later that he had not intended for me to open the envelope in his presence. Though I expressed my thanks, I was disappointed, and all I could think about were the unpaid bills that were waiting for me at home.

Though this event took place several years ago, the lesson I learned that evening would forever affect my life. In retrospect, every emotion and feeling that I had been previously cautioned about from a friend were now surfacing. The word HALT—an acronym for hungry, angry, lonely, tired—came to mind. I was hungry from not having eaten all day, angry because of unfulfilled expectations, lonely because I had no one to share my burden with, and tired from two days of speaking and ministering.

An addiction is a mood-altering experience. The mood I was facing begged to be altered with some of the practices from my past. Approaching a large city as I continued to drive through the night, pictures of past pornographic materials started flooding my mind. I felt powerless before the temptation and knew that without the grace of God and his intervention, another failure was certain.

"Oh, God," I cried out in desperation, "please help me." The Scripture from 1 Peter l:13 kept coming to my mind: "Gird your loins for action, keep sober in spirit, and fix your hope completely on the grace which is to come to you at the revelation of Jesus." I had always thought this Scripture applied only to Christ's return, but now I realized that it also applied to anyone who called upon him.

The word *gird* in this verse refers to people who used a belt or girdle to draw loose, hanging clothing tightly around themselves as they prepared to travel by horse or camel. They did this to prevent their clothing from becoming snagged on tree branches and other objects. The apostle Paul uses this same symbolism, in Ephesians 6, to describe putting on the full armor of God. The first instruction concerning armor is "to gird our loins with truth." The word for truth in the Greek language is *alethia,* which means reality.

These two verses contain some incredible insight into conquering a sexual addiction. The loins of our mind are more than intellect; they are the imagination of the heart by which all actions and deeds are born. The imagination is the womb of our actions. The loins are the areas of passion and generative power. Therefore, it is essential that we put a belt of reality around our imagination as our own personal boundaries and convictions. Isaiah the prophet also describes this belt of righteousness as a gift of the Holy Spirit.

The result of this revelation and understanding was immediate. As I cried out to Jesus for help, I fixed my hope completely on his grace. It was then that the pornographic materials and bookstore lost their appeal because the Holy Spirit gave me a different picture: three huge scorpions that looked larger than the size of a man. I knew this picture was a symbolic warning that to go to such a place was to risk great danger and even death. As this picture faded, another one emerged, one in which I was speaking to a multitude of people. The surroundings were bathed in light and it was as though the Holy Spirit were saying, "If you will overcome by my grace, you will minister liberty and freedom to many."

The Holy Spirit had superimposed spiritual reality in place of what my natural senses craved. As I have come to respect spiritual reality as truth, I have seen more and more immediate deliverance from Satan's deception. Scriptures tell us that Lot vexed (tormented) his soul with all that he saw and heard. Notice that the three most powerful of natural senses were present: vexed (feelings), seeing (visual), and hearing (audio).

Natural senses versus spiritual senses

For every natural sense, God gives us a spiritual sense that replaces it or is superimposed on it. I have ministered to many people who are coming out of addictive lifestyles, and each one has shared one or more things that seem to trigger or remind them of old behavior patterns. These triggers always seem to be related to natural senses: touching (or feeling), seeing, hearing, tasting, and smelling. The following Scriptures also show that these natural senses are parallel to spiritual senses:

Feeling: The joy of the Lord is my strength

Seeing: Beholding as in a mirror the glory of the Lord

Hearing: My sheep hear my voice

Tasting: Oh taste and see that the Lord is good

Smelling: For we are a fragrance of Christ to God

Just as I prayed for the Lord to show me the reality of my temptations, we can all continue to pray in various situations for wisdom and understanding about the reality of a circumstance and where our boundaries and convictions should be. It is through prayer that we can know where to establish boundaries based upon the reality or deceptiveness of something. Reframing, which we discussed in an earlier chapter, is actually gaining a clearer and more defined perception. Regirding, or rebuilding, deals more with our response to the perception.

Regirding is putting a belt (boundary) around our minds and hearts for protection. Prayer for truth and reality further opens the door to establishing correct boundaries through the Scripture and godly counsel. The apostle Paul illustrates this through his prayer for the Ephesian church:

For this reason I too, having heard of the faith in the Lord Jesus which exists among you, and your love for all the saints, do not cease giving thanks for you, while making mention of you in my prayers; that the God of our Lord Jesus Christ, the Father of glory, may give to you a spirit of wisdom and of revelation in the knowledge of Him. I pray that the eyes of your heart may be enlightened, so that you may know what is the hope of His calling, what are the riches of the glory of His inheritance in the saints, and what is the surpassing greatness of His power toward us who believe. These are in accordance with the working of the strength of His might which he brought about in Christ, when He raised Him from the dead, and seated Him at His right hand in the heavenly places, far above all rule and authority and power and dominion, and every name that is named, not only in this age, but also in the one to come. And He put all things in subjection under His feet, and gave Him as head over all things to the church, which is His body, the fullness of Him who fills all in all (Eph. 1:15-23).

To demonstrate how this concept works in a practical way, I will illustrate how different people have experienced it. Not every person will have the same triggers and responses to particular stimuli of the natural senses. As I mentioned earlier, I knew several older boys while I was growing up who felt it their duty to teach me how to be "a real man." They thought this meant smoking, drinking, and chewing tobacco, among other things. Taking a large drink of straight liquor almost choked me to death and trying to learn to smoke nearly choked me to death again. When I tried to learn how to chew tobacco, I became the sickest of all. I thought one had to swallow as much as possible and then spit out what was left, a practice that left me feeling deathly ill. I think I decided at that point that it wasn't a matter of being a man or not; it was a matter of living or not.

Today, whenever I smell whiskey or tobacco or see someone chewing tobacco, my natural senses bring a quick recall of coughing, teary eyes, and nausea. Smoking and drinking are not temptations to me because I associate them with negative feelings and thoughts. However, in other areas of my life, I chose certain behaviors associated with natural senses that brought me pleasure, and the behavior was reinforced and recalled by the natural senses acting as triggers. By crying out to the Lord for spiritual rather than physical reality, I can regird my mind with truth, seeing reality from both the negative and positive aspects. The following illustrations clarify this notion.

Feeling. Zane, who had come out of a homosexual lifestyle, was a staff member of a large and growing church. His main responsibility was to oversee the ministry to others who were on a similar journey, and he stayed busy in personal counseling ministry. He led small support groups and handled the various crises arising in families and individuals related to those in his ministry. Zane was feeling swamped with his many responsibilities and was greatly disappointed upon discovering that the new church budget provided no increase in salary for his ministry; in fact, his salary was lower than the previous year.

His feelings of rejection, lack of affirmation, and abandonment triggered some of the old thoughts of his previous lifestyle. For just a moment, he told me, he thought about giving up his ministry and going back to his old life. He even thought about how he would announce to the church and the world that a ministry to former homosexuals doesn't work.

When Zane prayed, the Holy Spirit showed him the reality of his negative thoughts. They were rebellious and destructive, and reflected the same way he had acted because of his natural father's rejection, lack of affirmation, and abandonment. The Holy Spirit then showed him that the heavenly Father loved him and was his real resource. These feelings of love and closeness were so real that Zane started weeping. He realized that those in leadership were not rejecting him and his ministry. Perhaps they just weren't aware of his needs. He knew they were men and women of God, and that if the Lord had shown his love to them, surely they would not be insensitive to his leadership.

Zane approached the pastor and a church elder and asked for clarification of this possible misunderstanding. They were surprised because they had not intended to express disapproval or rejection of Zane. Because of some necessary budget cuts, they were trying to cut back in every aspect of church life. Through this important lesson, Zane realized that he could have gone beyond his own boundaries and convictions because of a lack of communication. But more importantly, because of a lack of prayer, he could have succumbed to negative feelings that did not reflect reality. Emotional triggers of this kind could be anger, disappointment, loneliness, and discouragement.

Seeing. Some people's old habits and behavior are triggered by sight; a magazine advertisement, a television program, blinking lights on a tavern, candles, or others stimuli can be associated with past fantasies and actions. Tom was addicted to pornography, and just the memory of some magazines and pictures resulted in a feeling of lust. Even driving past a book store with pornographic materials brought about a rush or high in his nervous system. These feelings caused him great concern because he felt out of control. Whether he saw images in the real world or in his fantasies, the results of obsession and addictive behavior were the same.

Tom's obsession with fantasy led him to an adult bookstore while he was away from home at a business conference. He had heard me speak about crying out to God during times like this and the importance of putting the belt of truth (reality) around his imagination. He felt like his own boundaries and convictions were no longer strong enough to hold him back and had, in fact, gone beyond them. He was clearly out of control.

"Oh, God, please help me," he cried out in his heart as he stood in the dingy book store, staring at pornographic magazines. Other men stood nearby staring at the same kinds of pictures. Tom noticed their faraway look and glazed eyes, and wondered if he looked the same way. "Oh God," he cried again from his heart, realizing that he was responsible for having gone beyond his own convictions. He felt trapped and hopeless.

As he continued looking at a magazine, a glossy picture of a nude woman changed into a little girl. She was crying and reaching out to her mother and father. Tom couldn't help but wonder whose little girl she used to be, and what went wrong in her life. Just as quickly, the picture reverted to its original form. Now all Tom could think about were his own children, a boy and a girl.

"Oh, God," he cried out again, "I don't ever want my little girl to be on a cover like this and I don't ever want my boy to someday be standing in a store like this one." Tom knew that the hand of the Lord was upon his children and that they had been dedicated to Christ at birth. Through the years he kept pictures in his mind of their happiness and wholeness. He had already begun praying for the person who was someday going to be his daughter's husband, and for the future wife of his son. He believed that God had allowed him to see in his own mind and heart potential blessings for his children.

It was obvious that the Holy Spirit, in this situation, was superimposing spiritual senses and purposes over the natural senses and the destruction they were succumbing to. That day, Tom learned the danger of crossing his personal boundaries and convictions, but by the grace of God he also learned the power of girding the loins of his mind (imagination) with reality.

Hearing. A Christmas hymn, a Scripture chorus, a soft, summer breeze, or a howling wind can bring various moods and memories to one's heart very quickly. Don once listened to hard rock music and indulged in drugs, partying, and sexual promiscuity at the same time. Even though he had become a Christian, he retained the music that represented so much of his old lifestyle. After a Christian friend convinced him to destroy the music, Don was surprised to discover that he was still affected by the memories associated with the music when he heard it coming from a car radio or in a restaurant.

When Don prayed for the Lord to show him the reality of the memories and temptations, he saw more clearly than ever before the attitudes and lifestyles behind the music. Scripture began to fill his mind as the Holy Spirit spoke to his heart. "Now the deeds of the flesh are evident, which are: immorality, impurity, sensuality, idolatry, sorcery, enmities, strife, jealousy, outbursts of anger, disputes, dissensions, factions, envyings, drunkenness, carousings, and the things like these, of which I forewarn you just as I have forewarned you that those who practice such things shall not inherit the kingdom of God" (Galatians 5:19-21).

Each time Don heard the sounds that triggered previous temptations, he recalled this Scripture, which he had memorized. His association with the worldly music changed from temptation to dislike.

Tasting. The most powerful associations seem to be linked to feeling, seeing, and hearing. But a powerful association can also develop with taste and pleasure. When God created man and woman and placed them in the garden, it is said that "the Lord God caused to grow every tree that is pleasing to the sight and good for food" (Gen. 2:9). Remember that natural senses are not harmful, in and of themselves. The Lord provided aesthetic value for enjoyment. The problem arises when these senses trigger a response that causes us to make a substitution for God's grace and ministry in our lives. Taste can cause us to violate our conscience in an attempt to meet a legitimate need in an illegitimate way.

Evelyn was addicted to food, especially sweets. She was obese, and her shame and embarrassment caused her to feel isolated and lonely. She fed her shame with more sweets, thus continuing the vicious cycle. She had prayed many times for God to take away her desire for sweets. Though she didn't realize it, she was really asking God to take away her sense of taste—something which he had given for enjoyment, protection, and benefit. Taste was not the problem. The problem was that she associated taste with her need for security, comfort, and a relationship. The apostle Paul specifically instructs us not to live to eat, but to eat to live.

One day Evelyn was reading an article about the "trash content" in candy and chocolate. She was shocked to learn that her favorite candy was among the trashiest ones listed. She felt nauseated about the possibility of a roach's leg being in one of the candy bars she had eaten. Thereafter, she was unable to eat that particular candy.

Then she asked herself a question: If nausea or pain could be associated with a certain taste, why couldn't it be replaced with something more meaningful and satisfying? As she began to study Scriptures, she was surprised to learn of the spiritual references to taste: "Oh taste the Lord and see that He is good." When she craved something sweet, Evelyn asked the Lord to replace the craving with himself. To her amazement, the Scriptures she selected spoke to her own feelings of loneliness or rejection. She began to find such fulfillment in the sweetness of fellowship with Christ that her old patterns weakened. The more she reinforced the reality of enjoying the Lord and his Word during the low times, the more she established a new pattern.

Other people have reported success in quashing a taste for alcohol, cigarettes, and fried food. The answer is not simply to rely on mental gymnastics and human willpower, but to ask the Lord to give reality, in his grace, to the natural sense.

Smelling. One of the most effective deterrents is that of repulsive smells, such as bad breath, body odor, rotten flesh, vomit, and burned food. Just reading about repulsive smells can trigger a feeling of repulsion. Just as compelling are the memories of attractive odors, such as fresh flowers, freshly plowed soil after a spring shower, a light perfume, and a cinnamon apple pie baking in the oven. On and on these lists could continue, dependent upon our experiences and associations.

One day I felt an almost overpowering draw to a pornographic bookstore I had to pass by on my way to the airport. Even though I had shared this temptation with my wife, and we both prayed against any demonic power, the pull became stronger and stronger each time I drove by the establishment. In my spirit and heart, I knew this was not a place I wanted to go to, so why did this temptation persist?

After careful examination and prayer, I realized that the temptation seemed to occur when I was returning home late at night, when I was tired, and sometimes when I was drained emotionally. One evening, feeling almost powerless, I again cried out to the Lord to show me the reality of what I was dealing with. I did not see any pictures as I had before, nor did I hear any specific voice. But I suddenly remembered a putrid smell I had associated with a similar place I had gone to years before. I could feel the muscles in my face tighten, as if I were trying to keep from smelling the offensive odor. From that point on, I recalled the smell each time I drove by the bookstore, until the very sight of the place became repulsive to me. Now I realize that the natural sense of an offensive odor paralleled the offensive odor in my spirit.

Several months following these events, I was praying in our bedroom and kneeling beside the bed. I visualized the bed as an altar to the Lord, and, as before, presented my body to him as a living and holy sacrifice that would be acceptable to God (Rom. 12:1). In the middle of my prayer, I was startled by the most beautiful aroma. At first I was sure it must have been a new perfume my wife had bought. However, I soon discovered that it was the aroma that comes from the Lord's presence.

It is not my intent to sensationalize. I do not know if the fragrance was a real, natural sense or if it was a product of my imagination and spirit. But I do know that the memory of the fragrance during that special prayer far outweighs anything imaginable that the world offers.

In Revelation 4, many of the natural senses described are superimposed over the spiritual:

Feeling: Immediately I was in the Spirit.
Seeing: And He who was sitting was like a jasper stone and a sardius in appearance.
Hearing: I heard a voice like the sound of a trumpet, talking with me.

When we pray for the Lord's kingdom to come and for his will to be done on earth as in heaven, we should not be surprised that his kingdom also includes spiritual senses that give us reality over the temptations of falsehood. It is a powerful thing to pray during a temptation and see the reality of what the temptation is really about. However, even more powerful and necessary is to prepare ahead of time by establishing firm convictions and boundaries in our spiritual, emotional, and physical responses.

Brad contacted me by phone after having been arrested for indecent exposure in an adult bookstore. His voice quavered as he spoke. He had not yet told his wife about the incident, even though it was possible that the arrest would appear in the local newspaper. "Brad, maybe my wife and I could meet with you and your wife tomorrow for breakfast and we could discuss this situation and any steps necessary to dealing with it in the best possible way," I suggested.

By that time, Brad had told his wife about his arrest. Even though tension and fear filled the air, they were able to begin getting the help they deserved and needed because Brad had broken his silence and had begun to deal with his denial. The charges were dropped because Brad agreed to get professional help, and a period of probation was established to ensure that he would not repeat the offense.

Brad and his wife were both Christians who had been very active in lay Christian ministries. Brad's wife had not been aware of his addictive sexual behavior, which had been going on for most of their married life. She had been concerned about his outbursts of anger and isolation, but she did not link them to anything. Brad's secret world had been interrupted and he received counseling, became part of a support group, and established accountability with his minister. But one of his deepest concerns was how he could establish new patterns and boundaries that would help him from failing again.

I continued to meet with Brad for a period of time and helped him establish some new boundaries and convictions that would prepare him to stand against any future temptation. Of course, as I told Brad, without the grace of God, mental agreements and willpower will not suffice. As we admit our inability to overcome temptation and submit to total dependency on God's grace, the following boundaries can become powerful bulwarks of protection.

Since we will all face temptations, it is important that we be prepared for them. I suggest that we visualize and review each possible crisis and the boundaries to be established so that resistance becomes an immediate response.

1. The crisis of need. Since most temptations are attempts to meet legitimate needs in illegitimate ways, boundaries and convictions should be established ahead of time. Our most basic needs include our sense of being (who we are), our sense of belonging (why we are here), and our sense of becoming (where we are going). When needs have not been adequately met, and the meeting of any one of them becomes associated and attached to something or someone, the object of meeting the needs becomes a powerful drive.

131

For example, if someone's sense of being and belonging is attached to approval from peers, then the temptation to get that approval is more than a temptation to "just do something." It is a crisis of need. If someone's sense of being is attached to material possessions, then the temptation to acquire is more than an act of stealing, dishonesty, or taking advantage of others. It is a crisis of being. If someone's sense of becoming is attached to holding a position of power and prominence, then the temptation to control, manipulate, and even demoralize others is more than an act of violence or aggressiveness. It is a crisis of becoming.

The four crises that each person faces in making life changing decisions were acknowledged by Jesus when he conversed with the Samaritan woman at the well, as recorded in the gospel of John 4:5-30. A careful reading of this section of Scripture will reveal the different levels of conversation that Jesus had with the woman as she responded by making life changing choices. What each level or aspect of conversation acknowledged was really a crisis of temptation in the woman's life that she had to deal with.

The first level, the crisis of need, occurred when Jesus asked her for a drink of water. This first question appealed to her need to be needed. Probably one of the reasons that she came to draw water in the hot sun was to escape the accusatory and judgmental glares of the other women. They viewed her as a woman of poor reputation because she tried to fill her own thirsty soul in the wrong way.

When Jesus appealed to her sense of need, he appealed to her basic needs as wife and mother. What wife does not want to please and encourage? What mother is not willing to get up during the night to feed or give a drink of water to her child? Though Jesus did not portray himself as a husband or child, he appealed to a desperate need within her. It was during this appeal that Jesus told her of the living water she could drink and never thirst for again. He also gave her hope that her basic needs could be met in legitimate and deeply satisfying ways.

Many of our temptations are really attempts to meet our needs. A friend of mine was once faced with some continuing temptations during business trips. I suggested to him that he prepare some questions ahead of time that he could automatically ask and answer during these crises of temptation. There are some valuable questions that we can ask ourselves when tempted to meet one of our needs in an unhealthy way: Is this a *need* or a *want?*

The Lord has promised to meet our needs according to his riches in glory. In other words, we may be trying to fulfill a want more than a need. Instead of saying, "I must have this to be fulfilled," we can see the temptation for what it is: selfish ambition and greed. If we see a want as a need, then we assume a mentality of, "I deserve this because I'm entitled to it." Rather, we should be confident that our basic needs have been met or will be met in God's way and in his timing (Matthew 6:19-34).

Another important question to ask is, "Should this need be met now or later?" If meeting a legitimate need now would violate our conscience, then we can be assured that the timing is wrong. When king David's army suggested that he kill Saul, who was asleep in a cave that David was hiding in, they even quoted the word of the Lord to David; he was to be King over Israel. After all, Saul was in pursuit of David in order to kill him, and this would be the perfect time for David to save himself from Saul's hand, to save his own men from further running, and to become king now and not later. David followed their suggestion just so far, even to the point of taking a knife and cutting off the edge of King Saul's robe to show him how vulnerable he was. David's heart was convicted by the Lord and he repented. He was tempted to fulfill a legitimate need to protect his army and to become king, but the wrong timing would have meant violating his conscience (1 Samuel 24:1-7).

A final question to ask is, "Am I attempting to meet my needs in my way or in God's way?" This was the question David had to ask his own heart and one that we have to ask ourselves. The end does not justify the means. There is a way that seems right unto man, but the ways thereof are the ways of death.

If we focus on making decisions and forming responses only to meet our needs, then we become self-centered. It is important, therefore, that we review the second crisis of temptation.

2. The crisis of conscience. After Jesus appealed to the Samaritan woman's basic need for acceptance and approval, he asked her, "Go call your husband, and come here." The woman answered, "I have no husband." Jesus said to her, "You have well said, I have no husband; for you have had five husbands, and the one whom you now have is not your husband; this you have said truly" (John 4:16-18). The woman responded by declaring Jesus to be a prophet. The conscience is appealed to by appealing to the sense of responsibility. Jesus opened the door to the woman's heart by appealing to her sense of need, but appealed to her sense of conscience to deal with her responsibility. We can also prepare for temptations by asking questions ahead of time that deal with the crisis of conscience.

When Tim called and shared his frustrations after having come out of a lifestyle of multiple addictions, he blurted out in frustration, "I don't know who I am anymore. All the things I did to occupy my time I know were wrong, but now that they are gone, I just don't know who I am."

"Tim," I responded, "you are a new person and creation in Christ. Man was originally created in God's image. The apostle Paul says that Christ who is God's exact image is in us and that we are being transformed back into his image from glory to glory. Tim, who you are has to do with your new heart and character that is the result of Christ now living in you through the Holy Spirit. To violate your conscience is to violate your own character and integrity."

"I never understood it like that before," Tim responded with a new sense of hope and joy. "I guess that I thought that who I was depended on others' responses to me. That's the reason I spent so much of my time at bars. I wanted to be around people who I thought liked me because I was fun to be around, and when I was drunk and I was generous with my money, I was in that kind of a mood."

Like Tim, we too need to ask ourselves the question, "Who am I?" when we are faced with temptations. After reviewing this question in my own life over a period of time, my immediate response to temptations became, "This is not who I am. I am a new person in Christ, and the temptation to yield to this temptation violates my integrity, my conscience, and my sense of self." The more I understand "who I am" and "who Christ is in me," I know that to violate this is to violate my being.

Another question we should ask ourselves when dealing with the crisis of temptation is, "How will I feel tomorrow?" As one person put it, "I need to see the end results from the beginning." At first, the feeling of excitement and anticipation of temporary pleasure is very tempting, but all of us have experienced the emotional hangover of guilt and shame that lingers over us like a dark, heavy cloud.

When David told me how he had been tempted to steal from his company, he said that asking himself how he would feel about the theft the next day acted as a deterrent. David had become a Christian about a year before and had begun walking in new freedom in his life. Stealing and dishonesty had been a part of his old life, and he had gone through the process of asking forgiveness and making restitution to former employers since becoming a Christian. "Boy, I don't want to have to go through that again," he said, referring to making restitution and seeking forgiveness. David knew that he could have gone to prison, but his employers were so impressed by his honesty and sincerity that they allowed him to make restitution. One man even forgave him and released him from any repayment. The memory of this alone was a deterrent, but to live with a clear conscience was so meaningful to David that thinking about how he would feel afterward became a powerful new boundary in his life.

This second response, the crisis of conscience, continues to reinforce the boundaries and convictions needed to overcome temptations. However, following only the first two steps can result in legalism. Legalism means depending mostly on a set of rules and disciplines and the consequences of how we might feel to control our actions. Jesus appealed to the Samaritan woman next by probing her relationship to God.

3. The crisis of relationships. Interestingly, the woman began to divert her focus to a place of worship instead of the person of worship. "Our fathers worshiped in this mountain; and you people say that in Jerusalem is the place where men ought to worship" (John 4: 20).

Jesus said to her, "Woman believe Me, an hour is coming when neither in this mountain nor in Jerusalem shall you worship the Father. You worship that which you do not know; we worship that which we know, for salvation is from the Jews. But an hour is coming, and now is, when the true worshipers shall worship the Father in spirit and truth; for such people the Father seeks to be His worshipers. God is spirit, and those who worship Him must worship in spirit and truth" (John 4:21-24).

Addictions and compulsive behavior are an attempt to forge a relationship. Relationships and bonding are the deepest needs of the human heart, as we have discussed. The Samaritan woman had certainly attempted to form meaningful relationships; her five husbands and her present living arrangement with a man who was not her husband revealed her desperate search for a connection with someone. It was at this point that Jesus introduced her to the possibility of a relationship with God the Father. I call this level of appeal the crisis of relationships.

Nancy reminded me of the Samaritan woman when she came to talk with me. Though she had not been married five times, she had been involved with several men in promiscuous relationships. Nancy was in her mid-forties and was obsessed with the fear of growing old. Her mentality and false belief system of happiness were based on a personal appearance of youthfulness and her attractiveness to younger men. At first she tried to fulfill this need by flirting, but over a period of time, she became involved in multiple adulterous affairs.

Nancy, like the woman at the well, had experienced a new and vital relationship with Christ. She had joined the staff of a church, but it had only been a job to supplement the family income. However, when she really came to know Christ as Lord, she also began to understand God as her Father. The needs she had longed to fill from various men in her life—needs that were almost totally unfilled by her earthly father—were now being fulfilled in a deeper way than she had ever imagined by the heavenly Father, as well as by healthy relationships with both men and women in her local fellowship. Her relationship with her husband and children had begun to take on new meaning and were becoming deeply satisfying.

Still, some of the old temptations resurfaced, especially when Nancy felt rejected and disappointed. She said she did not want to return to the old lifestyle of deception and guilt. She was very concerned about the seemingly overwhelming draw of these temptations.

"Nancy," I said, "you are facing the crisis of relationships in your life. Before these temptations come, and they probably will continue to come until you become stronger in Christ and the renewal of your mind has taken place, you will need to establish boundaries and responsibilities in your responses."

I suggested several questions she could review beforehand and, with the grace of God, prepare for any forthcoming temptation: "How will my response to this relationship affect my relationship to God?" Nancy had deeply tasted the love and forgiveness of the heavenly Father, and any possible interruption of that love was unthinkable. The more we place a premium on knowing and experiencing God as our Father, the more we will place a premium on maintaining that relationship. It is important to understand God's unconditional love for us; it is knowing his love that causes us to respond to him. We love him because he first loved us.

A second question we should ask is, "How will my response affect my relationship with my family?" Any inappropriate relationship outside of our family will produce guilt and secrecy. The fruit of shame is always isolation, and the fruit of guilt is always judgmental. Not only do inappropriate relationships take away from the basic needs of a spouse and children, but they hinder intimacy and oneness with them. Our unhealthy responses to temptation do not affect only us, but our spouse, our children, and even our grandchildren. It is of great importance to realize that others can be affected in positive or negative ways by our lives and actions.

A third question we need to ask is, "How will my response affect my relationship with others?" This is similar to the question about our family, but it involves friendships, jobs, and our general response to people. Rage and angry outbursts often stand as proof of guilt in a person who offends and hurts other people.

The focus on the crisis of relationships, especially the relationship with God the Father, results in a Christ-centered perspective. To be God-centered also means to focus on people in regards to meeting their needs out of an overflow of love and fullness in our own lives. Thus the fourth approach to any crisis of temptation is the crisis of purpose.

4. The crisis of purpose. Jesus continued his conversation with the Samaritan woman and declared himself the Messiah who was to come. It was at this point that the woman had to face the issues of her future: to continue in her own adulterous and addictive behavior, or to share her love for the Christ whom she had encountered through a divine arrangement that she could not deny. Truly she had drunk deep from the water of life that he had offered and was becoming "a well of water springing up to eternal life."

The woman's response is very clear in Scripture: "So the woman left her waterpot, and went into the city, and said to the men, 'Come see a man who told me all the things that I have done; this is not the Christ, is it?' They went out of the city, and were coming to Him" (John 4:28-30).

Here is a woman who brings a city to Christ. Only an hour or so before, she had to come to the well at the hottest part of the day when no one else was usually there in order to escape the shame of their glares of disapproval. Now she appears before the very people who had shamed her to tell them of her quest and discovery of Christ. A life must back up a message, and obviously she had enough confidence in this brief, life changing encounter with Jesus to make an impression on those who had known her. The result: they began coming to Christ.

The apostle Paul tells us that every Christian has received a gift according to the measure of faith (Rom. 12:3). This covers the breadth and width of our ministry, as well as the depth and focus. Since one's ministry is a part of God's plan and purpose in our lives, any response to a difficult test or temptation should have the purpose of ministry in mind.

Some time ago in my own life, I was faced with several major disappointments at once. Now, looking back, I can see that if I had perceived these events through the eyes of the Holy Spirit, they would not have been disappointments, but challenges. The disappointments came during the Christmas season, and all of them together exerted an enormous pressure and drain on my emotions. One disappointment stemmed from a failed financial plan that I believed would have provided the resources needed for our ministry. The plan was a scam, and had it not been exposed when it was, I would have lost a considerable amount of money.

The second disappointment involved a failed partnership with another ministry. Because of a lack of finances, the other ministry backed off from the original agreement. The third disappointment stemmed from a person who had made hurtful remarks about my ministry and my attempt to help others. I had spent several hours on the phone and had driven more than four hours round-trip to counsel a married couple. I had done this at my own expense, but it resulted in their reporting distorted information to a third person, who told a friend, who then told me. Of course I called each person immediately to correct the information, but the disappointment and hurt lingered in my heart.

Then came two more major disappointments, and it became clear that my pride was playing a role in my reaction. Instead of being strengthened in the

Lord, I felt sorry for myself and allowed self-pity and lack of forgiveness to gain ground.

I began to isolate myself from others, an old ritual of mine. "Why be hurt again?" I thought. "I really can't trust others." These were some of the old tapes I began to play again in my mind. In my isolation, I would leave the house and drive around or go for walks to think about what was happening. My guard was down, and the lessons I had been teaching were not alive and abounding in my heart. It was then that some of the greatest temptations I faced during my recovery began to take place. Only in retrospect can I see the diabolical scheme to destroy again.

God is faithful, and the intercession of others, I am sure, was the redeeming factor in my crisis of ministry. As I worked through each crisis and even recorded what God was doing, I realized that this fourth crisis was very important. In the context of ministry and purpose, we must be careful not to place a ministry or job at the center and core of our lives. It is, however, important to see that our ministry is part of our joy and fulfillment in God's design for us to have dominion. During a crisis of temptation, which is also a crisis in ministry, we should ask, How will my response to this temptation affect my ministry?

We often believe that we are affected by a temptation only if we are caught or others learn about our failure. Otherwise, "what others don't know won't hurt them." What a false conclusion! What others don't know *will* affect us and other people. Any guilt and dishonesty in our lives will limit our ministry.

Jesus was filled with the Holy Spirit, and then was led by the Spirit into the wilderness to be tempted. It was after the temptation that he went forth in the power (authority) of the Spirit (see Matt. 4). Even so, it is through our obedience and overcoming that we minister with true authority and freedom. I knew, even in the times of my own temptations, that to give in would be to dilute the power and authority that was meant to help others. My message would lack genuine confidence and power. Words and messages can affect the minds of others, but only a pure heart and a clear conscience can touch their hearts.

Another question we might ask during temptation is, Do I truly want to help people in my ministry, or do I just want to impress them? We may impress others with our personality, humor, and abilities by teaching a Bible class and giving a sermon, but only through overcoming the temptations of life can we truly help them. The apostle Paul says this in Romans 15:18-19: "For I will not presume to speak of anything except what Christ has accomplished through me, resulting in the obedience of the Gentiles by word and deed in the power of signs and wonders, in the power of the Spirit."

Within the crises of need, conscience, relationships, and ministry are core belief systems that activate the cycle of addiction and unhealthy behavior patterns. We disengage the lies as we understand each false belief and expose it to the truth.

The crisis of need

False core belief: If God doesn't meet my needs now, on my terms, or in my way, then I cannot trust him. I will take control of the circumstances myself.

The truth: God is so concerned with our character, attitudes, and inner being that he may allow circumstances and tests to help bring us to maturity. "Consider it all joy, my brethren, when you encounter various trials; knowing that the testing of your faith produces endurance. And let endurance have its perfect result, that you may be perfect and complete, lacking in nothing" (James 1:2-4).

The crisis of conscience

False core belief: If I make one mistake or feel a temptation, or even begin the process of acting out my temptation, then it is proof that I am basically a bad person. I might as well continue. What's the use?

The truth: It is always beneficial to resist the devil and to immediately stop acting out our temptation. To continue will only bring further ruin and death. To humble ourselves and acknowledge our need for help will result in receiving grace and power to overcome. James 4:6-10 says, "But He gives a greater grace. Therefore it says, 'God is opposed to the proud, but gives grace to the humble.' Submit therefore to God. Resist the devil and he will flee from you. Draw near to God and He will draw near to you. Cleanse your hands, you sinners; and purify your hearts, you double minded. Be miserable and mourn and weep: let your laughter be turned into mourning, and your joy to gloom. Humble yourselves in the presence of the Lord, and He will exalt you" (James 4:6-10).

The crisis of relationships

False core belief: If others make a mistake or disappoint me, then it only proves that I cannot trust others. They will only hurt or betray me again.

The truth: The circumstances of people, places, and things do not make us happy or unhappy. We choose our state of mind by the way we view life and circumstances. Our judgment and condemnation of others is a reflection of ourselves. "Therefore, you are without excuse, every one of you who passes judgment, for in that you judge another, you condemn yourself; for you who judge practice the same things. And we know that the judgment of God rightly falls upon those who practice such things" (Rom. 2:1-2).

The crisis of ministry

False core belief: My ministry and purpose in life are not affected by what I do or say, as long as others do not know my failures or sins. My private life can be different from my public life.

The truth: Our ministry and purpose in life *is* affected by our private life. Guilt and dishonesty will affect our relationship and ministry because they cause us to practice deception and manipulation. "But we have renounced the things hidden because of shame, not walking in craftiness or adulterating the word of God, but by the manifestation of truth, commending ourselves to every man's conscience in the sight of God" (2 Cor. 4:2).

Once we have begun to see God's reality, decisions and events in our lives take on new meaning and importance. In terms of eternal and long lasting results, we will began to re-prioritize our lives as we continue the process of replacing old behavior patterns through repositioning.

Study questions

1.) Think about the feelings of anger, disappointment, loneliness, or discouragement that cause you to consider indulging your addictive behavior. How can you ground these emotional triggers in reality and confront these feelings rather than assuage them?

2.) Think about the powerful visual images that put unhealthy thoughts in your mind. How can you gird the loins of your mind with reality?

3.) Reread Galatians 5:19-21. How can this passage change your association of temptation with pleasure to temptation with dislike?

4.) Think about a craving that is triggered by the sense of taste or smell. How can you ask the Lord to give that craving reality so that you can substitute it with something healthy?

5.) Think about the last time you faced a temptation. Ask yourself these questions: Was it a need or a want? Could my need have been met then or later? Was I attempting to meet my needs in my way or in God's way?

6.) The next time you face a temptation, ask yourself: Who am I? Who is Christ in me? How will I feel the next day? How will my response to this temptation affect my relationship to God? How will my response affect my relationship with my family and others?

NINE

REDIRECTING

*Repositioning relationships and plans to fulfill God's
purpose*

"What is the most important thing in the world to you?" I asked Jerry. He
quickly replied, "Friends, family, and money, in that order." Without knowing it, he was revealing his value system to me. During our discussion, Jerry
came to see that his values were based on what he had considered to be important and to have lasting benefit. However, the more questions I asked
him, the more he realized that many of his present friends were not really
friends. He began to see that he had been used and had used others, resulting in a violation of his own conscience and destruction of his Christian walk.

Jerry began to change his value system by refocusing on the reality of lasting benefits and what is genuinely important. When we begin to ask ourselves questions like, "What is the most important thing in my life?" and
"Why is it important to me?" and "Will I consider the same things important
five or ten years from now?" our focus may began to change. This change results in a repositioning of our priorities and values.

Jerry valued friendship because of the rejection and loneliness he felt during childhood. He never had any close friends, and considered himself a
loner during high school. After graduation, he moved to another city to en-
roll in a university. He was determined to start over. One of his most important goals was to make friends and feel like part of a group. Jerry's value
system was developed out of pain, and it focused on meeting his needs.

Jerry was in his early thirties when we met, and he was becoming tired of
"the games," as he called most of his relationships. They were not as satis-

fying as he had hoped, and he was now disillusioned, believing that his life was hollow and lacked meaning. Part of Jerry's reasoning concerning the need for friendship and bonding was correct, but his focus was wrong. Rather than seeking God's kingdom and doing his will, Jerry really just wanted to fulfill himself.

I asked Jerry's permission to read Matthew 16:24-26. "Then Jesus said to His disciples, 'If anyone wishes to come after Me, let him deny himself, and take up his cross, and follow Me. For whoever wishes to save his life shall lose it; but whoever loses his life for My sake shall find it. For what will a man be profited, if he gains the whole world and forfeits his soul? Or what will a man give in exchange for his soul?'"

Jerry was visibly shaken. Even though he had been a Christian since the age of twelve, he had never seriously read the Bible or sought the Lord. The deep hole inside of his soul had become all-consuming. He was beginning to see the reality and vanity of his self-centeredness. He realized that his value system was out of order, and he was ready to refocus on lasting and fulfilling values.

Values will determine our actions, and what we believe is really important to us will determine our values. "For where your treasure is, there will your heart be also" (Matt. 6:21). If a man believes that money will make him happy, then his value system will be based on financial security. If he believes that good looks will bring him happiness, then his value system will be based on outward appearance. If he believes that a professional position of recognition and respect will make him happy, then his value system will be based on obtaining an important position. We set up our value system to accommodate those things that we think will bring us happiness.

When I asked Jerry why he put such a high priority on friendship, he realized that his emphasis was on the temporal and not the eternal. One of Jerry's closest friends had died in an automobile accident, and after his friend's death, Jerry began to realize that he had had very little effect on his friend's life. He had only been interested in being accepted by who he knew, not in making a difference to the kingdom.

When I asked Jerry about his potential priorities five or ten years from now, I was a little surprised by the tears in his eyes. I thought our conversation had been rational and straightforward. I did not expect this kind of emotion to surface so quickly. Jerry explained, "You know, I have always kind of felt that if something happened to me that caused me to be disabled or crippled, or if I lost my job and was in financial crisis, my present friends would not be there for me, especially five or ten years from now." He continued, "I was so focused on having friends, no matter what, that I compromised my convictions and real values, and now I really don't have anything or anyone that is secure."

Jerry recommitted his life to Christ, and the last several years have been ones of growth and refocusing his passions on those things that are eternal. After his recommitment to Christ, I asked him what was now the most important thing in his life. He replied, "I just want to know God and serve him with all my heart, and to show others his love."

"You know what you are saying, don't you?" I said. "Your response is to love the Lord your God with all your heart, all your soul, all your strength, and all your might, and your neighbor as yourself. That's not a bad value system." We laughed and shared in the joy of the Lord. As long as Jerry walks in the spirit of the Lord, his priorities will remain focused on God's kingdom and his righteousness.

How do we prioritize our value system and fulfill the desires of our heart? I hope the following system will be as helpful to you as it has been to me.

Write down your present values on a piece of paper. They may be general to start with. Don't try to list them in order of importance at first, but as they come to mind. After each value, list some of the goals that may be necessary to express the value, like this:

Spiritual values:	To have a passion for Christ.
Spiritual goals:	To have an intimate relationship with the Lord and to develop Christ-like character in every area of my life.
Psychological values:	To have a passion for life.
Psychological goals:	(Emotional) To be well balanced and respond to life situations with maturity and peace.
	(Mental) To be mentally alert and to continue the learning process.
	(Volitional) To be keen and precise in making decisions.
Physical values:	To enjoy physical vitality and energy.
Physical goals:	(Body) To reach and maintain a healthy body weight.
	(Health) To maintain good health through eating, exercise, and preventive measures.
Family values:	To have a happy family.
Family goals:	To have and maintain a healthy marriage, to develop and maintain a good relationship with my children, and to develop a growing relationship with my brothers and sisters.

Occupational and/ or ministry values:	To help others.
Ministry goals:	To focus on the restorative ministry of Jesus, to equip the body of Christ to restore, and to help develop a national center for sexual trauma and addiction recovery.

After you have listed the values in your life, prioritize them. In my list above, I kept the first one in its original place and then put "family values" second until I found the correct place for each value. One way you might determine the priority of a value is to list under each one the loss and gain related to living by it or not living by it.

Value: To have a passion for Christ

Loss	*Gain*
Lack of eternal perspective	An eternal perspective
Lack of spiritual power	Spiritual power
Lack of purpose	Purpose and creativity

I listed only a few of the losses and gains, but in my own mind, it became clear that without the first value, all others would be incomplete. The more importance we attach to a value and the more continuance that it has, the greater priority it should have in our lives.

When you have listed your values and prioritized them, then you may want to follow the outline I used to help express their relative value in your life. We may have a value system, but if we are not clear about it, then it becomes very easy for our passion and focus to be off center. I will use my first value priority to illustrate this point:

Spiritual value:	To have a passion for Christ.
Goal:	To have an intimate relationship with Christ.
Obstacle to goal:	Lack of time spent on a personal relationship.
Plan of correction:	Disciplined time for prayer and Scripture devotions. This involves a regular time of prayer and a plan to commit a section of Scripture to memory.
Growth and evaluation:	Share commitment with wife and ask her to ask me how my efforts are progressing.
Goal:	To develop Christ-like character in every aspect of my life.

Obstacle to goal:	Blind spots that are most glaring to others; pride would keep me from knowing this.
Plan of correction:	Ask people close to me to share my blind spots.
Growth and evaluation:	Take notice myself and ask others to tell me how I relate to difficult situations, how quickly I forgive, and how willing I am to receive correction.

Once we have determined our value priorities, we may then need to reposition some of our relationships, ministries, schedules, etc. Remember, some of our value priorities may change, but some will and should forever remain intact. For example, my value priority for spiritual wholeness and a passion for Christ should always be first, since all other values will flow from it. However, other value priorities may change in emphasis as needs arise, or as we adjust them through reevaluation of what is more important to us.

Repositioning relationships

About two years into my own recovery and restoration, I began developing an emotionally dependent relationship. The emotional dependency was similar to the old ritual and patterns of my past addictive behavior. Since I had not written out or even considered my value system, I assumed my number one value and goal in life would be my own healing and wholeness. Mixed with this self-focused value system was a goal to develop healthy and healing relationships.

It was this emotional relapse that actually prompted me to seek professional Christian counseling for the next year and a half, during which time I also attended a clinic for addictive sexual behavior. When I told the Christian psychotherapist about the relationship, the counselor firmly and lovingly responded, "Don, you are having a fix. You are doing the same thing a cocaine addict would do, except you are experiencing the high in a relationship. What are you going to do about it?"

"I guess I'll try to change it," I said. "Are you going to try to change it," she said, "or will you reposition this relationship for your own wholeness as well as that of the other person?"

It was at this point that I discovered I needed to change my value system, and form a passionate and loving relationship with Christ as well. Somehow the focus wasn't so much on my need, but on my relationship with Jesus. With this discovery, my value system took on a new focus: a value priority for a passionate relationship with Christ and then my family, before the value priority of relationships with others. Healing and wholeness followed in line with the right value system. "Seek you first the kingdom of God and all these things will be added to you."

Upon arriving home from the counselor's office, I conferred with my wife and then called the other person in the relationship. We both agreed to help each other because of our similar background and problems, but in doing so, we were harming each other. I reaffirmed my interest in the person's spiritual and emotional growth, but I expressed that I no longer believed that I had the spiritual maturity or understanding to give the help that person needed and deserved. However, the person was welcome to call my wife and me whenever we might be of help. I also offered the names of three Christian counselors.

As you can see, this type of repositioning did not involve a rejection of the person, but a repositioning toward a healthy and helpful direction for assistance. It also led me to reposition my relationships and refocus my passions toward God and his kingdom, and then to my wife and family.

There may be other relationships in our lives that will need to be repositioned. Relationships that are draining and unhealthy will need to repositioned by spending less time on them or eliminating them altogether. Relationships that need to be strengthened, especially within our family, will need a repositioning that results in positive growth.

Repositioning ministry

Every believer has a mandate to minister. The apostle Paul says that everyone has been given a gift according to the measure of faith:

> For through the grace given to me I say to every man among you not to think more highly of himself than he ought to think; but to think so as to have sound judgment, as God has allotted to each a measure of faith. For just as we have many members in one body and all the members do not have the same function, so we, who are many, are one body in Christ, and individually members one of another. And since we have gifts that differ according to the grace given to us, let each exercise them accordingly (Rom. 12:3-6).

I believe that one of the best reasons for restoration and recovery is so that we can exercise our gifts and calling more effectively. Restoration is not an end in and of itself, but the means by which a person may become and express the fullness of Christ and glorify God. The apostle Peter certainly emphasizes the importance of sound judgment (having value priorities):

> The end of all things is at hand; therefore, be of sound judgment and sober spirit for the purpose of prayer. Above all, keep fervent in your love for one another, because love covers a multitude of sins. Be hospitable to one another without complaint. As each one has received a special gift, employ it in serving one another, as good stewards of the manifold grace of God. Whoever speaks, let him speak, as it were, the utterances of God; whoever serves, let him do so

as by the strength which God supplies; so that in all things God may be glorified through Jesus Christ, to whom belongs the glory and dominion forever and ever. Amen (1 Peter 4:7-11).

I believe the testimony of Kenneth further illustrates this call to ministry. When Kenneth pulled me aside during a conference, he asked if I could meet with him sometime during my stay. I agreed and scheduled a meeting for the next morning at breakfast.

Since I had shared my personal testimony about my restoration and recovery from sexual addiction, Kenneth felt at liberty to share with me and seek counsel. He had already told his present pastor about his early childhood sexual abuse and of the following years of his addictive sexual behavior. Kenneth had engaged in pornography and some anonymous sexual contacts, but that had occurred several years before. He had received Christian counseling and participated in a small support group. He had also begun sharing his personal testimony in several groups that were designed to help believers who were dealing with sexual addictions. Kenneth met with the pastor to discuss the possibility of sharing his story with the congregation and starting a restoration ministry through a church fellowship. His wife and family were excited about this possibility.

The pastor, however, felt very uncomfortable about the idea. He did not want his church associated with that kind of problem. Kenneth was disappointed, but he tried to understand. It was for this reason that Kenneth sought my counsel. Should he, he wondered, continue at his present church and try to help others who had come to him on a personal basis, or should he go into another ministry where he would have greater liberty to minister out of his own burden and heart?

I suggested that he stay with his present ministry and illustrate a servant's heart. We read Nehemiah, chapters 1 and 2, and after fervent prayer, began discerning God's direction for his life. A year later, Kenneth met with me again and excitedly reported his new direction, which met with the full approval of his family and his pastor. He resigned from his staff position at the church, but with the blessing and approval of the pastor and congregation, he was going to a new church where he would serve in a similar position. It included a ministry to those he had a special understanding for.

A biblical guideline is always helpful when we begin to reposition our lives and ministries. The example of Nehemiah going to Jerusalem to rebuild its ruins is an excellent and helpful example for doing this. I will outline the steps that Nehemiah took in fulfilling the burden God had given him. I trust that you will receive help for your own direction in ministry.

The report of need

> Hanani, one of my brethren, came, he and certain men of Judah; and I
> asked them concerning the Jews that had escaped, which were left of the cap-
> tivity, and concerning Jerusalem. And they said unto me, the remnant that are
> left of the captivity there in the province are in great affliction and reproach;
> the wall of Jerusalem also is broken down, and the gates thereof are burned
> with fire (Neh. 1:2-3).

Ministry comes from a burden and a call. Usually the burden begins with either hearing about or seeing a need. Several years ago my wife and I ministered to homeless children in Guatemala. Seeing their needs forever left an impression on our hearts. Thereafter, we led ministry groups to that country and still have a desire to spend more time in the future in Central and South America working with homeless children. The same thing happened in the early part of my ministry after I spoke at a missions conference in India. The needs and poverty that I saw became a burden that finally resulted in a ministry that helped purchase land and build a medical clinic and a college.

The ministry of restoration I am involved in now came out of my own awareness, but also out of the needs of many others who called on me for help. Out of the need for ministry will come the burden to minister.

Hearing or seeing a need does not necessarily constitute a call to meet the need, though it is a call to pray or to give. We should always pray about everything and never close our hearts to those in need. When I see a need that I cannot personally fulfill, I can pray at that time and thereafter as the Lord brings it to my mind. I will give whenever possible, and if I am asked to give, I will give as Jesus instructed: "Give to him who asks of you, and do not turn away from him who wants to borrow from you" (Matt. 5:42).

Jesus' instruction to give may include money, food, clothing, or even counsel. This verse is not necessarily teaching us to loan to someone who wants to borrow, but if someone asks for a loan and we cannot fulfill the request, we still must give something.

The apostle Paul also shows how hearing of a need does not necessarily translate into a call for action: "And they [Paul and Barnabas and their team] passed through the Phrygian and Galatian region, having been forbidden by the Holy Spirit to speak the word in Asia; and when they had come to Mysia, they were trying to go into Bithynia, and the Spirit of Jesus did not permit them" (Acts 16:6-7).

In the very next verses, however, a need does become a call: "And a vision appeared to Paul in the night: a certain man of Macedonia was standing and appealing to him, and saying, 'Come over to Macedonia and help us.' And when he had seen the vision, immediately we sought to go into Macedonia, concluding that God had called us to preach the gospel to them" (Acts 16:9-10).

When the need becomes a burden

When the burden for a need can no longer be released through prayer and giving, it may be that God is calling us to help meet the need through some more personal contact. As I speak of a burden, perhaps it is important to clarify its meaning. In Galatians 6:1-2, Paul instructs the church to restore those who have been overtaken in a fault. He concludes with the call to bear one another's burdens and thus fulfill the law of Christ. The word for burden here is *baros,* and it means a heavy or pressing problem. The pressure from this burden may be financial, emotional, spiritual, etc. This is a call to a ministry of mercy that focuses on a moment of pressure that can be alleviated at that time (though some people will experience a call to the restoration ministry of a person or persons on a more long-term basis).

A second word for burden is *phortian,* which is found in Galatians 6:4-5: "But let each one examine his own work, and then he will have reason for boasting in regard to himself alone, and not in regard to another. For each one shall bear his own load [burden]." In this case, burden means a light task. Ministry in this case corresponds to the words of Jesus in Matt. 11:30 when he said, "For My yoke is easy, and My load [burden] is light."

Hearing of a need that is from the Lord should not seem like a heavy, oppressive weight. It should bring a sense of lightness and joy. Even though we may not be able to complete the task or alleviate the burden ourselves, the joy of the Lord becomes our strength, and his adequacy is present to complete the calling.

Through prayer and fasting, we can discern more clearly God's call as Nehemiah did: "And it came to pass, when I heard these words, that I sat down and wept, and mourned certain days, and fasted, and prayed before the God of heaven" (Neh. 1:4). During this same prayer, Nehemiah cried out to God and made an appeal to his covenant, confessed his sins, and appealed to God's mercy. As Nehemiah prepared his own heart to hear God, we too should cleanse our hearts before the Lord in order to hear him with a pure heart and respond to his call.

The call is in accordance with his Word

Nehemiah based his call to rebuild the walls of Jerusalem upon his understanding of the purposes of the Lord and in accordance with Scripture:

> Remember the word which Thou didst command Thy servant Moses, saying, "If you are unfaithful I will scatter you among the peoples; but if you return to Me and keep My commandments and do them, though those of you who have been scattered were in the most remote part of the heavens, I will gather them from there and will bring them to the place where I have chosen to cause My name to dwell" (Neh. 1:8-10).

It is obvious that Nehemiah knew the Scriptures confirmed God's desire for his people to dwell where he had chosen: Jerusalem. I believe he also knew that the Word of the Lord to him personally was that he should be the one to lead the process of rebuilding and regathering. Thus his prayer in Nehemiah 1:11, asking for God's favor in seeking permission from the king to return to Jerusalem to rebuild: "'O Lord, I beseech Thee, may Thine ear be attentive to the prayer of Thy servant and the prayer of Thy servants who delight to revere Thy name, and make Thy servant successful today, and grant him compassion before this man.' Now I was the cupbearer to the king."

In my own journey in ministry, these two beliefs have been of the utmost importance: that a ministry would be in accordance with Scriptures, and that the Word of the Lord had come to my heart personally. During the days following my resignation from the pastorate, I spent much time researching the subject of personal restoration. The more I studied and cross-referenced the Scriptures, the more it became obvious that God's heart is a heart of restoration. In the prophetic books of the Bible that I had considered the harshest in regard to sin, I found a heart for restoration.

Receive counsel from authority

We are all probably aware of stories of the perversion of both spiritual and civil authority. The purpose of this point is not to explore these issues, but to reemphasize that our ultimate authority should come from God (Acts 4:18-20). When our decisions affect the lives and investments of others, we should seek their authority and counsel (Proverbs 15:22). If we submit to proper authority, God will accomplish his will more effectively, more quickly, or more safely. Nehemiah experienced this:

> And it came about in the month Nisan, in the twentieth year of King Artaxerxes, that wine was before him, and I took up the wine and gave it to the king. Now I had not been sad in his presence. So the king said to me, "Why is your face sad though you are not sick? This is nothing but sadness of heart." Then I was very much afraid. And I said to the King, "Let the king live forever. Why should my face not be sad when the city, the place of my father's tombs, lies desolate and its gates have been consumed by fire?" Then the king said to me, "What would you request?" So I prayed to the God of heaven. And I said to the king, "If it please the king, and if your servant has found favor before you, send me to Judah, to the city of my fathers' tombs, that I may rebuild it" (Nehemiah 2:1-5).

A careful reading here reveals the wisdom with which Nehemiah appealed to the king: he had been faithful in his service and his attitude; he had earned the respect and opportunity to share; he focused more on the king's needs than on his own; he shared a desire based on others' needs; he answered the king's question, "What would you request?" with careful prayer and consideration; he desired to please the king in his request and placed himself before him as his servant; and he responded within the limits requested by the king, which did not violate God's Word to him.

The result of Nehemiah seeking counsel was the delivery of letters to various governors granting them permission to pass through the territory. In addition, the king provided timber to make beams for the gates and the walls of the city.

One day a minister told me that he had crossed nearly every authority figure in his life. His life had been a long story of sorrow and disappointments, mostly related to disagreements with former senior pastors and employers. His conclusion in sharing this information was to confirm how correct he had been to fight and strive. After all, he proudly exclaimed, "Look where I'm at now." He was referring to his position as pastor of the largest church in the city. My only comment was, "You probably are where God intended you to be, but I wonder if the journey wouldn't have been easier and taken less time if you hadn't fought and resisted so much." His expression was blank, but somehow I knew the message had sunk in.

I too am learning the value of wise counsel and authority in my life. During my restoration process, it has been a blessing to experience the value of wise counsel from my wife. We have agreed to walk together in agreement in those things that relate to and affect each other—and that's most things. Though I know that God is my final authority, the wisdom of counsel from my wife has been invaluable.

Other sources of counsel that have helped me make major decisions include a group of godly Christian leaders whom I have submitted my life and ministry to for accountability.

Allow for God's timing

We have all seen a dream or desire get delayed—when no matter how much manipulating and pushing we exert, we feel stuck. I believe there is a time to knock, a time to push, and a time to be aggressive in moving forward. There is also a time to be aggressive in waiting before God in prayer and spiritual warfare. I have often ended up being thankful for those occasions when the timing of something wasn't what I thought it should have been, because when a door finally opened or an opportunity did come about, I was ready and better prepared, whereas before it would have been premature for me to act.

This same experience is illustrated in Nehemiah's vision and ministry to rebuild the walls. He responded as circumstances changed: "Then I came to the governors of the provinces beyond the river and gave them the king's letters. Now the king had sent with me officers of the army and horsemen" (Nehemiah 2:9). Nehemiah did not attempt to fulfill his plans when he felt the time was right. He followed the king's schedule, which was really God's schedule.

Investigate and validate a need. Ministry is designed to meet needs. Jesus came to seek and save that which was lost. Even so, in repositioning a ministry, we should investigate whether the location, organization, church, or opportunity is a place where the ministry will fulfill our call or burden. "He who gives an answer before he hears, it is folly and shame to him" (Prov. 18:13). Some possible areas of investigation include:

• Explore the past history. How did the ministry begin? Was there division and dissension at its roots? Are there any past offenses to be cleared up? History will affect the future of any ministry. The seeds of good fruit or bad fruit will produce after their kind.

• Define responsibilities. Don't wait until you are on board before finding out what the authority structure is and what your responsibilities are. Undefined responsibilities, expectations, and goals are the foundations of destruction.

• Define your future goals and vision. Does the vision God has given you complement the one in place, or will you have to suppress your vision? If you are the one in leadership, can the vision of the church or organization be raised to meet your vision, or do you need to go somewhere else to implement your vision?

Even though Nehemiah went to Jerusalem with the burden of the Lord, he still investigated the need before plunging in.

> And I arose in the night, I and some few men with me; neither told I any man what my God had put in my heart to do at Jerusalem; neither was there any beast with me, save the beast that I rode upon. And I went out by night by the gate of the valley, even before the dragonwell, and to the dung port, and viewed the walls of Jerusalem, which were broken down, and the gates thereof were consumed with fire (Neh. 2:12-13).

Confirm your ministry with coworkers. I believe that men are first called to be a team, then to minister. Jesus called men together, trained them to be fishers of men, and sent them forth into ministry. I do not seek out a ministry in a particular city or area. Rather, I seek the relationships that the Lord has for me in that city. The ministry flows from those relationships. Nehemiah waited for the same kind of response and common vision among the people:

> Then said I to them, "You see the bad situation we are in, that Jerusalem is desolate and its gates burned by fire. Come, let us rebuild the wall of Jerusalem that we may no longer be a reproach." And I told them how the hand of my God had been favorable to me, and also about the king's words which he had spoken to me. Then they said, "Let us arise and build." So they put their hands to the good work (Neh. 2:17-18).

In obtaining a common vision and enthusiasm, Nehemiah raised the vision of the people. First, he related to their needs and associated with their pain of being a reproach. Second, he shared how the hand of God had been with him. And third, he talked about how the circumstances had worked out.

The people's response was to rise in unison to the challenge. This is the basis for working together: a common need, a common goal, and a common inspiration.

Continue with boldness and confidence in God's purposes and power. Once we have repositioned our ministry to reflect our true value priorities, we can be sure that opposition, tests, and trials will arise. This is the message of the Epistle to the Ephesians. Once their priorities were corrected and their lives were empowered by the Holy Spirit, they had to be strong in the Lord and in the strength of his might, and stand firm against the schemes of the devil. Paul describes the full armor of God, and then concludes by entreating them to pray. Nehemiah encountered this same type of test and opposition, but he stood firm in the power of God:

> But when Sanballat, the Horonite, and Tobiah the Ammonite official, and Geshem the Arab heard it, they mocked us and despised us and said, "What is this thing you are doing? Are you rebelling against the king?" So I answered them and said to them, "The God of heaven will give us success; therefore we His servants will arise and build, but you have no portion, right, or memorial in Jerusalem" (Neh. 2:19-20).

It is one thing to experience passions out of control; it is quite another to feel no passion at all. Fortunately, the people under Nehemiah had a passion and a vision that was based upon God's will.

When a pastor friend called me one day, he sounded lonely and depressed. I kept trying to describe God's will for ministry, but I soon discovered that this was not his need. What was the use of knowing God's will for ministry if one didn't have the passion and desire to even continue? After a lengthy conversation, it was obvious that my friend had been doing what others expected of him. He was going through the motions, with no passion in his heart. Because of a lack of passion, he had become passive, and his life had become bland and dull.

We have discussed repositioning our ministries and refocusing our passions, but you may not feel any passion at all to rise up with enthusiasm to God's call in your life. Like my pastor friend, your problem—or perhaps the problem of someone close to you—isn't just a matter of refocusing passion. It is a matter of experiencing passion.

Let's look next at how we can, by God's grace, experience a resurgence of passion of the right kind.

Study questions

1.) What is the most important thing in your life? Why is it important to you? Will you consider it important five or ten years from now?

2.) Write down your own spiritual, psychological, physical, family, and occupational values and goals on a piece of paper.

3.) Next, prioritize your values.

4.) Then write down the obstacles to your goals, how you plan to correct those obstacles, and a method for evaluating your progress.

5.) Is there a relationship in your life that needs to be repositioned? How might you accomplish this to refocus your passions toward God and his kingdom?

6.) Think about the last time you rejected a call to fulfill someone's need because it seemed to be beyond your capability. How could you have made even a partial effort to fulfill it?

7.) Who might you turn to for wise counsel? What qualities does this person possess that will help you in your restoration?

8.) What are the common needs, common goals, and common inspirations of the people in your ministry?

TEN

OVERCOMING PASSIVITY

Roy told his wife, Betty, how unhappy he had been for the past several years. "I'm just not fulfilled," he softly uttered under his breath. Realizing how he had hurt his wife, and seeing the pain and hurt on her face as we continued to talk, Roy tried to hide his growing frustration. Then he blurted out, "All my life I've wanted to be a minister or missionary, but I knew that Betty wanted a different lifestyle. She wouldn't be satisfied with a lower income or maybe living in a smaller house until we could get better established." By now, he couldn't even look at his wife.

Betty responded with total surprise. "I didn't know that you wanted to be a minister. If I had only known, I would have done anything to help and encourage you." Tears welled up in her eyes, and all too vividly I witnessed again the results of a person going on for years and years with hidden dreams and plans, not doing anything about them and, like Roy, projecting frustration and blame on a spouse.

The couple received some ongoing help in communication, but for Roy, help in overcoming passivity was the key to a more fulfilling life and future. Even though he and Betty did not enter Christian ministry on a full-time basis, they were able to make some decisions and arrangements that allowed them to express their hidden desires and plans for a part-time ministry. They later agreed that a part-time ministry was probably the best arrangement since they were now in their early fifties with grandchildren. Short-term ministry trips and special projects allowed them to fulfill a lifelong dream together as well as spend time with their children and grandchildren.

The last time I spoke to Roy, he reminded me of our conversation and how close he had come to leaving his wife and family. "Boy, can you imagine what a mistake I almost made? I am so happy," he said. "I only wish that I had understood about overcoming passivity years ago. Thank God that Betty and I can still experience a new passion for the Lord and each other." I understood how Roy felt. I too had been in a place of passivity—frustrated and unhappy and projecting the blame for my own inadequacy on my wife and other people.

What is passivity?

Passivity is the lack of courage, confidence and persistence to accomplish what God has called us to do. A few years before talking with Roy and Betty, my own life consisted mostly of sleeping too much to escape my own boredom and shame. Overeating was another way I tried to fill the vacuum inside of me. More painful than the outward signs of depression and frustration was the pain of anxiety, fear, and insecurity.

After I resigned from the ministry because of a moral sin, I submitted myself to a group of godly Christian leaders for accountability and restoration. After about a year and a half, they released me back into public ministry. Speaking engagements were sparse at first, and my wife and I had to live off our savings. But as more people heard my testimony and teachings on personal restoration, the speaking engagements increased, and I was soon travelling throughout the United States.

Instead of being fulfilled, I became increasingly tired and unhappy. The demanding schedule was draining, and I was not accomplishing the real vision I believed God had given me. It was like being on someone else's track and racing downhill toward an unknown destination.

"What has gone wrong?" I kept asking myself. My passion for life and the message God was working in me were almost gone. Anger was building up inside me, and so was my resentment over what I saw as others' failure to fulfill my expectations of them. It was then that I began to realize that I was really angry with myself and my own passivity; I was not pursuing the goals and dreams in my heart, but letting other people set my schedule and agenda. These people had no idea of my feelings, and their intent was certainly not to take away my dreams. They simply didn't know what my dreams and plans were because I had never shared them.

Passivity is really a lack of passion or, at most, passion suppressed. When the passion in our heart is not expressed in creative ways, eventually it begins to die out. It was for this reason that the apostle Paul encouraged his son Timothy "to kindle afresh the gift of God which is in you through the laying on of my hands" (2 Timothy 1:6). In the following verse Paul continues, "For God has not given us a spirit of timidity, but of power, and love and discipline."

It was while reading this account of Paul's words to Timothy that my heart began to cry out to God to show me how to overcome passivity and begin living out the dreams and visions he had given me. The first step in the journey to a more passionate heart and life was to identify the characteristics and causes of my own passivity.

Characteristics of passivity

Procrastination: Talking and thinking about plans and dreams, but not taking action. Several plans were in my heart, but they had remained just that for several years: plans. I had plans to write a book, plans to begin a seminar on restoration, plans to work with fallen pastors and leaders, plans to begin a teaching ministry through cassette tapes, and plans for a radio ministry and possibly a television ministry. But I had failed to act on even one of these plans. They remained in the attic of my mind with all the things that I wanted to accomplish someday. It became much easier to make new plans than to do something about the ones I had already made.

Ted was the same way. He was an older man whom I had always admired for his witty and intelligent mind. He never lacked for creative ideas and suggestions. His office was stacked with magazines and articles he had cut out of newspapers to use for special projects. The only thing was that the special projects never came to fruition, and the only evidence of any passion at all were well-intended plans that never moved beyond a stack of clippings.

When Ted died, a friend called me and told me of the impending funeral arrangements. My heart felt saddened for his family and their loss, but I was also saddened that he had died with so many dreams and plans in his heart that were unfulfilled. The experience left a deep impression on me, for I too had put things off. It influenced me to stop procrastinating.

Dependency: Expecting others to take care of us and do for us what we should do for ourselves. It is certainly valuable to look to others as role models and seek counsel and help. But many people, like me, may have consciously or subconsciously been looking to someone else to fulfill their plans for them.

The Lord kept sending outstanding people into my life, and I was always left with a feeling of gratitude for having met them. Yet I often wondered, "Is this the person God is going to use to open the doors for my future plans and help me accomplish what he has called me to?" The Lord may use people to open a door, but I have learned that ultimately it is God who opens and shuts doors: "He who is holy, who is true, who has the key of David, who opens and no one will shut, and who shuts and no one will open" (Rev. 3:7).

To have expectations of others without ultimately placing those expectations on the Lord will set one up for disappointment. Whatever someone else may do for us should be enough. Whatever someone else does not do for us should be enough. God is our resource and, as David says in the Psalms, my expectations come from thee, oh God. Dependency on others actually takes away from our trust in God and prevents us from spiritual and emotional growth.

Dependency is necessary while we are babies, but as we become more mature it is healthy and normal to begin taking care of ourselves. Of course, I am not talking about a kind of self- sufficiency and independence that is unhealthy, but an interdependence that is cooperative.

Shame: The faulty belief that "I am a mistake" instead of "I made a mistake." A mistake can be corrected and a sin can be forgiven, but to believe that you *are* a mistake causes you to feel less than unredeemable. Passivity is a result of unhealthy shame and continues as an ongoing cycle in the passive personality. Unhealthy shame does not feel that it deserves to be blessed, but that it deserves death.

The attitudes that reinforce passivity are:

• Submission to others' views, decisions, and actions that may affect our own selves in an unfavorable way without questioning or stating another point of view or option. In the past, my wife would often question why I would work under certain circumstances or not say something about a wrong. My reply would be, "I'm not in a position to do anything about it," or "I don't have an option." The truth is that I could do something about it. I could have changed jobs or ministry, or I could have gone to the one in leadership and shared my views. Some things are unchangeable, but many situations can and should be changed. Moreover, we may need to remove ourselves from a situation if it cannot be changed.

• Nonaggressive planning (or a lack of planning) for the future or letting others plan for us. For a long time my response to life was that it was okay for others to be blessed, but I did not deserve to blessed and even felt guilty about receiving benefits. It was after I read Ephesians 1:3 that my attitude began to change: "Blessed be the God and Father of our Lord Jesus Christ, who has blessed us with every spiritual blessing in the heavenly places in Christ."

This is not to suggest at all that we are to benefit from others' mistakes or to disregard the benefit and blessings of others. Rather, we are to receive blessings as well as give blessings.

Several years ago I began shopping for a car with money given to me as a gift. It was important to the salesperson to sell me a car since he said he had not yet sold a car that month. After some negotiation, I was ready to make an offer that was below his price; it would have resulted in a fairly low commission for him. It was then that the Holy Spirit reminded me that I had been blessed and that I should bless the salesperson by allowing him to make a fair commission. Shame may prevent a person from receiving a blessing, but greed may keep one from giving a blessing.

Another result of shame in a person's life is what I call the victimization syndrome. That is, because a person has been a victim of past abuse—sexual, physical, or emotional—he or she keeps living life as a victim. The victimization syndrome represents an attempt to complete the past and somehow fix it, creating new scenarios as opportunities to bring closure. However, the new scenarios only continue the vicious cycle of shame and passivity. It is necessary to release the past, learn from it, and recognize that in Christ we are no longer victims, but victors.

Isaiah the prophet gave a special promise to God's people who were victims by encouraging them to rise above the victim mentality: "Therefore, please hear this, you afflicted, who are drunk, but not with wine: Thus says your Lord, the Lord, even your God who contends for His people, 'Behold, I have taken out of your hand the cup of reeling; the chalice of My anger, you will never drink it again. And I will put it into the hand of your tormentors, who have said to you, lie down that we may walk over you. You have even made your back like the ground, and like the street for those who walk over it'" (Isa. 51:21-23).

Blaming: Placing responsibility on others for our losses and failures. It is so easy to blame others for our circumstances, and much less painful than holding ourselves responsible. Passivity finds a way to justify why we haven't done certain things, or worse, why we can't because of what someone has done to us. As long as we blame others for our failures, we allow them to control our lives. After all, passivity is giving control of our lives to others. Through forgiveness and assuming responsibility, we give control of our lives to God. Lack of forgiveness and blame is actually a form of unbelief. Notice the connection between forgiveness and faith in the following section of Scripture:

> And Jesus answered saying to them, "Have faith in God. Truly I say to you, whoever says to this mountain, 'Be taken up and cast into the sea,' and does not doubt in his heart, but believes that what he says is going to happen; it shall be granted him. Therefore I say to you, all things for which you pray and ask, believe that you have received them, and they shall be granted you. And whenever you stand praying, forgive, if you have anything against anyone; so that your Father who is in heaven may forgive you your transgressions. But if you do not forgive, neither will your Father who is in heaven forgive your transgressions (Mark 11:22-26).

When a person has a forgiving heart, he or she is affirming that he or she trusts God to work everything together for his good, for his glory, and for our benefit. It is passion that allows us to move forward in spite of the offenses and circumstances of the past. When a person has an unforgiving heart, that person is in unbelief. He or she is in fact saying, "I don't believe that God is just or fair, so I will take matters into my own hands to make sure that the other people get their due punishment and I receive my due justice." This view totally disregards God. Scripture says, "Never take your own revenge, beloved, but leave room for the wrath of God, for it is written, 'Vengeance is mine, I will repay,' says the Lord. 'But if your enemy is hungry, feed him, and if he is thirsty, give him a drink; for in so doing you will reap burning coals upon his head.' Do not be overcome by evil, but overcome evil with good (Rom. 12:19-21).

One can live for years in a state of resentment and distrust, feeling unable to do the good he or she was called to accomplish and overcome with the evil of passivity and distrust of God and others. We are not responsible for the actions of others against us, but we are responsible for our actions and re-actions toward them. Passivity is focusing on the offenses of others to explain our hurt and pain, and diverting our passion and energy away from our hopes and dreams.

Discouragement: Becoming easily diverted from dreams and plans by discouragement and negative circumstances. When my wife and I began the seminar ministry, we believed the Lord wanted us to provide for all the expenses through the registration fees of those attending. This meant that our transportation (mostly by air), lodging, office, personal salary, etc., would not be a burden to the churches. Of course, in many areas the churches cooperated and were very gracious. In some areas there was hardly any cooperation, and it would cost us more to do a seminar than we received. Added to this was the problem of unpaid bills from a monthly tape ministry that sometimes reached several thousand dollars.

My initial response was to focus on the breakdown of our ministry and how it wasn't working. Even though we were receiving many letters from people we had helped, my tendency was to become discouraged instead of feeling challenged. (Helen's tendency was to break through the problems and work on a solution, which I have also begun to do.)

Many times, I wanted to quit instead of looking at the challenge and re-adjusting. Fortunately, the Lord led me in a breakthrough to change strategy, seek counsel, and move from passivity to a new passion for him and his ways. My focus had been on getting "my ways" to work instead of on working "his ways."

Discouragement will always result when we set our hearts on fulfilling our plans and seeking temporal things. God may use human plans and allow temporal results, but when our heart is set on him and his purpose, temporary failures and losses will be just that: temporary. If we live our life in a mode of, "If I had only . . ." instead of "Next time . . .," we fail to see God's design for our growth and maturity. Past mistakes and failures are opportunities for breakthroughs in our own character development and for finding creative solutions. God's ultimate design is, "Christ in Us, the Hope of Glory." To have Christ in us is to have his wisdom, his power, his love, his passion, etc. After all, heaven and earth will pass away, but his Word will abide forever.

Intimidation: Comparing ourselves with others and living with the fear that they can succeed but we cannot. When others become our final standard of comparison, then passivity easily occurs, especially when we realize that we can never become just like someone else (when, in fact, we were never intended to).

One characteristic of intimidation is the lack of ability to negotiate and confront. We may be the kind of person who signs the bottom line of a contract without having read it carefully. We may reason, "Who am I to question an authority or an expert?" Or worse, we may sign the contract or agree to some action and later explode in an outburst of anger. Like children, we learned how to get our way by crying, but we may not have learned to negotiate and confront like adults.

Another characteristic of intimidation is the fear of asking others for help. A false pride—thinking that we have all the answers—may keep us from seeking help. The fear that others would not want to be bothered with helping us is also a painful force in the passive person. "Who am I to ask for help?" we may think. The truth is that some people will not want to help or be available; however, some of the most fruitful decisions I have made resulted from seeking counsel from others.

Causes of passivity

John was a young businessman in his early thirties. He had been laid off from his job as an engineer and worked part time in a fast food restaurant. For five years he struggled with depression and spent most of his time after work sleeping. His wife and children adapted to his passive behavior, but not without pain and loss. When I asked John what dreams were in his heart and what he would really like to do with his life, I was surprised at the creativity and ideas that emerged.

"What are you going to do about it?" I responded with excitement and encouragement.

"Nothing," he said.

"Is that all?" I asked. "What about the dreams and plans you've mentioned? You're still a young man, and if the Lord permits, you have years to grow and succeed."

"I don't know. I guess nothing."

I decided to ask John a question that would probe his passivity and possibly unlock his reasons for closing down. "What do you fear most about stepping out to fulfill your dreams for yourself and for your family?"

"I'm not sure," he responded.

"If you could start a business or obtain a job today that you knew would succeed, would you do it?" I asked. With a dim twinkle of hope in his eyes he said he would. "Then, if you knew that you would not fail, would you be encouraged and excited about life and your future?"

"Yes," he responded, with more boldness.

"Then it's fear of failure that has been keeping you back," I reasoned. John agreed and was eager to respond to the steps of overcoming passivity.

Fear of failure. I was fifty years old when I decided to begin a seminar ministry, write a book, and start a teaching ministry through cassette tapes. As long as I responded with a spirit of fear, especially to the possibility of failure, I could not act on my dreams. The fear of failure produced pain that reminded me of past loss. For me, like John, the risk seemed too great. As I realized that there would be more loss by not taking a risk and by not living out God's plan, the fear began to subside and creativity started flowing.

Why are people like myself, John, and others so paralyzed by a fear of failure? John's response to this question was answered by deep memories of a childhood during which he was criticized daily for being too slow, too lazy, and too stupid. He had not been able to separate these accusations from his father from the reality of his true abilities and skills.

Some people have a fear of failure because they have never tasted the joy of success and accomplishment. Suzy was an example of this type of person. She had never been allowed to complete a task as a child without her mother accusing her of being too slow and taking over. Suzy remembers making toast and letting it burn before realizing it was overdone. Her mother nearly flew into a rage and said that anyone who couldn't make toast had to be stupid. Her father laughed at the whole episode and often reminded Suzy in front of guest and friends that she knew how to make "burnt offerings." Each criticism increased Suzy's fear of failure and her inability to complete a task.

Fear of rejection. Anthony desperately wanted his father's approval, but he just didn't have the build and natural talent to compete with the other guys in football. His father had been a high school football star and had expected the same from his son. Anthony could see the look in his father's eyes when he didn't make the football team, and the distance between them grew.

It reminded Anthony of an incident years earlier when his father tried to teach him how to throw a ball. Because he didn't measure up to his father's expectations, his father became angry and lashed out, "If you can't play any better than a sissy, I'm through trying to show you." He walked away, and Anthony remembers that his father never again tried to teach him how to play a sport. These experiences in Anthony's early years laid the groundwork for the faulty belief system that he developed later in life: that we are accepted based on our performance rather than our being.

Performance is important, and competition and skills are a reality in the world we live in, but to base acceptance on our performance is to distort our heavenly Father's love for us. God's design in creation is that a baby is accepted and loved, not for what it can do or perform, but because it is and has great value. It is precious because it exists.

Fear of death. When Glen's wife called me to come visit her husband because of depression, I was a young minister who did not have much of an understanding of how to deal with this kind of a problem. I do remember being surprised that Glen was in such an emotional state. He had a beautiful family, a nice home, and a successful job. He and his family were active in church and, by all outward signs, they were very happy.

Glen had spent a week or two in a psychiatric clinic and was seeing a counselor on a weekly basis, but somehow he didn't seem to be able to pull out of the depression that plagued him for months. I visited him on a regular basis to pray and give him hope.

Several years after I had moved from the area, I heard that Glen had committed suicide. My heart sank when I heard part of the reason for his depression: he had been passed over for a promotion at work and began the deep road downward into hopelessness. Though there may have been other factors I was unaware of, it was clear that Glen, like many other people, did not distinguish between who he was and what he did.

This same experience is all too common among successful businessmen who, after losing a job, descend into a depression and commit suicide. Their identity is not in Christ and based on who they are as a person, but in their job or position and based upon recognition from others. When they lose their job and the accompanying prestige, they believe their life is over.

When we tie our identity and ultimate value to what we *do* instead of who we *are*, the result will be either an aggressive performance orientation or a passivity that dares not risk taking action for fear of death.

When the apostle Paul wrote to Timothy, "For God has not given us the spirit of timidity, but of power and love and discipline [sound mind]," he must have understood the causes of passivity. We could put the word "passivity" in place of "timidity" in this passage, in that the result of timidity is passivity. One only has to read between the lines of Timothy's life to see the potential for failure and passivity. Yet because of a praying grandmother and mother, Timothy had become a man of respect and spiritual growth.

In fact, the apostle Paul chose Timothy to travel with him in the ministry and later gave him important responsibility and authority in the early church. Paul further encourages him not to let others look down on his youthfulness (1 Tim. 4:12) and not to be ashamed of the testimony of the Lord and of Paul's being in prison (2 Tim. 1:8). It is in this context that Timothy is reminded of the power of the Holy Spirit in his life and the accompanying grace that overcomes fear and passivity.

The spirit of power

To understand the meaning of power here, one has to consider not physical strength, but rather the ability to choose, to decide, and to take action. The spirit of power is not about brute force, but spiritual authority and the ability to take control of one's own life and destiny by giving control to the Lordship of Christ and walking in his power and authority.

With the reader's patience, I am going to share my own experience with overcoming passivity. I had often dreamed of starting a teaching ministry through cassette tapes. This would mean recording a teaching and distributing it to those interested in the content, which would be on the restorative ministry of Christ and related subjects.

I had earlier made wisecracks about those producing a "tape of the month" and was a little embarrassed by my former attitude. So I decided to call my tape ministry "a monthly teaching tape," not a tape of the month.

I found it easier to dream about the tape ministry than to do something about it. As long as it remained in my heart and mind, it seemed safe from disappointment and possible failure. But it also remained only a dream without any reality and joy of fulfillment. One day I decided that if I didn't do something about it, this part of my dream could die. It was then that I took one of the most important steps into my future: I made one simple phone call to a minister who had a "tape of the month" and sought his counsel on how to get started. He was more than helpful, and his counsel was crucial to the entire project. I believe the information he gave me saved me years of learning what to do and what not to do.

At my friend's suggestion, I made another phone call to a company that duplicated tapes in large quantities and learned the cost of doing such a project. Since I was beginning with no orders, it was not possible to use this particular company; they required a minimum order of two hundred tapes. But at least it was information that could be used in the future. (In fact, it has been used; today we send out hundreds of "tape of the month" cassettes.)

Each phone call and/or other step seemed to lead to another phone call and another step. We had a nice recording machine to record the "teaching," but realized that we would need envelopes for mailing, a permit from the post office, and a mailing list. Helen quickly went to work obtaining the permit and shopped around until she found the best price for mailing envelopes. The only remaining step was to get a mailing list and a small duplicator to reproduce the master tape until we needed a quantity large enough to have it reproduced professionally.

Everything seemed to be falling into place, and I planned to present the opportunity to receive my monthly teaching tape at my next scheduled speaking engagement, which was a men's retreat of about two hundred people. The leadership for the retreat had given me permission to talk about signing up for the teaching tape. The men responded very positively to my ministry and even asked about additional materials. This made it easier to present the monthly teaching tape ministry, but a lump still seemed to stick in my throat when I tried to explain it.

The leader of the retreat had introduced my presentation about the tape ministry by calling it my "tape of the month" club. My face turned red as I remembered the fun I had made of others. I wished I had repented sooner. Nonetheless, recognizing the Lord's humor in gently rebuking me, I gladly took hold of the opportunity to take another step in this venture and excitedly explained to the group what would be forthcoming in the teaching ministry.

Now it was time to have those interested fill out a card indicating their commitment to be a part of our monthly teaching tape series. A lump bigger than usual seemed to fill my throat and the fear of failure almost paralyzed me. I never would have won a salesman of the year award, and probably did everything wrong while asking the men to sign up: "You may not be interested," "Please do not feel pressured to do anything," "You may not even need this, but just in case you do, you can fill out one of the cards and we will mail our tape to you on a monthly basis." Afterward, I could hardly believe how noncommittal my presentation had been, but to my surprise, thirty-five men signed up.

The whole process was beginning to move more quickly than I realized, and it was definitely time for another step. I had a mailing list of thirty-five men, but desperately needed a small duplicator machine to reproduce the necessary tapes. (Remember, each step requires another step. If you are thinking of starting something entirely new for you, I would encourage taking small steps at first.)

The first step—making a phone call—didn't seem to take much faith (at least for me), but each step thereafter got bigger and a new dimension of faith became necessary. Another way I found to describe faith is "risk." However, the more we are assured that our dreams and plans are from God, the less a risk faith seems to be. The risk factor feels more risky when our discernment is a little fuzzy about which parts of the plan are God's will and which parts may not be.

The next big step definitely involved risk: buying a small duplicator machine and the number of tapes necessary to begin. I call this a risk and a step of faith because money was not available at the time for the purchase. But another speaking engagement was forthcoming, and my plan was to use the love offering from that source to purchase the machine. Since our only salary and livelihood came from these love offerings, it seemed to me a little risky to forgo salary to buy a machine. Since no one had yet paid for the tape ministry, the worst that could happen, I reasoned, was that I would send the orders back explaining my dilemma.

The Lord had planned for me to take another step of faith that was bigger than I had planned. During the aforementioned speaking engagement, the pastor announced that a fire had destroyed the home and all the belongings of a church family. One of the family members was in the hospital with serious burns. The still, small voice of the Holy Spirit kept telling my heart that my offering was to be given to this family and that those giving were to be challenged to give even more than they had planned.

"God, are you sure this is you?" I tried to reason. "What about the duplicating machine?" I asked, as though he had forgotten. But the duplicating machine didn't seem to be on his mind, and the voice of the Holy Spirit gently and firmly continued to nudge me to give the offering to the family. I wish I could say that I gave the offering without any hesitation. But quite honestly, I gave it out of obedience and was fearful that my dreams to begin the tape ministry were gone. Not only did the Holy Spirit prompt me to give the love offering, but when the collection plate was passed, he also prompted me to give the twenty dollar bill that was neatly tucked away in my billfold for a "special need."

The next day when I arrived home, I knew Helen wouldn't be bothered that I had given the offering to the family; she is more likely to do that sort of thing than I am. Moreover, I had a deep, growing joy about the family and was realizing that their loss was an opportunity to pray for them and to focus on someone else's need for a change, not just mine.

When Helen opened the door for me, I had a suitcase in one hand, a small box of books balanced on the other hand and a satchel with my Bible and notes barely clinging by the strap on my shoulder. Her eyes were bright with hope, and one of the first things she said was, "Guess who we got a gift from today?" I responded with very little excitement, as I supposed it was some candy or a gift of appreciation from someone. I was more concerned about the duplicator and our living needs.

When she explained that the gift was in the form of a check, and from a person who had not yet given to our ministry, I was overtaken with gratitude to the Lord and joy for the person who had been sensitive to the Lord's prompting. The amount of the gift was more than enough to purchase the duplicator machine, the tapes, and other necessary items to get started. In fact, it was more money than the Lord had prompted me to give away.

We have already mentioned that having power is the ability to make choices and decisions and to take action. When the Holy Spirit expresses his power over the spirit of timidity and passivity, the following three qualities, among others, will always be present.

1. Creativeness. The spirit of God hovered over the surface of the waters in the creation as recorded in Genesis 1. The same Holy Spirit is always associated with the creative work of God. The Scriptures tell us that that which was conceived in Mary, meaning Jesus, was of the Holy Spirit. The Gospel of Matthew says very clearly that she was found to be with child by the Holy Spirit (Matt 1:18). This same Holy Spirit raised Jesus from the dead and empowered the early church to be a witness throughout the world.

Even so, as we are filled with the Holy Spirit and the gifts of God are released in our life, creativity will flow naturally like a river from our innermost being. The apostle Paul says that each believer has received a gift according to the measure of faith (Rom. 12:3). Creativity and vision for purpose may vary from one believer to another in accordance with our ministries, but the Holy Spirit does produce creativity for our lives and ministries. Wherever true New Testament Christianity flourishes and expresses the fullness of the Holy Spirit, civilization will, in time, rise to higher levels of morals, education, medicine, economics, family values, science, etc.

People often ask how to tap into this creativity. Ask yourself these questions: What is in my heart? What are the dreams that I would like to see fulfilled before I die? Habakkuk the prophet put it this way: "I will stand on my guard post and station myself on the rampart; and I will keep watch to see what he will speak to me" (Hab. 2:1). The prophet did not say he would *hear*, but *see* what God would speak. The Lord does indeed speak to his people, but another way of hearing God is to look around and see what the needs are, what is already being blessed in your life, where you are the most effective, and what areas of your own life produce the maximum results.

Several years ago I was earnestly seeking the Lord about direction for ministry and was discouraged when there seemed to be no clear answer from the inner voice of the Holy Spirit. It was then that I read this in Habakkuk and realized that God was already speaking. I also needed to "hear with my eyes." It had become obvious that the message and ministry of personal restoration was that which was being blessed and resulted in fruit. I just needed to "see" what God was saying.

2. Initiative. Dreams and visions that are not implemented will remain dreams and visions. When Jesus gave a command to someone for healing, he often asked them to *do* something: "take up your bed and walk," "stretch forth your hand," "go wash in the pool," etc. In the Old Testament, we often find the same pattern: faith required a person to take a step, to do something that required action.

So when we believe that God has given us an idea, a dream, a plan, DO SOMETHING ABOUT IT. I am not suggesting that you leap in the dark without seeking counsel, counting the cost, or planning carefully. Faith is walking in the light, but it does involve taking a step. It may not be a leap of faith, but it can be a step of faith. When the apostle Peter walked to Jesus on the water, he had to step out of the boat.

A step of faith does not necessarily mean selling your home, business, and other possessions and going to some faraway country as a missionary. If the Lord has put missions in your heart, you may need to seek counsel with your church leadership, pastor, elders, etc., and obtain information about possible opportunities. A short mission trip of a week or two to the area you are interested in may be the first step. Further training may be another step. As you take each step, the goal and fulfillment will become clearer. Of course, if you have already walked in a dream or plan for a while, then much bolder steps may be required by the Lord.

3. Effectiveness. How well I remember a certain man who had a great business idea and put it into effect. His merchandise was creative and very much in demand. However, as the demand for the product increased and he was pressured to fill the orders, he paid less and less attention to quality. Soon the product became sloppily and carelessly made. When his business went bankrupt, he seemed very surprised and blamed it on the economy. The truth is that his product lacked quality. People will not pay maximum prices for minimum standards. Remember that not only products but services, such as a ministry, can lose their effectiveness if quality is sacrificed to quantity.

While traveling by air to a speaking engagement, I was talking with a gentleman seated next to me. He was a national manager for a well-known fastfood chain and spent part of his time making unannounced calls on various restaurants to check on their quality and effectiveness. I asked him to list the most important things that customers looked for in a food service such as his. He quickly replied, "Cleanliness, quality of food, and service."

Should the Christian world do less in terms of quality? I am not talking about luxury, but being effective in what we do. It may be that resources are unavailable to be as immediately effective as you dream of, but if only a small percentage of improvement takes place every few months, or even once every year, just think of what could happen over five or ten years.

Staying effective may involve seeking counsel, having role models, and making adjustments. A friend recently reminded me of the acronym KISS:

Keep It Simple Stupid. I'm not in favor of calling anyone stupid, but I got the message.

Recently my wife was discussing childhood memories with a friend who talked about the poverty of her childhood years. "We had dirt floors in our house, but they were clean. We swept them every day." I admire that kind of effort. That's being effective with what you have.

The spirit of love

The essence of love is giving. The most well-known passage in the Bible is John 3:16, about God giving his only begotten son. When a friend asked me if I thought it was wrong for him to want to prosper in his business, I said that it depended on his motives. If his motives were to get rich and hoard things to himself, then it was indeed wrong, not to mention selfish and greedy. One of the strongest warnings in the New Testament concerns the rich:

> Come now you rich, weep and howl for your miseries which are coming upon you. Your riches have rotted and your garments have become moth-eaten. Your gold and your silver have rusted; and their rust will be a witness against you and will consume your flesh like fire. It is in the Last Days that you have stored up your treasure! Behold, the pay the laborers who mowed your fields, and which has been withheld by you, cries out against you; and the outcry of those who did the harvesting has reached the ears of the Lord of Sabaoth. You have lived luxuriously on the earth and led a life of wanton pleasure; you have fattened your hearts in a day of slaughter. You have condemned and put to death the righteous man; he does not resist you (James 5:1-6).

I further explained to the friend that if his motives for prospering were to give to others, then indeed he understood the basis for prosperity. The apostle of love, John, puts it this way: "Beloved, I pray that in all respects you may prosper and be in good health, just as your soul prospers" (3 John 2).

The apostle Paul also speaks of prosperity:

> Now this I say, he who sows sparingly shall also reap sparingly; and he who sows bountifully shall also reap bountifully. Let each one do just as he has purposed in his heart; not grudgingly or under compulsion; for God loves a cheerful giver. And God is able to make all grace abound to you, that always having all sufficiency in everything, you may have an abundance for every good deed; as it is written, "HE SCATTERED ABROAD, HE GAVE TO THE POOR, HIS RIGHTEOUSNESS ABIDES FOREVER."
>
> Now He who supplies seed to the sower and bread for food will supply and multiply your seed for sowing and increase the harvest of your righteousness; you will be enriched in everything for all liberality, which through us is producing thanksgiving to God. For the ministry of this service is not only fully supplying the needs of the saints, but is also overflowing through many

171

thanksgivings to God. Because of the proof given by this ministry they will glorify God for your obedience to your confession of the gospel of Christ, and for the liberality of your contribution to them and to all, while they also, by prayer on your behalf, yearn for you because of the surpassing grace of God in you. Thanks be to God for his indescribable gift!" (2 Cor. 9:6-15).

Perfect love casts out fear; love and passion go hand in hand. To have love is to have passion and to have passion is to have love. Perfect love is the kind of love that gives without receiving. The apostle John describes this kind of love:

> Whoever confesses that Jesus is the Son of God, God abides in him, and he in God. And we have come to know and have believed the love which God has for us. God is love, and the one who abides in love abides in God, and God abides in him. By this, love is perfected with us, that we may have confidence in the day of judgment; because as He is, so also are we in this world. There is no fear in love; but perfect love casts out fear, because fear involves punishment, and the one who fears is not perfected in love. We love, because He first loved us (1 John 4:15-19).

When we have experienced the love of God as a result of regeneration or new birth, God's love in us is then perfected in every part of our lives. This perfect love happens when a believer is so in union with Christ that he or she becomes the expression of God's love to others. This love is not dependent upon the recipient, but simply on abiding in God's love and allowing the natural outflow of his divine nature in us. Paul describes this process in Romans 5:5: "And hope does not disappoint, because the love of God has been poured out within our hearts through the Holy Spirit who was given to us."

The fear of failure no longer has its hold because God will not abandon us as we abide in him. The fear of rejection no longer weighs us down because our acceptance is from him. The fear of death no longer torments because his life is in us.

To have God's love in us and to be free of fear results in a passionate love for God and others. This passion translates into everyday life and into everyday experiences. It is when we focus on getting instead of giving that the fear of loss grips our souls and our passion becomes fear.

Am I saying that we should not expect to receive? No, we are blessed with all spiritual blessings in heavenly places in Christ Jesus. It isn't wrong to have expectations, but when these expectations are aimed at people and not at God, disappointment is certain. Look to the Psalmist as an example: "My expectations come from thee, Oh, God." Expectations may be, and often are, met through others, but ultimately our hope is in the Lord.

Develop a disciplined mind. Passion that is not directed or disciplined toward a purpose is like a geyser that may be admired for its power display, but has no other purpose than to release steam or pressure. God's passion is given for a purpose: "But you shall receive power when the Holy Spirit has come upon you; and you shall be My witnesses both in Jerusalem, and in all Judea and Samaria, and even to the remotest part of the earth" (Acts 1:8).

The power of the Holy Spirit upon the early disciples, coupled with a new intense passion for Christ, was directed toward a mission: to be witnesses. This mission also had direction, and a careful reading of the book of Acts will reveal a threefold division: in chapters 1 through 7, the mission is focused on Jerusalem and is basically an apostolically led church whose primary goal is to establish the new believers in the Christian community; in chapters 8 through 15, the focus is on Judea and Samaria, especially Antioch, and the mission involves equipping believers to carry the message beyond; beginning in the last part of chapter 15 and to the end of the book, the focus is on the regions beyond and establishing churches and elders in every city.

The purpose of this observation is not to give a detailed outline of the ministry of the early church, but to emphasize their plan and strategy coupled with their love and passion. How can we individually give direction to our passion and energy? I hope the following outline will help you get started.

Set goals. We can begin planning our future by setting goals. Of course, God is sovereign and all of our plans are in his hand. Setting goals was a powerful method that helped me to move out of passivity into direction, out of fear into confidence, and from vagueness into greater clarity.

I believe that it is important to write down goals and share them with your spouse. Goals involving your spouse should be agreed on together. By writing out our goals, we not only clarify them for ourselves, but also for others.

As the seminar ministry that I am involved in began to grow, I would passionately share my dreams with others. But when I heard these same people describe my ministry to others, I was disappointed that they either shared only a part of my vision or missed it altogether. Even those closest to our ministry were unsure what I was doing until I wrote out the vision and goals.

After I shared my vision and goals with one close friend, and even wrote them out for him, he exclaimed, "Don, I've been there for you because you're a friend, but now I'm excited about your ministry. I believe that others would be excited to help you if they understood what it really involved."

Habakkuk understood the process of writing out his vision. "Then the Lord answered me and said, 'Record the vision and inscribe it on tablets, and the one who reads it may run. For the vision is yet for the appointed time; it hastens toward the goal, and it will not fail. Though it tarries, wait for it; for it will certainly come, it will not delay'" (Hab. 2:1-2).

As you think about writing out your goals, note that I also used the word "vision." The vision or mission is the larger desired result or destination. I began writing out my visions and goals by dividing my life into different areas and writing out simple, attainable goals for each one. I review these goals on a regular basis and make changes and adjustments as needed. If you have never done this before, you may also want to begin in a simple way. The following example from my own life might be helpful:

1. List of personal goals
Spiritual goals
Marriage and family goals
Physical and health goals
Occupational or ministry goals

2. Vision for each goal
(Example) Spiritual—To become Christ-like in character and actions

3. List goals under each heading
(Example) Spiritual goals
Develop a father's heart
Deal with blindspots
Develop a consistent prayer life
Effectively share my faith with others
Memorize the book of Romans

4. Develop a strategy for each goal
(Example) Memorize the book of Romans

Memorize one verse about every three days and one chapter every three months. Share each chapter with your spouse and review with accountability. Time frame: four years.

The reason I want to memorize the book of Romans is because this goal has been the most difficult for me to attain. At first I tried to complete the process in one year and became discouraged with interruptions and not being able to recall some of the chapters. So I learned that the next step in developing a disciplined mind is to readjust.

Learn to readjust. Never set goals and plans in cement without allowing for adjusting the time schedule, strategy, or even the resources necessary for fulfilling them. In my goal for memorizing Scripture, I readjusted the time schedule to something more reachable that would give me more joy, not pressure.

The same process for readjustment carries over into any goal that we feel we are stuck in without making progress. Helen and I have been readjusting our ministry goals and creating new strategies. As an example of this, we had conducted our six- to seven-hour seminar, "A Journey Toward Wholeness," on an all-day Saturday schedule. I would lead the seminar on a Saturday and stay over on Sunday to speak in a morning church service. Often after the morning service, many people would ask when we would return to the area. "Oh, we were just here yesterday," I would say. Maybe they hadn't read the announcement or listened carefully, but after two years of this, we finally realized that we were doing things backwards. We have readjusted our seminars to include speaking in a church on Sunday morning, beginning the introduction on Sunday evening, and continuing each evening through Tuesday night.

We make other adjustments as we seek counsel and discern needs. Sometimes even the adjustments need adjustment. Do not attach personal feelings to formulas. If the formula or method for reaching our goals and visions isn't working, which is more important: completing the formula or reaching the goal?

How does one know how to readjust? Seek counsel. The Proverbs tell us that there is safety in the multitude of counselors. When I began to ask the Lord for wisdom and counsel, it was amazing how he began to bring people into my life. Counsel has come to me while sitting next to someone on an airplane, talking with a friend, attending a seminar, or after asking someone directly for help. Some of the best counsel will often come from someone who has already succeeded in the area in which you need help. Find a role model and ask for counsel. I have found that most people are very willing to help, taking into consideration their time and schedule.

Keep learning. One of our family goals has been in the area of personal finances. This has involved getting out of debt, establishing a savings program, buying a home, and setting aside sufficient money to give to others in need. After resigning from the pastorate several years ago, we lived mostly on our savings and equity from having sold our home. Now that I have rejoined the ministry and am past the age of fifty, these goals have to be quite rigorous.

We have just recently begun trying to buy a home for the first time since my resignation. This meant attending seminars and joining a financial consulting organization to learn all that I could about meeting my goals in financial matters.

It should never be too late to have goals and to learn how to meet them. Whatever your goals are, plan some time to learn the skills and information that will help you fulfill them. Browse through the library, attend seminars and conferences and, by all means, ask others who have succeeded in your area of interest.

Be persistent. There are two times in moving forward with any project that we may face the need for persistence and perseverance: when things are going so well that we let our guard down or become careless, and when pres-

175

sure and stress results in discouragement. More often than not, it is the stress and pressure that cause some of us to lapse back into passivity. Understanding the causes of discouragement and pressure may help you overcome these hindrances and move on in passion and with a disciplined mind.

Lack of resources. The lack of money, personnel, and skills may all be a reason for discouragement. It is during this time that we should ask ourselves some questions: Is the lack of money God's way of redirecting my ministry or occupation? Can I cut down on some unnecessary spending? Am I trying to do too much? Do I need to put some projects on hold and create a stronger base of resources? Is this need a prompting to pray?

By asking these questions, we put our mind and heart in a position to more easily hear an answer from the Holy Spirit.

Wrong timing. I am grateful that some of the seminars I led did not begin with large attendance. If they had, I would have continued teaching with the same materials and using the same format. Now I realize that I needed more time to develop and better define some of the content. Remember the word of the Lord to Habakkuk: "The vision is yet for the appointed time; it hastens toward the goal, and it will not fail. Though it tarries, wait for it; for it will certainly come, it will not delay."

There are two important questions that we need to ask the Lord when our plans and visions seem delayed: Is this project or goal from the Lord? Has he called me to accomplish it? If we can answer yes to these questions, then we need to heed the words of the apostle Paul to "not become weary in well doing for we will reap if we faint not."

After we have addressed these questions, we can ask the third: Is there something yet in my character or strategy that needs to be changed?

Lack of understanding of the process of growth. Some of the pressures we feel in pursuing a goal are from normal growth changes and signify that it is time for a different approach or strategy. A friend recently shared with me the four stages of a growing ministry or organization. He called the first "forming." This is the stage where our ideas, dreams, and goals become defined on the way to sharing and accomplishing. He called the second stage "storming." This is the stage where the ministry or project has grown beyond the "mom and pop stage" and the pressures of demand and growth mean letting go, readjusting, delegating, and brainstorming. Old ways of doing things may not work for the future.

The third stage is "norming," when change and delegation begin to become normal, adjustments have been made, and the ministry or organization becomes more tranquil. The final stage is "performing," when maximum results occur.

After talking about these stages, Helen and I recognized that we were in the "storming" stage of our ministry. It had grown beyond our ability to adequately manage it without further help, change, and resources. Understanding this new level helped us see that there was nothing wrong; we were just in the middle of a process. Then we knew what to do about it.

If you recognize passivity in yourself, I trust you will pray, as I did several years ago, for a new and fresh touch of the Holy Spirit to empower you to accomplish the dreams he has given you.

I was past fifty when I asked the Lord to show me how to overcome passivity. The first year after saying this prayer and experiencing the truths I have shared in this chapter, Helen and I began the seminar ministry, "A Journey Toward Wholeness," I wrote my first book (by the same name), and recorded a mini-seminar on video cassette and a series on releasing shame.

We also began the monthly teaching ministry by cassettes (the infamous tape of the month) and the ministry continued to expand beyond what we had dreamed. We have seen some of these same sorts of accomplishments in our family members as they, too, have begun to overcome passivity and receive a new passion and empowerment in their lives.

Passion is not just creating new programs and projects, but having the love of God flow through us to accomplish his will for our lives. The programs, projects, and ministries are only byproducts of his power.

Study questions

1) Everyone is guilty of putting things off, but procrastination can lead to passivity over time. Why do you tend to put things off? What steps can you take to overcome procrastination and fulfill your dreams?

2) It is often easier to blame others for a loss or failure than to hold ourselves responsible. How can you move beyond this stagnation to gain control of your life?

3) Think of someone you consider strong and successful. How can you benefit from his or her example rather than feel intimidated by it?

4) Fear of rejection can be a powerful but debilitating cause of passivity. Identify the fears you need to overcome to succeed at something important to you.

5) Make a list of your personal goals and then a strategy for reaching each goal.

6) A lack of resources—time, money, skills, equipment—can result in passivity. What resources do you lack to reach your goals? How can you obtain these resources?

ELEVEN

FINDING A HAVEN

What is a haven? A place where you will not be hurt physically, mentally, emotionally, or spiritually is how one person I know described it. But finding a haven, a safe place, does not mean that you will feel no pain. Part of recovery and restoration involves dealing with pain and ending denial of past events. A safe place is where there is no *intent* to bring additional hurt. A safe place is as essential to the process of healing and restoration as any other.

A safe location

When Brian talked about his voyeuristic problem, it became obvious that his present location near the beach presented all kinds of temptations that, at this point in his life, made it very difficult for him to walk in freedom. Brian had been ensnared in pornography, and his sexual addiction had escalated to the point that he followed women on the beach and made sexual overtures to them. After one woman reported his impropriety, Brian became more aware of his problem. Breaking the cycle of his addiction required him to change jobs and move to a new city.

I am not suggesting that simply changing jobs or locations is the only answer, or that it will work for everyone. I am saying that when our addictive behavior is so strongly influenced by our environment, it would seem that our healing and future well-being is more important than a job or a place where we live.

This same consideration might be given to people whose behavior is greatly influenced by continuous and unhealthy contact with people, places of temptation, or threats of danger. This is not to say that we should run from problems. Rather, we should place ourselves in safe places so that the restorative process may have a greater chance for success.

A safe church

The most important element of a new location is a church or a community of believers. A wounded church cannot heal a wounded person. When a church has been wounded by fallen leaders, whether pastoral staff or laymen, a spirit of suspicion and judgmentalism may hang over the church like a dark cloud until healing and restoration have occurred. People who try to become a part of that particular fellowship will come under that cloud if they are subject to any past failure.

A healthy church is a place where grace and truth are evident. By grace I mean an understanding of the sovereignty of God and his mercy. Grace bestows the wisdom and ability to see a person through the eyes of God's heart so we can see not only the problem, but hope and redemption for the future. Truth is the ability to present reality and confront both errors and falsehood in love and with a view that correction may bring about genuine change.

A safe church is a congregation of believers who understand and believe in personal restoration as well as restoration to ministry. This does not mean placing a person who needs restoration back into ministry prematurely, but in God's time and with accountability.

A safe church is a place of spiritual protection. The character and spiritual maturity of the leadership is of great importance.

A safe person

When Steve called me long distance on the phone, he kept saying over and over that he believed he could count on confidentiality. Steve was really saying, "Please be a safe person whom I can trust, someone who will not betray me."

Steve had once shared his history with a pastor friend. In only a few days, Steve's confidence had been shattered by reports that his talks with the pastor had become part of the pastor's grapevine of gossip. Fear of betrayal seems to most often explain why people do not share their hurts and failures when they search for help.

How can we know when a person is safe as a confidante and as a friend? These thoughts may help:

• A safe person is a spiritually growing Christian who is recognized by others in the church for strength and character.

• A safe person is someone who is there for you more than you are there for that person.

• A safe person is someone who can keep a confidence but shows discretion when it comes to sharing information with the appropriate people. For example, most state laws require the reporting of child abuse and molestation. Therefore, some information may not be legally withheld from the proper authorities when danger and harm have been done or may occur.

• A safe person is usually someone of the same sex. Shared information and secrets often bond two people, but it could result in inappropriate bonding with sexual connotations.

• A safe person is someone who does not assume improper authority over your life. Remember that your loyalty rests not with the person who is helping you, but with God the Father. A true friend and confidante will continue to point you toward a trust and devotion to the heavenly Father rather than demand loyalty to himself or herself.

People often ask me about the importance of being open with one's spouse, especially with information that involves sexual unfaithfulness. My personal opinion is that it's not a matter of *if* you should share the information, but *when* and *how*.

A spouse usually feels angry and betrayed when he or she hears of the infidelity. That's why it's important to have a counselor or friend guide the unfaithful partner through the steps of restoration, including when and how to have that painful discussion.

Though hurtful and disappointing, infidelity is often not as surprising as the unfaithful partner supposed. Spouses are intuitive; they can sense when something is wrong even when they don't know exactly what it is. Hearing the confession, at the very least, may make them feel as though they are not going crazy after all.

A safe counselor

For almost two years after my resignation from the ministry, it was very difficult for me to share my deepest thoughts and feelings with anyone else, especially a counselor. The events leading up to my resignation included the experience of having a counselor betray my confidence. It left me with a distrust of almost everyone, and being able to trust again took time. It was only after a year and a half of tentative discussions with a Christian psychotherapist that I was able to trust again, especially a counselor. My personal restoration and healing began to solidify.

How can we find a safe counselor? I follow these two guidelines:

(1) *A safe counselor can keep a confidence.* Information shared with a competent counselor will not be shared with other people without your permission, either in verbal or written form.

(2) *A safe counselor is Christ-centered.* Since our ultimate goal is to grow in every aspect in Christ (see Eph. 4:15), the following principles from Matthew 5:3-12 will be reinforced, not violated, by a safe counselor:

Blessed are the poor in spirit, for theirs is the kingdom of heaven—

This verse is a recognition that man is powerless in his own ability and unable without God's grace to be fully restored. This involves breaking denial and admitting our sins.

Blessed are those who mourn, for they shall be comforted—

People deal with their own grief and sorrow by releasing the past (not covering it up or ignoring it) and by genuinely experiencing godly sorrow that leads to repentance. This involves helping a person to become sensitive to those things that grieve the Spirit of God.

Blessed are the meek, for they shall inherit the earth—

This verse reminds a person to view every event and circumstance in life as being under the lordship of Christ and to see God's sovereignty and grace. This means submitting our will to Christ and trusting him to work out everything in our life for his glory and our benefit, in his timing, and in his way.

Blessed are those who hunger and thirst for righteousness, for they shall be satisfied—

A person refocuses passions for righteousness by asking God's spirit to give him or her a new motivation and a renewed heart. This involves regeneration, being filled with the Holy Spirit, and walking in the Spirit.

Blessed are the merciful, for they shall receive mercy—

Jesus reminds us to forgive fully from the heart and to learn positive lessons from the offense or hurt. A true Christ-centered counselor will help one develop new boundaries and guidelines as a protection from offenders, allowing a spirit of forgiveness and mercy to prevail—not one of revenge and destruction. Vengeance belongs to the Lord and injustice that was done is dealt with at the cross.

Blessed are pure in heart, for they shall see God—

A person needs to identify systems, rituals, and motives that serve self more than they serve the kingdom of God. The focus will be on taking off the old man and crucifying the flesh, not fulfilling it. True joy and happiness come from love that flows out of a pure heart, a clear conscience, and genuine faith.

Blessed are the peacemakers, for they shall be called the children of God—

This verse reminds a person to develop a clear conscience before God and man. This may involve making amends with those who have been wronged and making restitution when necessary or possible. It also involves assuming responsibility and not blaming others.

Blessed are those who have been persecuted for the sake of righteousness, for theirs is the kingdom of heaven—

A person can deal with rejection and disappointment by seeking God's approval more than the approval of others. This requires the courage to stand alone when necessary, developing an eternal perspective and showing a clear discernment between a martyr's complex and a genuine love for God's kingdom.

Blessed are you when men cast insults at you and persecute you and say all kinds of evil against you falsely, on account of me—

A person should deal with false accusations, assume responsibility for character faults, and respond in wisdom to the accuser through prayer and spiritual warfare. Since persecution seems to follow kingdom service, we can assume that part of the restorative and healing process is to become whole so that we, in turn, may help bring the ministry of healing and restoration to others. All healing and restoration should aim to bring a person to understand and fulfill the purpose of Christ in us. God's call also includes serving in his vineyard. A counselor who manipulates a client to stay sick for the selfish, emotional reason of monetary gain is a hireling and not a true servant of Jesus with a shepherd's heart.

Methodology and expertise may vary from counselor to counselor. These are general guidelines to keep in mind as a framework for truth. A non-Christian counselor may be of benefit in specific and specialized areas of help, but only in the context of truth that Jesus presented to his first disciples at the Sermon on the Mount.

A safe support group

The safe places discussed so far should be like islands of love and restoration in the process of recovery. The support group is another island that I believe is essential to the restorative process. It differs from a church service, Bible study, or prayer group in that it is made up of fellow strugglers who are in varying degrees of recovery. It should be a place to share honestly and openly, but with accountability and love. A person unprepared for this type of openness and honesty would not be ready for this kind of group. Also, an unprepared and untrained group leader could be detrimental to the group's process.

There are various types of support groups that meet needs at different levels. In most situations, I would strongly lean toward a closed group.

One of the most powerful dynamics that takes place in a support group is that of bonding and trust. Once a group has begun and continued for several weeks or months, introducing a new person or persons will slow the group down because the new members have not experienced some of the dynamics necessary for trust. Through personal experience, I have observed that more is lost than gained when such new members are admitted.

Another restriction that helps build bonding and trust are groups in which men meet exclusively with other men and women with women. Since sharing and openness produce a bonding, a safe place is provided when people don't have to deal with inappropriate bonding. This guideline applies to the more personal type of support groups. A group for married couples in recovery would be different.

Here are some other considerations to keep in mind:

An effective leader. The best leader would most likely be one who had been a member of the support group, though this is not absolutely necessary as long as he or she has acquired training in leadership skills. The leader is not there to control but to guide the discussion and follow the prompting of the Holy Spirit. The best way to describe this leader would be "spiritual," or one who is filled with the Holy Spirit and faith.

Interviewing applicants. A support group is best begun by interviewing applicants. An hour is plenty of time to hear a person's story, background, and his or her reason for wanting to join the group. I ask each applicant to agree to a one-year commitment.

Evaluating applicants. By evaluating each applicant's request for a small group, members can be placed in a group of people who share levels of need and risk. A minister in sexual addiction should be placed in a group with ministers who exhibit the same risks. By risk, I mean the courage it takes to open up and share one's history, feelings, failures, struggles, etc. People with similar risks and ministries would all be at the same level. This will provide part of the safety for confidentiality.

A commitment to confidentiality. Each person in the group must take a pledge of confidentiality. One may tell his or her spouse what one has talked about in the group, but not the names or information shared by other group members. Information is power, and it is necessary to maintain this pledge for the protection and safety of the group and the restorative process in general.

Service to others. Every person in a support group can serve others through his or her own growth process. A support group is not a garbage dump where fallen persons decay and rot away in the midst of other garbage. A support group is more like a greenhouse where even damaged plants become strong and get replanted. Jesus said he would not break a bruised reed or put out a smoking lamp. Neither should a support group.

Finding a haven through a safe location, church, person, counselor, and support group will buoy your restorative process.

Study questions

1.) How might your present environment instigate your addiction? How could you change your environment to propel your recovery and restoration?

2.) What characteristics do your church possess that make it a place of spiritual protection?

3.) Confidantes are more than friends; they are soul mates. What qualities do you prize in a confidante?

4.) How would you go about choosing a safe counselor?

5.) Why is it important that a counselor be Christ-centered?

6.) How can a support group restore you in ways that a church service, Bible study, or prayer group cannot?

TWELVE

REDISCOVERING CHRIST

It isn't a plan of action, a new discipline, or any other method or theory that finally changes the human heart and refires our passions for more noble and higher ideals. It is the discovery that the ideals themselves have value and eternal meaning. This discovery, or rediscovery, changes the human heart and refocuses our energies to pursue them.

Reading about parenting and how to raise children didn't give me passion and love for a child; it was when our own children were born that we discovered the wonder and beauty of a newborn baby and embraced the responsibility of rearing children who had eternal destiny. Passion is more than *learning about* something or someone; it is *discovering* something or someone that has profound meaning and continuance in one's own existence and purpose.

A new plan of action, a new discipline, or another method may come as a side product from our new discovery, but it is in experiencing our new discovery as being of value and importance and fully enjoying it that our passion is truly focused and directed.

People may learn for years about Jesus Christ and his kingdom and may be consumed with a passion for study about him in the Scriptures. But they may not feel a genuine passion until they discover and experience him in the deepest part of their being. Jesus himself warned of this intellectual pursuit: "You search the Scriptures, because you think that in them you have eternal life; and it is these that bear witness of Me; and you are unwilling to come to Me, that you may have life" (John 5:39-40).

How does a person make such a discovery? I believe the answer is simple: ask. The discovery itself is unfathomable. The joy and wonder of discovery is a paradox: we have the fullness of Christ, yet his fullness includes an eternity that we are yet to fully experience; we are complete in him, yet our completion is yet to come; we shall know as we are known, yet we know only a part.

A host of Scriptures and examples illustrate the importance of asking and continuing to ask questions. One of the most striking and pointed is recorded in Luke 11:1-13:

> And it came about that while He was praying in a certain place, after He had finished, one of his disciples said to Him, "Lord, teach us to pray just as John also taught his disciples." And He said to them, "When you pray, say: Father, hallowed be Thy name. Thy kingdom come. Give us each day our daily bread. And forgive us our sins, for we ourselves also forgive everyone who is indebted to us. And lead us not into temptation." And He said to them, "Suppose one of you shall have a friend, and shall go to him at midnight, and say to him, 'Friend, lend me three loaves; for a friend of mine has come to me from a journey, and I have nothing to set before him;' and from inside he shall answer and day, 'Do not bother me; the door has already been shut and my children and I are in bed; I cannot get up and give you anything.' I tell you, even though he will not get up and give him anything because he is his friend, yet because of his persistence, he will get up and give him as much as he needs. And I say to you, ask, and it shall be give to you; seek, and you shall find; knock, and it shall be opened to you. For everyone who asks, receives; and he who seeks, finds; and to him who knocks, it shall be opened. Now suppose one of you fathers is asked by his son for a fish; he will not give him a snake instead of a fish, will he? Or if he is asked for an egg, he will not give him a scorpion, will he? If you then, being evil, know how to give good gifts to your children, how much more shall your heavenly Father give the Holy Spirit to those who ask Him?"

In conjunction with this and many other passages that instruct us to ask for our needs, also consider those who came to Jesus and asked for a miracle of healing, for salvation, or for an answer to some specific need. The most basic response to the need for a new passion for Christ is to ask him for such a heart. David the psalmist and king made such a request: "Create in me a clean heart, O God, and renew a steadfast spirit within me" (Ps. 51:10). Should we, today, ask anything less from God who sees the heart of man?

I suppose that most of us, at some time in life, become tired of our own hypocrisy, pride, and self-centeredness. It was at such a time in my own life when I cried out to God in a desperation, "Please cleanse my heart and do whatever it takes to purify me." What I *really* meant was that he should do whatever it took, but in the most private and least painful way. However, the Lord began to move very swiftly following that prayer in the late summer of 1985. In only a matter of days and weeks my secret sin had been exposed, and I had resigned from the ministry. After a lifetime of building a ministry,

I saw that all that was wood, hay, and stubble was in ashes and had fallen around me.

Once again, several years later, a prayer from deep within my heart seemed to ascend to the heavenly Father when the still, small voice of the Holy Spirit had asked, "What do you want the Father to do in your life?" I answered hesitantly and cautiously, "O God, I want to be like the psalmist David and have a heart after you."

There were times when I almost forgot that prayer, but then the presence of God would seem to cover my very being—sometimes for only a few brief moments and other times for several weeks at a time, but never on an ongoing basis. Memories of my childhood conversion would often replay in my mind, and the desire to regain that intimacy with and joy in Christ would resurface. Even though I was only twelve years old then, the Scriptures became like daily food to me. Sometimes I would memorize entire chapters. Late at night on warm summer evenings, I would often slip outside of our house to walk through the fields of grain and cotton to worship and pray. Though my emotions and mentality may have been that of a twelve-year-old boy, the intimacy with God and awareness of his presence would seem awesome.

My boyhood "secret altar" was associated with another memory of intense and deep intimacy with Christ. When I felt disappointment and rejection, it was easy for me to escape to the secret altar I had built underneath an old mesquite tree on our west Texas farm. The altar was only a large block of wood that had been discarded. I had dragged it to the far corner of the pasture and arranged it so that it wouldn't be discovered by anyone else. There, day after day, I would pray, pour out my heart to him, and seek him. How often I would hear his voice in my heart but not understand how to interpret what I had heard. Sometimes I would feel immersed in his love, while other times I would feel a sense of anticipation—that some event was going to take place either in my life or someone else's. And often it would, precisely as I had seen and heard.

These experiences continued into my early adult life, but again I did not know how to interpret them to others. I shared them with Helen a few times, especially when they involved the two of us. Always, they would happen precisely as I told her, even to the day and year.

I would tell myself that perhaps these memories were a means of escape or some subtle form of denial. However, my deep longing for closeness and fellowship with him would continue. I could easily identify during those times with the words of Solomon: "On my bed night after night I sought him whom my soul loves; I sought him but did not find him. I must arise now and go about the city; in the streets and in the squares I must seek him whom my soul loves. I sought him but did not find him."

Reading the Psalms always gave me renewed hope for the passion and intimacy that I was longing for. Psalm 42 became a constant reminder of this possibility:

> As the deer pants for the water brooks, so my soul pants for Thee, O God. My soul thirsts for God, for the living God; when shall I come and appear before God? My tears have been my food day and night, while they say to me all day long, "Where is your God?" These things I remember, and I pour out my soul within me. For I used to go along with the throng and lead them in procession to the house of God, with the voice of joy and thanksgiving, a multitude keeping festival. Why are you in despair, O my soul? And why have you become disturbed within me? Hope in God, for I shall again praise Him for the help of His presence. O my God, my soul is in despair within me; therefore I remember them from the land of the Jordan, and the peaks of Hermon, from Mount Mizar. Deep calls to deep at the sound of Thy waterfalls; all Thy breakers and Thy waves have rolled over me. The Lord will command His lovingkindness in the daytime; and His song will be with me in the night, a prayer to the God of my life. I will say to God my rock, "Why hast Thou forgotten me? Why do I go mourning because of the oppression of the enemy?" As a shattering of my bones, my adversaries revile me, while they say to me all day long, "Where is your God?" Why are you in despair, O my soul? And why have you become disturbed within me? Hope in God, for I shall yet praise Him, the help of my countenance, and my God.

I read this Psalm over and over until I felt it was my own. Soon, insights and hope would well up inside of me. The Holy Spirit was beginning to show me the doorway, and hope in God was the key. The feeling of hope was a deep, abiding trust that he is sovereign and causes all things to work together for good to those who love him and who are called according to his purpose (Rom. 8:28).

The apostle Paul doesn't say that everything is good, or that God causes everything to happen, but he does say that God will work everything together for good. We may not be responsible for what has happened to us or what will happen to us, but we are responsible for responding to God's grace in relation to events in our lives.

The second key was praise. That is, to acknowledge and establish his glory and presence in every place and situation. The psalmist further states that God inhabits the praises of Israel (or his people). Praise enthrones God in our midst as we not only acknowledge his sovereignty, but give glory and praise to him for what he has done and for who he is. After seven years of mental distortion and madness because of pride, Nebuchadnezzar entered the door of sanity and restoration through these very same avenues.

> But at the end of that period I, Nebuchadnezzar, raised my eyes toward heaven, and my reason returned to me, and I blessed the Most High and

praised and honored Him who lives forever; for His dominion is an everlasting dominion, and His kingdom endures from generation to generation. And all the inhabitants of the earth are accounted as nothing, but He does according to His will in the host of heaven and among the inhabitants of earth; And no one can ward off His hand or say to Him, "What hast Thou done?" At that time my reason returned to me. And my majesty and splendor were restored to me for the glory of my kingdom, and my counselors and my nobles began seeking me out; so I was re-established in my sovereignty, and surpassing greatness was added to me. Now I Nebuchadnezzar praise, exalt and honor the King of Heaven, for all His works are true and His ways just, and He is able to humble those who walk in pride (Dan. 4:34-37).

The greatest expression of praise and thanksgiving may be found in heaven itself.

After these things I looked, and behold, a great multitude, which no one could count, from every nation and all tribes and peoples and tongues, standing before the throne and before the Lamb, clothed in white robes, and palm branches were in their hands; and they cry out with a loud voice saying, "Salvation to our God who sits on the throne, and to the Lamb." And all the angels were standing around the throne and around the elders and the four living creatures; and they fell on their faces before the throne and worshipped God, saying, "Amen, blessing and glory and wisdom and thanksgiving and honor and power and might, be to our God forever and ever. Amen" (Rev. 7:9-12).

In Scripture, the key of praise seems to result in at least two things: the presence and purposes of God in a person or people's lives, and judgment upon the enemy and circumstances that prevent his people from his blessings and purposes (see Psalm 149).

The third key found in Psalm 42 is the key of his presence, resulting from praise. In his presence is the fullness of joy and at his right hand are pleasures forever more (Psalm 16:11). It is the Lord's presence that gives life and sustains. It is also through the Lord's presence that we reign over our circumstances. Every obstacle to his purposes will melt before us. "The Lord reigns; let the earth rejoice; let the many islands be glad. Clouds and thick darkness surround Him; righteousness and justice are the foundation of His throne. Fire goes before Him, and burns up His adversaries round about. His lightnings lit up the world; the earth saw and trembled. The mountains melted like wax at the presence of the Lord, at the presence of the Lord of the whole earth" (Psalms 97:1-5).

The presence of the Lord directs, protects, and sustains us. This is the reason his presence is called the "help of his presence." Moreover, the presence of the Lord changes us: "Now the Lord is the Spirit; and where the Spirit of the Lord is, there is liberty. But we all, with unveiled face beholding as in a mirror the glory of the Lord, are being transformed into the same image from glory to glory, just as from the lord, the Spirit (2 Cor. 3:17-18).

In Psalm 42, David responded to despair in his soul by remembering the goodness in days past. Even so, I too continued to remember the days of youth and even early adulthood and the goodness of God in my life. Oh, how I longed for him again—to know him in the "power of his resurrection and the fellowship of his sufferings" as the apostle Paul described to the Colossian church.

The Lord began to answer my heart's cry (and probably much earlier than I realized) in a very tangible way one evening while I was attending a conference in our local fellowship. The speaker for that evening was ministering in a prophetic way, and he turned to Helen and me and said, "For God did not send the Son into the world to judge the world, but that the world should be saved through Him" (John 3:17). These words became like a brilliant light in my soul, and I immediately realized that my "first love" had eluded me because of fear.

After my resignation from ministry, much of my relationship with God was based on a fear of his judgments and not on a love of his person. The apostle John says that "there is no fear in love; but perfect love casts out fear, because fear involves punishment, and the one who fears is not perfected in love. We love, because He first loved us" (1 John 4:18-19).

The fear that had been in my heart was not a "fear of the Lord" that resulted in wisdom—that is, a concern that my actions would bring reproach on his kingdom and cause others to stumble—but a spirit of fear of punishment that resulted in isolation and distance from intimacy.

"O God," I cried out, "forgive me for my believing a lie about your love and character. Now I understand that much of my motivation has been to escape punishment, and not a response of love to your love in sending Jesus to save." That evening, my focus began to change from responding to a fear of punishment to responding to the Father's love through Jesus Christ as the one who came to save me, not condemn me. "O God," I continued, "give me a new passion for your son, Jesus, my Lord and my savior. Restore unto me the joy of your salvation and renew my first love."

That evening I rested my head on the soft pillow in our bedroom next to my wife and went to sleep. Early the next morning, at about 4 a.m., I was awakened. Even though this had happened many times in the past, this time it was different. I was crying, and soon sobbing, with hot tears washing my face. Pressing my lips together tightly, my concern was to keep from waking Helen with the shaking of my body and the sound of my sobs, but the sobbing grew louder as though it was coming from deep inside of me.

The sobbing was not from fear or sorrow, but rather like a wellspring that had just been opened and was flooding every part of my soul. Once again in prayer I cried out, "Lord what is happening?" Even though I didn't want this wonderful experience to end, I was still overcome by surprise at the continuous wellspring of cleansing and refreshing that was taking place.

Then the small, gentle voice of the Holy Spirit spoke within my heart: "I am renewing your heart like that of a twelve-year-old boy. Now you will have a new opportunity to make new choices to follow me."

I must confess that the inner voice was so clear that it startled and even frightened me. When the Lord spoke about having the heart of a twelve-year-old, I reasoned he meant the mind of a twelve-year-old. "Lord," I thought, "are you sure this is you?"

Suddenly it began to dawn on me that the Lord was answering my prayer and renewing my heart—restoring my first love for him as it had been when I became a Christian as a twelve-year-old boy. I was experiencing an answer to the prayer of Jesus for his disciples: "O righteous Father, although the world has not known Thee, yet I have known Thee; and these have known that thou didst send Me; and I have made Thy name known to them, and will make it known; that the love wherewith Thou didst love Me may be in them, and I in them" (John 17:25-26).

How incredible that the love that the Father has for his son can be in us. What passion and intimacy is possible for those who believe in his son. The refocusing of our passions finally results when we come to know him and abide in him.

Some time had passed by the time Helen was awakened by my experience. She quietly asked, "Don, what's happening?" When I explained, she knew that this was indeed the Lord and rejoiced with me. The results of that early morning experience have not diminished. Though the emotions may vary, the wellspring in my own spirit keeps flowing like a river of living water.

The experience and discovery of this new passion and intimacy continued to bring new discoveries and revelations of his love and grace. I believe that it is these discoveries of truth that continue to set us free and renew our hearts to follow him. Some of the truths that have affected my life are shared in the following excerpts. Even though books could be written about each one, I trust that the introduction of these basic concepts and revelations will be a part of the transformation in your own life, as they have been in mine.

We are a new creation in Christ. The apostle Paul clearly states, "Therefore if any man is in Christ, he is a new creature; the old things passed away; behold new things have come" (2 Cor. 5:17). How astounding, but true, that as believers we are now in Jesus Christ. Paul also declares this truth: "No man should boast before God, but by His doing you are in Christ Jesus, who became to us wisdom from God, and righteousness and sanctification, and redemption, that just as it is written, "'Let him who boasts, boast in the Lord'" (1 Cor. 1:29-31). Our very acceptance by God and basis for going to heaven is that we are accepted in God's beloved son, Jesus Christ (Eph. 1:6).

The dilemma that most believers face is described and solved by Paul in Romans 6. That is, when we do things we do not wish to do, it is not us doing them, but sin that dwells in us. This is not an excuse for us to dwell in sin, but rather a fact that as believers we have a new nature. The old man has been crucified with Christ and we have a new nature. But the sin principle may still be present, and the extra baggage of old behavior patterns may still be hanging on, so we are instructed to take off the old man in reference to the former manner of life and put on the new man.

It is important to recognize that our spiritual man was born again (John 3:5), and that our soul (mind, will, and emotions) is being transformed into his likeness (Rom. 12:1-2; James 1:21). In our regeneration experience, God gave us at least three new things: a new heart, a new spirit, and a new mind (Ezek. 36:26; 1 Cor. 2:16). Therefore, the real us, the inner man of the heart, is a new creation. God has given us a new passion—a passion for his son, Jesus Christ, and a passion for his kingdom and righteousness.

Please notice how, in the words of the apostle Paul, the regeneration experience of the new birth gives us a new character resulting in new behavior.

> For the grace of God has appeared, bringing salvation to all men, instructing us to deny ungodliness and worldly desires and to live sensibly, righteously and godly in the present age, looking for the blessed hope and the appearing of the glory of our great God and Savior, Christ Jesus; who gave Himself for us, that he might redeem us from every lawless deed and purify for Himself a people for His own possession, zealous for good deeds. These things speak and exhort and reprove will all authority. Let no one disregard you. Remind them to be subject to rulers, to authorities, to be obedient, to be ready for every good deed, to malign no one, to be uncontentious, gentle, showing every consideration for all men. For we also once were foolish ourselves, disobedient, deceived, enslaved to various lusts and pleasures, spending our life in malice and envy, hateful, hating one another. But when the kindness of God our Savior and His love for mankind appeared, He saved us, not on the basis of deeds which we have done in righteousness, but according to His mercy, by the washing of regeneration and renewing by the Holy Spirit, whom He poured out upon us richly through Jesus Christ our Savior, that being justified by His grace we might be made heirs according to the hope of eternal life (Titus 2:11–3:7).

The more we recognize who we are in Christ, the more the old patterns will seem unnatural and unbefitting our new nature. We are not our old nature, and our old nature is not us. Our old self was crucified with Christ so that our body of sin might be done away with, and so that we would no longer be slaves to sin (Rom. 6, 7, and 8). We are in Christ and, therefore, his new creation. With a growing revelation and understanding of this new self, we are instructed: "As you therefore have received Christ Jesus the Lord, so walk in Him, having been firmly rooted and now being built up in Him and established in your faith, just as you were instructed, and overflowing with gratitude" (Col. 2:6-7).

Christ is in us. It is almost beyond thought to comprehend that we are in Christ. It is even more glorious to know that Christ is in us. No wonder the apostle Paul describes this new relationship of our being in Christ and Christ being in us as a mystery that God has made known to his own:

> I was made a minister according to the stewardship God bestowed on me for your benefit, that I might fully carry out the preaching of the word of God, that is, the mystery which has been hidden from the past ages and generations; but has now been manifested to His saints, to whom God willed to make known what is the riches of the glory of this mystery among the Gentiles, which is Christ in you, the hope of glory. And we proclaim Him, admonishing every man and teaching every man with all wisdom, that we may present every man complete in Christ. And for this purpose also I labor, striving according to His power, which mightily works within me (Col. 1:25-29).

People who finally come to the place of brokenness recognize their inability to save themselves and how powerless they are over sin and addictive behavior. Unless a power greater than us intervenes, we stand hopeless and powerless before the onslaught of Satan and our own sinfulness. But thanks be unto God, Jesus Christ, who was crucified and raised from the dead, is our living Lord who lives in us and through us by faith.

When Paul speaks of "Christ in us the hope of glory," we understand that our only hope for completion and wholeness according to God's image and glory is through Christ. "For we through the Spirit, by faith, are waiting for the hope of righteousness" (Gal. 5:5). "But we all, with unveiled face beholding as in a mirror the glory of the Lord, are being transformed into the same image from glory to glory, just as from the Lord, the Spirit (2 Cor. 3:18).

The possibility and reality of wholeness and victory in this life are the result of Christ living his life in us and through us. "I have been crucified with Christ; and it is no longer I who live, but Christ lives in me; and the life which I now live in the flesh I live by faith in the Son of God, who loved me, and delivered Himself up for me" (Gal. 2:20).

To know Jesus Christ is to know the Father. One of the heart cries I hear throughout the nation is a longing for a father. Because of their own wounds, fathers often wound their sons and daughters. They, in turn, wound their sons and daughters in the same way, and the vicious cycle goes on and on until it is stopped by the healing and wholeness that comes through our heavenly Father's love.

Jesus told his disciples:

> "I am the way, and the truth, and the life; no one comes to the Father, but through Me. If you had known Me, you would have known My Father also; from now on you know Him, and have seen Him." Phillip said to Him, "Lord, show us the Father, and it is enough for us." Jesus said to him, "Have I been so long with you, and yet you have not come to know Me, Phillip? He who has seen Me has seen the Father; how do you say, 'Show us the Father?' Do you now believe that I am in the Father, and the Father is in Me? The words that I say to you I do not speak on My own initiative, but the Father abiding in Me does His works. Believe Me that I am in the Father, and the Father in Me; otherwise believe on account of the works themselves" (John 14:6-11).

It is through the natural mother that a child first experiences acceptance, nurturing, security, and unconditional love. The father affirms the child through continuing expressions of love and thus gives the child a deepening sense of identity, value, direction, and courage. The apostle Paul told husbands to love their wives just as Christ loved the church and gave himself up for her (Eph 5:25). He continues his discussion of the husband/wife relationship, concluding that this is a great mystery, but that he was speaking with reference to Christ and the church (Eph. 5:32).

I believe that part of this mystery involves the relationship that the Father and the son had with one another, thus Christ could love the church and give himself up for her. This is part of the mystery—that the love of the Father for His son gives us the ability to love another without expecting anything in return.

When we experience the love of our heavenly Father, and his love is shed abroad in our hearts by the Holy Spirit, we become channels of that love to others. Whatever they give back is enough and whatever they do not give back is enough. The Father's love, quite simply, is enough.

John, the apostle of love, declares in 1 John 4:8 that "God is love" and proclaims with breathtaking clarity that "we love because He first loved us" (1 John 4:19).

To know the Father through Jesus Christ is to experience his love and to desire that others experience the same. "By this all men will know that you are My disciples, if you have love for one another" (John 13:35). In turn, his love refocuses our passions on his son, Jesus Christ, and on others.

Study questions

1) Discovering Christ means asking questions about him. What do you want to know about Christ? How can you find the answers to your questions?

2) What does Psalm 42 tell you about the prospect of intimacy with Christ?

3) Addictive behavior seems more unnatural as we begin to recognize who we are in Christ. How do you see yourself in Christ?

4) How has refocusing your passion brought you closer to God?